THE DARK PATTERN

THE DARK PATTERN

THE HIDDEN DYNAMICS OF CORPORATE SCANDALS

GUIDO PALAZZO AND
ULRICH HOFFRAGE

New York

Trigger warning: Two chapters (7 and 10) discuss suicide and suicide attempts. If you find this disturbing, please skip these chapters. If you or someone you know is suicidal, please contact your physician or call the suicide prevention hotline.

Copyright © 2025 by Guido Palazzo and Ulrich Hoffrage

Cover design by Chin-Yee Lai
Cover image © huzu1959/Moment Open via Getty Images
Cover copyright © 2025 by Hachette Book Group, Inc.

Hachette Book Group supports the right to free expression and the value of copyright. The purpose of copyright is to encourage writers and artists to produce the creative works that enrich our culture.

The scanning, uploading, and distribution of this book without permission is a theft of the author's intellectual property. If you would like permission to use material from the book (other than for review purposes), please contact permissions@hbgusa.com. Thank you for your support of the author's rights.

Basic Venture
Hachette Book Group
1290 Avenue of the Americas, New York, NY 10104
www.basic-venture.com

Printed in the United States of America

First Edition: June 2025

Published by Basic Venture, an imprint of Hachette Book Group, Inc. The Basic Venture name and logo is a trademark of the Hachette Book Group.

The Hachette Speakers Bureau provides a wide range of authors for speaking events. To find out more, go to hachettespeakersbureau.com or email HachetteSpeakers@hbgusa.com.

Basic Venture books may be purchased in bulk for business, educational, or promotional use. For more information, please contact your local bookseller or the Hachette Book Group Special Markets Department at special.markets@hbgusa.com.

The publisher is not responsible for websites (or their content) that are not owned by the publisher.

Print book interior design by Sheryl Kober.

Library of Congress Cataloging-in-Publication Data
Names: Palazzo, Guido, author. | Hoffrage, Ulrich, author.
Title: The dark pattern : the hidden dynamics of corporate scandals / Guido Palazzo and Ulrich Hoffrage.
Description: First edition. | New York : PublicAffairs, 2025. | Includes bibliographical references and index.
Identifiers: LCCN 2024049067 | ISBN 9781541705302 (hardcover) | ISBN 9781541705326 (ebook)
Subjects: LCSH: Corporations—Corrupt practices. | Business ethics.
Classification: LCC HV6768 .P345 2025 | DDC 174/.4—dc23/eng/20250218
LC record available at https://lccn.loc.gov/2024049067

ISBNs: 9781541705302 (hardcover), 9781541705326 (ebook)

LSC-C

Printing 1, 2025

Dedicated to
—the countless victims of the dark pattern
—those who have the courage to speak up

CONTENTS

INTRODUCTION: Good Managers Gone Bad **1**
CHAPTER 1 Ethical Blindness **9**
CHAPTER 2 The Power of Context **35**
CHAPTER 3 The Dark Pattern **51**
CHAPTER 4 Theranos—the Empress's New Clothes **85**
CHAPTER 5 Uber—an Embattled Unicorn **105**
CHAPTER 6 Wells Fargo—Sell Like Hell **125**
CHAPTER 7 France Télécom—a Fatal Change Management **143**
CHAPTER 8 Boeing—the Price of Cutting Costs **161**
CHAPTER 9 Volkswagen—Cheating in the Name of Fairness **181**
CHAPTER 10 Foxconn—Welcome to the Machine **199**
CHAPTER 11 The Bright Pattern **219**
CHAPTER 12 After the Fall **249**

EPILOGUE **265**
ACKNOWLEDGMENTS **271**
NOTES **273**
INDEX **309**

INTRODUCTION: GOOD MANAGERS GONE BAD

> You squeezed your employees to the breaking point so they would cheat customers and you could drive up the value of your stock and put hundreds of millions of dollars in your own pocket. And when it all blew up, you kept your job, you kept your multi-multimillion-dollar bonuses, and you went on television to blame thousands of $12-an-hour employees who were just trying to meet cross-sell quotas that made you rich.
>
> —Senator Elizabeth Warren[1]

John Stumpf, the CEO of Wells Fargo and one-time "Banker of the Year," had navigated the biggest US retail bank almost unharmed through the storm of the financial crisis that devastated the globe. Now he was sitting in a congressional hearing, looking small and pale in his chair, forced to listen to a fuming Senator Elizabeth Warren denounce his "gutless leadership." Since taking over the

170-year-old bank, Stumpf had led it to a higher stock value year after year. This success story ended in 2015, when the Los Angeles city attorney initiated legal proceedings against the bank, in the course of which Wells Fargo finally had to admit that it had opened a total of 3.5 million bank accounts and half a million credit cards for its customers without their knowledge or consent. Trust was gone, the bank's reputation was lost, and the damage was immense. John Stumpf, the banker of the year, went from hero to villain and had to resign. Wells Fargo laid off 5,300 employees and paid a total of around $20 billion in fines, settlements, and consulting fees.

Scandals aren't new. They've been around forever and have happened across all geographical, cultural, and national boundaries and in most, if not all, sectors, whether it's banking, commerce, medicine, sports, or politics. It seems like almost every day we find another big corporate scandal in the news. Some make global headlines. Enron, Theranos, and Purdue Pharma have become household names. But there are countless smaller scandals that have received little attention beyond the local news. And then some never surface, silently buried by the companies themselves to avoid any bad publicity. But whether they become public or not, whether they are on a massive scale or not, they all cause damage.

Scandals are expensive. The companies involved can lose their money, their reputation, and in some cases even their existence. WorldCom, Lehman Brothers, Arthur Andersen, Theranos, and FTX, to name only a few, collapsed under the weight of their moral failures and became history. Others survived but at a high price. Some scandals, like the ones at Wells Fargo, Boeing, or Volkswagen, have price tags between $20 billion and $60 billion. After the fallout, these companies struggled for years to get back on track—and indeed some continue to struggle as we write this book. Others had to pay less but still had their PR nightmares, lost talent, and tied up the energy of those who might be innovating but instead had to clean up the mess of their predecessors.

Scandals outrage us. They shake our belief in a good and just world, at least with regard to the world *as it is*. But they also remind us of how the world *should be*. We restore our moral ideals by instinctively distancing ourselves from such terrible and immoral events. We consider ourselves the good guys, and we are horrified by evil. Accordingly, scandals are usually narrated in the news like Hollywood movies: There are villains and heroes. Often, the villains are once-celebrated leaders who fell from grace. The *Economist* called the former CEO of Enron, Kenneth Lay, the "Messiah," and many hoped that Elizabeth Holmes, the founder of Theranos, would be "the next Steve Jobs." Somehow, these once-great CEOs move to the dark side and then are stopped by the heroes—the (very few) employees who stand up against them and blow the whistle. Netflix is full of these Hollywood renditions. In them, the villains are found and punished, and justice is restored. After that, the world is a better place again.

The treatment that Wells Fargo CEO John Stumpf received at his hearing before the Senate can serve as a real-world example of this kind of narrative. By the way, the term "hearing" is somewhat misleading in this case, as Senator Elizabeth Warren barely gave him a chance to speak. She publicly pilloried him in front of the cameras and, visibly agitated, heaped accusations on him, all of which amounted to him being solely responsible for the entire fraud scheme and having orchestrated it all to enrich himself personally.[2]

So, is John Stumpf a bad apple? Sure, as the CEO of Wells Fargo, he bears responsibility for this colossal system of fraud. However, the sales strategy had already been invented by his predecessor. He just continued it (and yes, increased the pressure on his salespeople). Then, there were all the risk and compliance experts and his team of top executives, including Carrie Tolstedt, head of community banking, who repeatedly downplayed the extent of fraudulent sales practices when the problem was brought to their attention. They attributed it to isolated instances of misconduct by a few individual employees, on the order of 1 percent of the company's workforce. They were not willing or able to see that the problem was systemic. But it was. As later investigations revealed, there were over 100,000 (!) employees involved in these fraudulent activities. The fact that the board of directors did not recognize the problem is astonishing enough, but the fact that so many went along with the fraudulent practices is at least as astonishing. It is hard to imagine that 100,000 bad apples applied to Wells Fargo because, for whatever reason, they thought that this was the best place to unleash their criminal energies. The vast majority of them were presumably normal people, people like you and me, who take care of their loved ones at home, have hobbies, and maybe walk the dog in the evening or go to church or a sports event on Sunday.

When it comes to corporate scandals, what we often do not realize is that when bad things happen, usually people like us are doing it. Good people, or at least average people, with decent values and no bad intentions. And it happens again and again. In 2001, *CFO* magazine awarded their annual Excellence Award for CFOs for the last time because the previous three winners had ended up in prison. And it does not just happen to CEOs and CFOs—anyone can break the rules or behave unethically.

This book is about good people doing bad things. Under certain circumstances, they may lie, cheat, bully, and commit fraud. But to understand their behavior, we should not just focus on their character flaws but examine the context in which they make their decisions.[3] Context can be stronger than reason and stronger than values. It can distort people's perception of reality to such an extent that they can no longer see the ethical or legal dimension of their decision. They become what we call *ethically blind*.

In Chapters 1–3, we will lay out this rationale. Through a mix of psychological research, case reports, and organizational anecdotes, we illuminate the driving forces and hidden dynamics that explain why individuals—and entire organizations—fall over the moral cliff. In Chapter 1, we focus on the individual decision-maker and show how people can manage to maintain a positive self-image despite doing ethically borderline things. In Chapter 2, we discuss the role of context in people's moral failure. In Chapter 3, we introduce the nine building blocks of a context that can make ethical dimensions disappear from the radar screen of decision-makers and thus pave the way to hell, suffering, and catastrophe. We call such constellations the *dark pattern*. Its building blocks are *rigid ideology*, *toxic leadership*, *manipulative language*, *corrupting goals*, *destructive incentives*, *ambiguous rules*, *perceived unfairness*, *dangerous groups*, and a *slippery slope*.

In Chapters 4–10, we present seven scandals. They span the last two decades and include examples from a variety of organizations, industries, and countries. These scandals are well known, but they have rarely been analyzed in terms of the psychological forces that drive good people to actively (or passively) engage in misconduct. How did we get there? To avoid being blinded by our own theoretical approach, we first wrote the case descriptions with an attempt to ignore this framework. In these pure descriptions, we built on thousands of pages of court documents, insider reports, videos, and documentaries, as well as books and articles written by investigative journalists or scholars. In our accounts of what happened, we used as many direct statements from people within these organizations as possible. Most of the cases were then read by one, two, or even three insiders who not only were there, in those organizations, when the scandal happened but also witnessed the developments beforehand. We asked them to check whether our case narratives were accurate, complete, and realistic. Some of them helped to correct elements and (mostly anonymously) added insider knowledge to enrich some aspects of our narrative. Only then did we search for overlapping elements using existing research—including our own—from social and cognitive psychology, behavioral and environmental economics, and related disciplines. In parallel to our own theoretical reflections, compliance practitioners, master students, and executive MBA students received our pure case descriptions, and we asked them to find explanations and uncover the hidden dynamics. Note that we did not inform them of our conceptual framework, so we had independent judgments. Their interpretations were in line with ours. In a final step, we interwove our pure descriptions of the cases (such as the scandals of Volkswagen, Boeing, Theranos, and Wells Fargo) with the analyses we conducted using our conceptual lenses.

In Chapter 11, we take the nine building blocks of the dark pattern as a starting point and show how managers can turn each of them around to create an ethically robust business that is better protected from moral failure. In Chapter 12, we explore what can be done "after the fall" if a company is involved in a scandal.

Over the last decade, we have conducted research on unethical decision-making in organizations, and the *dark pattern* is the result of what we have learned from looking into dozens of scandals. For the last twenty years, we've been professors at the University of Lausanne in Switzerland on the Faculty of Business and Economics, specializing in business ethics and corporate responsibility, and judgment and decision-making. And we've joined forces to develop a theoretical approach that explains why good people in organizations do bad things. We call our concept *ethical blindness* and, together with our colleague Franciska Krings, have established it within the business community as an important element in corporate failure.[4]

Before we ever wrote down our conceptual ideas about good people doing bad things, we had created a course for our master students in what we called *unethical decision-making*. More than 2,000 students have participated in it so far. A bit later, we've created an online version of the course that has been taken by more than 50,000 people.[5] In addition, over the years more than 100,000 managers in companies worldwide have been trained in the dark pattern approach. This book has benefited greatly from our interactions with students and managers through these courses and trainings.

A warning up front: this book contains disturbing subject matter and is not always a pleasant read. Indeed, we delve into the dark side of power. It is not a book about success, but about failure—about moral failure, often with disastrous consequences. Hundreds of people have lost their lives because of the events described here, whether because of avoidable accidents or because they were driven to suicide. Still others have been humiliated or lost their money or jobs because of them.

It can also be disturbing what you learn about others and yourself. Yes, we belong to the league of the "good guys," or at least we like to think we do. But so did many of the people who inflicted harm and suffering on others, committed fraud, or engaged in other types of illegal behavior. And maybe, one day, we may find ourselves in a situation where the dynamics described in this book can unfold and tempt us to do things that we may later regret. When that moment comes, you will be better prepared.

What can you gain from this book? First, we will take you on a fascinating journey into the psychology of human behavior, or more accurately, of bad human behavior, and we promise an interesting read. Second, you can then, hopefully, relate all this to your own social environment, both professional and private. This can be useful in terms of diagnosis, therapy, and prevention. As you read our analysis of the scandals we have selected, you can try to *diagnose* the situation in your own organization. We selected some of the biggest scandals of the last decade to illustrate the power of the dark pattern, simply because they are well-documented and thus easier to analyze. However, any organization can fall prey to it, whether small or big, for-profit or not-for-profit. If you see problems in your environment that bear certain similarities to what we present here, you can ask yourself how you as a *therapist* could act and address these problems with the help of what is discussed in this book. Of course, it is even better not to let it get that far in the first place, so we hope that our insights, stories, and case analyses can help you avoid slippery slopes in the first place and thus *prevent* bad things from happening in the future.

Finally, you can look in the mirror, or more precisely, you can try to look at yourself with the conceptual glasses that this book offers—and this is probably the hardest part. It is easier to see the shortcomings of others than our own. Similarly, it is easier to see the ethical blindness of others than our own blindness. Seeing our own blindness—that's quite a paradox. And indeed, this book is about nothing less than shedding light on areas that are normally dark and hidden, and this explicitly includes precisely those areas that are in our own blind spots. The attempt to bring light into the darkness places this book in the tradition of the Enlightenment. At the same time, it challenges important tenets of the Enlightenment by pointing out that context can be stronger than reason.

Welcome to our disturbing and exciting journey!

1
ETHICAL BLINDNESS

Imagine the typical white-collar criminal—one of those you occasionally see being handcuffed and taken away on camera. How would you describe these fallen top managers to others? Greedy? Cold-heartedly calculating? Narcissistic? Arrogant? Despotic? Now describe yourself: What are *your* predominant character traits? Presumably (and hopefully!), your two lists of traits are very different and do not overlap. There are at least two reasons for this.

First, there's the so-called illusion of superiority. We are all convinced we have above-average moral standards. We all believe we belong to the good guys—and believe it or not, this even applies to convicts of violent crimes.[1] Second, there's the so-called fundamental attribution error. When we explain the misbehaviors of others, we make a simple assumption: they do what they do because they are who they are—bad apples.[2] Interestingly, things are different when we talk about ourselves: we do what we do because of the circumstances and the situation we find ourselves in. And if we do something bad—which of course in our view rarely happens—then we have a good excuse and can explain it through the external factors that pushed us to act like this.[3]

Scandals are usually portrayed as a series of events triggered by bad apples, who are then discovered and brought to justice. This narrative plays out in three famous examples: Enron, the energy, commodities, and services company that met its end in 2001; the case of the ill-fated Ford Pinto car; and the trial of the German Nazi leaders after World War II.

Founded in 1985 and headquartered in Houston, Texas, Enron initially focused on the transport and distribution of natural gas but quickly grew into a giant dealing in all kinds of commodities, including electricity, telecommunications, and broadband services. In 1996, the company went public, and between 1999 and 2001 its share price rose from around $30 to around $90. But what looked like a success story from the outside had an ugly downside. While growing at an ever-accelerating pace, aggressively pushing its traders to do more and more deals, Enron was far from being profitable. Under its chief financial officer, Andrew Fastow, and with the help of auditors from Arthur Andersen, Enron was piling up debts and making unrealistic predictions about future profitability, thereby deceiving countless trusting investors about the dire financial state of the company. The fraud was exposed, which ultimately led to the collapse of Enron in 2001. Shareholders lost $74 billion.[4] CEO Jeffrey Skilling and Fastow were sent to prison. Arthur Andersen lost its license to operate, and thousands of highly skilled people lost their jobs. After that, the world was a better place again. Right?

In the 1970s, Ford hit the headlines when it became known that the Pinto, one of its best-selling cars, had an increased risk of catching fire in a rear-end collision due to its fuel-tank design. Over the years, sixty people died horrible deaths in car crashes because of this technical flaw. Ford could have easily fixed the problem with a recall and a retrofit for only $11 per car, but it would have added up to a total cost of about $137 million. Ford calculated that it was cheaper to pay out the survivors and the family members of those who had died due to the design flaw than to recall the Pinto. This calculation, in the so-called Pinto Memo, leaked to the public. The outrage was huge: Ford had coldly jeopardized the lives of its customers and betrayed their trust in the quality of the car, all for the sake of a few pieces of silver. The carmaker suffered enormous reputation damages and faced approximately 117 lawsuits related to rear-end accidents, one of them ultimately resulting in punitive damages of $3.5 million. On June 9, 1978, a few days before Ford expected a formal recall order, the company "voluntarily" recalled more than one million Pintos.[5] After that, the world was a better place again. Wasn't it?

One of the most famous efforts to punish evildoers was the Nuremberg trials from November 20, 1945, to October 1, 1946. The location was carefully chosen: Nuremberg, a city in southern Germany, was a stronghold of Adolf Hitler's National Socialist German Labor Party (the NSDAP). It was precisely there, in the center of evil, so to speak, that these evil people were to be accused and condemned before the eyes of a worldwide audience. Accused and on trial were twenty-one high officials of Hitler's regime that was responsible for bringing death and suffering to millions of people. Twelve were executed and six received long prison sentences, some of them for life. Parallel to this punishment at the highest level, the so-called denazification began in Germany, where millions were scrutinized for their relationship to Hitler's regime, and many lesser villains were excluded from socially relevant positions. After that, the world was a better place again. Correct?

THE HIDDEN DYNAMICS OF SCANDALS

In this book, we cut through the popular narrative that the media normally propose in the aftermath of a scandal: the manager going rogue, the villain whose behavior explains it all. Granted, there are bad apples, psychopaths, and criminals, and they may even play an important role in many scandals. However, focusing on these actors and their bad character usually explains next to nothing. The term "bad apple," the explanation given in many of these cases, is not an explanation at all, but rather empty jargon.[6] It is essentially a label on a black box that can easily prevent us from examining the underlying psychological forces and cognitive processes. And indeed, intriguing questions remain: How did they become such bad apples? In what context did they act, and what effects did this context have? How were they able to get their way when they were surrounded by so many good guys? How did the good guys contribute? But above all, could it be that many, perhaps even most, of these supposedly bad apples turn out to be people like you and me—normal people with values and good intentions? And vice versa: What would we have done had we been in their shoes?

With these questions, the strict dividing line between good and evil already begins to blur a little. Let us take a small step further along this path and go back to the three examples of Enron, Ford, and the Nazi trials. But this time, let us try to put these bad apples in the context in which they had acted, and let us try to see the world from their point of view.

Imagine we were in the 1990s, long before the Enron scandal broke out. It was the time of the so-called new economy, characterized by a shift toward a more technologically driven and globally interconnected economic system. This shift went hand in hand with the rapid growth of the internet and the related rise of knowledge-based industries such as information technology, software development, and biotechnology. The new economy was seen as a radical departure from the traditional manufacturing-based economy and was characterized by exploding innovation, buzzing entrepreneurship, and steep economic growth. Many experts believed that it would bring unprecedented prosperity and opportunities. It was the time of rapid speculation in internet-based businesses, when the dot-com bubble grew and grew and grew. It was the time *before* it burst and could then be called a bubble.

Enron was a poster child of the 1990s and can only be understood if this sociopolitical and economic context is considered. For six consecutive years, *Fortune* magazine named it "America's Most Innovative Company." By the late 1990s, it was one of the largest energy companies in the world, Wall Street's darling, and widely regarded as a leading example of the new economy.[7] Who would not want to work for such a company? And indeed, Enron attracted graduates from top US business schools such as Harvard and Wharton and hired them as traders—young and hungry people with an entrepreneurial and combative spirit, executing economist Joseph Schumpeter's (1883–1950) "creative destruction" at high speed. They started their new jobs shortly after the Reagan administration, inspired by neoliberal ideas, had deregulated the electricity market. This deregulation created a lot of new opportunities—and some uncertainty about what the new rules of the game were. Remember that a few years ago, in the early 1990s, terms like "internet" and "online platform" did not even exist!

Granted, the knights of the new economy, including leaders and traders at Enron, were driven by greed. But "greed is good" and "greed is healthy" is what they were taught during their business-school education.[8] How could it be wrong to be selfish after it had been legitimized by one of the founding fathers of economics, Adam Smith, by modern economists such as Nobel Prize winner Milton Friedman, and by political leaders such as US president Ronald Reagan and British prime minister Margaret Thatcher? In August 2000, Enron was worth $70 billion and had outperformed the S&P by more than 200 percent. In this seeming success story, were all these people, from the CEO to the CFO to the trader on the floor, bad apples? Weren't they trying to make the world a better place with the help of the invisible hand of the market that turns the actions of selfish individuals into general prosperity? And the accounting fraud? There was a gold-rush atmosphere, like in the Wild West. It was a time of deregulation, with economists and politicians loudly proclaiming from their pulpits that the state should stay out of the free market. Why should we be surprised if some people took this as an invitation to interpret the rules generously? And since the new economy would be totally different from the old economy, managers often believed in those totally unrealistic forecasts of future profits they were selling to their shareholders. Who was the victim here, and who was the perpetrator? Enron: a bunch of bad apples or a group of clever egoists who were attracted, driven, and legitimized by neoliberalism and inadvertently helped to reveal the dangers and design flaws of this ideology?

The story of the Ford Pinto might also be less straightforward than it seems: Dennis Gioia, a young engineer, played a central role in part of this scandal before he left Ford in 1977. He was a child of the highly politicized student generation of the sixties: an opponent of the Vietnam War, a critic of capitalist exploitation, a flower-power student who wore his hair long. He saw himself as value conscious and full of integrity.[9] Despite his critical attitude, he decided to take a job at Ford. Unlike many other representatives of his generation, Gioia was convinced that the system had to be changed from within, through reform rather than revolution. In German-speaking Europe at the time, this was known as the "march through the institutions," with the aim of transforming them and making the world a better place. With all this, Gioia was probably the exact opposite of a bad apple. So why did he pass up the chance to make the Pinto a safer car? How could it be that he did not realize at the time that Ford's cost-benefit analysis had an ethical dimension? Why did he not speak up?

Well, after he entered Ford, he changed. In small steps, bit by bit. The daily interactions between teams of engineers and managers, all of whom shared a functional-technical perspective and strove to increase Ford's profit, contributed to the narrowing of his perspective. The rebellious teenager of 1969 had become an adult manager who had since cut his hair. This bond with his colleagues, his in-group, must also be seen against the background of external pressure. Ford found itself in an aggressive international competition with Japanese car manufacturers—a constellation that, as Gioia put it, came with "a strong feeling of we-vs-them, where we (Ford members) needed to defend ourselves against them (all the outside parties . . .)."[10]

Gioia identified himself with Ford and played by Ford's rules. And the company had clear criteria for its recall team. The job was to identify faulty parts and recall affected cars to replace these parts. The Pinto had no such part. The problem was the design of the car itself. Based on the criteria defined at Ford, there was no reason for a recall. The engineers were also under great time pressure. Numerous decisions about potential recalls had to be made every day. Every positive decision entailed high costs for the company and might have caused reputational damage because quality defects are made public. The risks to vehicle owners therefore had to be weighed against the financial risks to the company. To make such a judgment, accident probabilities and possible damage sums were calculated. Recall teams used tables drawn up by insurance companies for this purpose: What was the cost of an arm, a leg, or a whole life if a company had to pay compensation? These costs could be calculated precisely, but the question of which risks were tolerable, and which required a recall, had to be weighed up by the engineers themselves. There were no precise guidelines for this. Not to mention that in the early 1970s, it was also generally accepted that driving a car was a risk per se. At that time, there were significantly more road deaths than today. Everyone who got into a car knew about this risk and accepted it. Incidentally, Gioia drove a Pinto himself at the time and had no problem selling one to other family members, too.

Regarding explosions, it should also be noted that car manufacturers were monitored by the National Highway Traffic Safety Administration. They were required by law to conduct crash tests. The Pinto complied with the legal limits. Later, the test conditions were tightened and the speed limit for rear-end collisions was increased. The Pinto failed these crash tests, but by then it was already officially approved for road use. From this point of view, no laws were broken. Gioia was convinced at the time that he had acted reasonably. It was only after he resigned from Ford, became a management professor, and began researching decision-making processes that he developed an understanding of his own decision-making and culpability in the situation. For him, at the time, his perception of the recall decision was driven by the elements described above. He simply didn't see the moral dimension of the calculation.[11]

If the bad apple narrative proves to be shaky for Enron and Ford, it at least applies to the Nazi perpetrators, right? One of Hitler's representatives who did not sit in the dock at the Nuremberg trials was Adolf Eichmann, the SS officer responsible for the logistics of the Holocaust. While many of his colleagues had committed suicide after the war and thus escaped the trial, Eichmann had managed to flee to Argentina. In May 1960, the Israeli intelligence service, Mossad, seized him and brought him to Jerusalem, where he was finally sentenced to death and executed.

One of the many trial observers in Jerusalem was the philosopher Hannah Arendt. As she later wrote, she expected to see a Nazi monster in the courtroom. Instead, she found a boring bureaucrat who even invoked his Kantian duty. Eichmann claimed that he was simply following orders and adhering to the duties imposed on him by the state, which he suggested was in line with Kant's idea that moral duties are binding and universal. What disturbed her most was that Eichmann seemed to be a person like many others. Frighteningly normal. As she wrote in an article for the *New Yorker* in 1963: "Half a dozen psychiatrists had certified Eichmann as 'normal.' 'More normal, at any rate, than I am after having examined him,' one of them was said to have exclaimed."[12] To her, Eichmann was simply a loyal subordinate, intelligent and, even by today's standards, an efficient manager and leader. If one were to anonymize his personnel file and include it in a present-day application process, he probably would have excellent chances of getting a leadership position. However, he was doing his job within the framework of the prevailing ideology of the time and did not have the strength or the motivation to resist it. Neither did millions of others, a moral failure on a colossal scale. Eichmann orchestrated the Holocaust—which is in a totally different dimension than the silent collusion of ordinary German citizens. Whether Arendt was right in her judgment of Eichmann or whether she was a victim of his acting has been contested, but the core idea of what she famously called *the banality of evil* has since been amply confirmed in countless experiments: average people can commit above-average immoral acts without any sense of disturbance. As Arendt wrote in a letter to Gershom Scholem in 1963: "Evil possesses neither depth nor any demonic dimension. It can overgrow and lay waste the whole world precisely because it spreads like a fungus on the surface."[13]

We hasten to point to the heated controversy between historians Christopher Browning, author of *Ordinary Men*, who blamed context for why ordinary people like you and me could be seduced into committing atrocious acts, and Daniel Goldhagen, author of *Hitler's Willing Executioners*, who argued that the Third Reich was only possible because antisemitism was deeply rooted in society and therefore also in people.[14] In our opinion, there is truth in both sides, and in fact it takes two to tango: on the one hand, context can be a strong determinant of behavior, but on the other hand, people also have their share of personal blame. Obviously, in any evil system, many people play the role assigned to them. Often, they feel that they have no other options. Some, however, and Eichmann is certainly one of them, do not just play a role; they help write the script. In this sense, a continuum of evil certainly exists—both for the character of those involved and the magnitude of their deeds. However, we are not so much interested in somehow placing Eichmann and millions of others on this continuum. Rather, we want to point out that we are not just dealing with people who we then categorize as good or bad apples, but that we must also consider the context in which people find themselves—and which they, in turn, create for others.

UNETHICAL BEHAVIOR

Jeff Skilling and Andrew Fastow: knights and willing executioners of neoliberalism from top business schools. Dennis Gioia: an idealistic flower-power child of the Woodstock generation. Adolf Eichmann: a boring bureaucrat serving under Hitler. It can hardly be assumed that they were born as bad apples or even monsters and set out to produce evil. How did they see themselves? In their compliance trainings, companies often advise their employees to apply a simple rule of thumb to assess the morality of their own decisions: Can I still look in the mirror tomorrow if I make this decision today? Will I still be able to look my children in the face? Would it be okay for me if what I did today was in the newspaper tomorrow? Today, Fastow tells his story as a speaker at corporate events. There, he points out that he was initially praised and honored for the same behavior for which he was later locked up as a criminal. He would probably have been able to answer the questions about the mirror, the children, and the newspaper with a clear and sincere yes. Today, Gioia also gives lectures on business ethics, and he too was convinced at the time that he was doing the right thing. Even Eichmann was proud to have fulfilled his Kantian duty well—for the good of the people and the regime he served. We can assume that our protagonists are interchangeable. Had they not been in their places, it would probably have been another graduate from a top university, another idealistic do-gooder, and another bureaucrat whose name we would know today. Who among us can say "it wouldn't have happened to me"?

For all these people, context played a significant role in driving them to do what they did. This is one of the core theses of this book: *context can be stronger than reason, stronger than values and morals, and stronger than the best intentions.* This is by no means an excuse. Psychology, the science of human experience and behavior, is no "excusiology."[15] We are not robots; we almost always have a choice. Context may exert a strong pressure, but ultimately, we are still responsible for what we do. Relatedly, people operate in contexts, but contexts are in turn made by people. Our analysis of corporate scandals does not minimize but, on the contrary, extends the responsibility of decision-makers in organizations: not only are we responsible for our own actions, but we are also responsible for what context we create for others.

It takes two to tango: the person and the context. Both must be carefully analyzed to understand what happened in a scandal. While our analysis will show how strong contextual pressures transform good people into unethical decision-makers, we first need to understand what exactly happens in the minds of people as they go through this process of transformation from good to evil before we can examine the context pressures that drive such a transformation.

We distinguish between two types of unethical behavior: the kind where the bad apples engage and the kind where we ordinary people potentially engage. In other words, we distinguish between bad things done by bad people and bad things done by good or at least average people.

The story of the bad people is rather simple. Some people want to harm other people or break some rules. Sometimes they want to take revenge or restore justice, and sometimes they simply enjoy doing harm. Many of them are psychopaths. Psychopathy is a clinical phenomenon that is studied and treated by psychiatrists. Perhaps such psychopaths have not received enough love or attention and now want to make some innocent people suffer so that they are not alone. Or they want to show themselves or others that they have power. We know that antisocial behavior is hardwired into the brains of some people.[16] However, a book on why bad people do bad things would be rather boring. And it's not particularly useful to understand the biggest scandals where *many people* are involved.

Our second category is much more important for understanding organizational evil. Evil done by good people might start as a kind of collateral damage: we harm others as a side effect of pursuing our own interests. According to capitalist ideology, this is who we are as humans: *Homo economicus*. Taken to the extreme: we are greedy—and some more than others. We maximize our own benefit or, as businesses, our profit, and the invisible hand of free markets in turn ensures that this selfishness leads to prosperity for all. As the CEO of Goldman Sachs said in 2009, when his company was criticized in the aftermath of the financial crisis for again starting to pay lavish bonuses to their traders: "I am doing God's work."[17] Armed with such a narrative, we develop a certain tolerance for collateral damage. It is regrettable but unavoidable on our way to increasing efficiency and ensuring prosperity for all—starting with ourselves. Although we may feel deep down that selfish behavior is morally questionable, the rhetoric of the invisible hand certainly has the potential to soothe our conscience. Over time, and embedded in a context where people think like us, our decisions turn into a habit; the ethical questions disappear from our radar screen. They *fade away*, and we simply do not see them anymore when we make our decisions.[18]

Some years ago, and together with our colleague Franciska Krings, we labeled this phenomenon *ethical blindness*.[19] It describes the state where people deviate from their own values or principles when they make a decision. Importantly, ethical blindness is context bound, which makes it slippery. It can be a temporary state that disappears again when the context changes. In a state of ethical blindness, people are not aware of their unethical behavior, often deviating from their own values without realizing it. Only later, when they have been made aware of it, do they wake up, so to speak, and regret their behavior. They ask themselves: How could I have acted like that, and why didn't I see it at the time? Dennis Gioia also asked himself precisely this question at some point after he managed to distance himself from the corporate culture at Ford—a culture into which he had previously immersed himself, thereby burying his ideals before he cut his hair. So the question becomes this: What happens in a person's mind when they choose to move down this slippery slope to the dark side?

THE CONSTRUCTION OF REALITY

In a state of ethical blindness, we do not see the ethical dimensions of a decision. It would be naive to think there is one objective reality out there and that we each simply perceive it. What appears as perception is essentially based on a construction. We play an active role in this construction process but are usually not aware of it—and precisely because we somehow sleep through our own part in it, we assume that "our" reality is objective. But it is not. Consider a group taking part in a city tour, for instance: an architect, her fifteen-year-old daughter, a historian, a real-estate agent, his five-year-old son, a burglar, a sociology student, and so on. Although they take the same tour, they will see and later remember completely different things. This process of selective perception, which ultimately results in what we consider to be reality, is controlled by what psychologists call *frames*. One can think here of a picture frame, the purpose of which is to help the viewer of a picture separate it from its surroundings and concentrate on what's inside.

When social scientists use the word "frames," they use it as a metaphor to refer to mental structures that simplify and guide our understanding of a complex reality.[20] Frames filter. They focus our attention. They force us to view the world from a particular, and limited, perspective. They structure the information that comes to us from outside. As a result, we only see a snippet of reality, a simplified representation, a very subjective interpretation. Frames inherently come with blind spots. In 1605, philosopher Francis Bacon described this phenomenon precisely when he wrote that "if you put the light in one corner, you darken the rest."[21] Focusing our attention on something necessarily means that we do not see something else. For example, you cannot look *at* a windowpane and *through* a windowpane at the same time. We also find such layers of reality in the navigation systems of our smartphones, where we are asked to tell the system whether we are traveling on foot, by car, or by public transport, as this determines which snippet of reality the system uses when it displays our surroundings and makes recommendations.

Framing is very important for understanding the hidden dynamics of a scandal: what an observer sees *from the outside* as immoral, irrational, or obviously wrong may be perceived as rational, morally right, or without alternative from the point of view of the decision-maker who is *inside* of the organization. In certain situations, it is obviously difficult for people to see beyond the boundaries of their own context. They are trapped in their respective frames and thereby limited in their perception of the world. Individuals then continue to act rationally, but only within the framework of their immediate situation and only in relation to the decision-making routine that they have developed, and which has been successful to date. They cannot see what lies outside this context and they themselves cannot adopt the role of the neutral observer of their own decision. In this state, they can easily become blind to certain dimensions of their decisions and, tragically, this also applies to the moral dimension. They then make wrong (that is, unethical) decisions but think they have done the right thing.

The construction of so-called reality can go wrong in two ways. While frames can prevent us from seeing certain things even though they are there, it can also happen that we are convinced we have seen things that were not there, or that we remember things that never happened.[22] Surprisingly, such "inventions" have even been demonstrated in autobiographical memory.[23] Imagine you are shown a photo of yourself flying in a hot-air balloon with your father. You are perhaps five or six years old in the photo. You are then asked whether you remember the flight and asked not to omit any detail, no matter how trivial. Fifty percent of the respondents who were shown just such a photo reported more or less clear memories of the flight. Well, the photos were photoshopped. The interviewees had never been in such a balloon as a small child. Their memories were wrong, but participants were not aware of this. One of the participants was even "pretty certain that mum is down on the ground taking a photo."[24] Psychologists call this phenomenon *confabulation*: the ability of our brain to add details—ultimately inventing them—so a coherent story emerges that we then believe ourselves.[25] This construction work can therefore also be interpreted as conflict resolution.[26] To these interesting insights into human cognition, we can add one more: in some extreme cases, we even invent the *entire narrative* that guides our decisions.

Dorothy Martin, a housewife from Chicago, regularly received messages from aliens who called themselves the "Guardians." Among other things, Sananda, one of these guardians, announced that on December 21, 1954, a great flood would wipe out all of humanity. Only Dorothy Martin and a small group of chosen ones would be saved, picked up by a spaceship on a hill that the Guardians announced as a landing site. On December 21, this small group set off to be flown out. Some of them had quit their jobs and given away their possessions and now sat on this hill waiting. Waiting with them was a psychologist, Leon Festinger, who had claimed to be a follower of Dorothy Martin's Guardian narrative but was actually using the situation as a social-psychology research project (today, such a morally dubious research method would no longer be possible).[27] To everyone's surprise—except Festinger, probably—no spaceship came. Not that day and not the next. And there was no flood either. Festinger's research question was a simple one: What happens when the narrative in which people believe collides with the facts that they observe? As children of the Enlightenment, we would expect people to decide in favor of the facts and against the narrative in such a case. On the hill, however, the opposite happened. The group began to *rationalize* and thus resolve the *cognitive dissonance*—this is what Festinger called the tension between beliefs and observable facts. As they told each other, the spaceship would come later. Dorothy Martin didn't get the message precisely right. The Guardians had decided to spare the Earth, and so on. The facts were interpreted in such a way that the spaceship narrative did not have to be abandoned.

As Festinger's report shows, the construction of reality in our minds not only takes place in relation to perceptions (What was seen on the city tour?), but also extends to *causal explanations* (Where did the inner voices that Dorothy Martin heard come from? Why did the aliens not come?). Indeed, the construction of reality goes hand in hand with the construction of narratives, and these narratives can be quite robust even if they are distorted: contradictory evidence is then turned around, information is selectively processed, and warning signals are ignored.[28]

If you now think that this can happen to individuals here and there, but that groups of people could help each other with a reality check: far from it. In the group around Dorothy Martin, the members tended to confirm each other in their narrative of the extraterrestrials. When the construction of reality takes place in a social setting, it is even stronger and can indeed very easily become dangerous. An extreme example would be the Peoples Temple Agricultural Project in northwest Guyana, founded by Jim Jones and secluded from the world, which tragically ended in a mass suicide (and several murders) in November 1978.[29] Among the much milder and more modern examples are the numerous echo chambers and filter bubbles in social media, in which people gather around a common narrative and support each other in their opinions and beliefs. The members of such a group become each other's context and thus create a microworld of mutually reinforcing shared beliefs that can differ considerably from the world outside. From an internal perspective, many things look very different than they do to outsiders. Conversely, it is often difficult for outsiders to understand why someone within the group has done this or not done that.

When social groups collaborate in the construction of a distorted reality, their cognitive dissonances might have an ethical dimension, too. Very often, they will deal with those inner conflicts. They will remove moral doubts and contradictions through rationalizations because, as we have seen, we all want to see ourselves as good people. The scandal of Purdue Pharma and McKinsey is a frightening demonstration to this effect.

Until a few decades ago, the only powerful treatment existing for chronic pain was morphine, which is highly addictive and was thus exclusively used to ease the pain of patients in palliative care. Then, in the early 1980s, Purdue Pharma invented a special coating technology for pills that could regulate the diffusion of a drug into the bloodstream. It started to coat morphine pills, selling them as MS Contin. Purdue started to market the drug in the United States. However, the Food and Drug Administration (FDA) had limited the sale of morphine solely to terminal cancer patients. What if their pain could be treated without side effects? Purdue developed a new painkiller, called OxyContin, with the intention to mass-market it, and claimed that it was nonaddictive.

Purdue found some powerful support. Russell Portenoy, professor of neurology and the head of a new center of pain medicine at Beth Israel Medical Center in New York, who was called the "King of Pain," argued live on CBS's *60 Minutes* that opioids were not addictive. In reality, no serious scientific studies existed. The main reference point for these bold claims was a short note published in the most prestigious medical journal, the *New England Journal of Medicine*, in 1980. This was not a peer-reviewed scientific article, but rather a few-sentences-long letter to the editor (!), in which the authors argued that in a hospital study, fewer than 1 percent of patients got addicted to opioids. This was not a serious clinical study, and claims were based on a short-term observation of a few patients during their (controlled) stay at the hospital. It had no value for the question of whether opioids were addictive if prescribed over the course of months or years. Amazingly, over the following years, hundreds of medical articles would cite this letter as evidence for the nonaddictive character of opioids.[30] In 1990, for instance, *Scientific*

American called it a "tragedy" that patients would suffer "needless pain" and argued that "contrary to popular belief," opioids were nonaddictive. And the *New York Times* argued that the problem was not the drug but the patients abusing it.[31]

Purdue convinced the FDA that OxyContin was nonaddictive. It was given the right to market the drug with this claim, and between 1996 and 2002 it financed 20,000 trainings on chronic-pain treatment where doctors learned that opioids were nonaddictive. In a promotional video patients could watch in doctors' waiting rooms, Purdue asserted: "The rate of addiction among pain patients who are treated by doctors is much less than one percent."[32] Elderly patients with arthritis, war veterans with chronic pain, and even teenagers were targets of Purdue's marketing efforts. In 2010, one in four teenagers with back pain were prescribed painkillers, and one in ten teenagers received opioids for headaches.[33] Doctors now felt obliged to routinely check for pain, next to blood pressure, pulse, temperature, and breathing, and OxyContin gave them a seemingly easy fix for their suffering patients.[34]

While Purdue was making billions in profit with their painkiller blockbuster, suddenly alarming letters arrived at its headquarters. "My son was only 28 years old when he died from OxyContin on New Year's Day," a mother wrote to the company. Rural states across the US were the first to face massive problems with addiction. It hit the working class: truck drivers, nurses, firefighters, and ironworkers would overdose on the painkiller. For Purdue, however, the problem was not the drug, but the abuse by some patients (more precisely, just 1 percent of them!). As the company's president, Richard Sackler, angrily argued, the solution was to "hammer on the abusers in every possible way.... They are the culprits.... They are reckless criminals."[35] Many OxyContin victims even shared this narrative themselves. Some of them felt ashamed of their addiction.[36]

Then, US authorities started to investigate. In 2007, Purdue settled the investigation with a fine of $634.5 million for having minimized the addiction risk of its painkiller to doctors, regulators, and patients.[37] This did not stop Purdue from producing and selling OxyContin. Nor did it change its aggressive marketing strategy. It even hired McKinsey to boost OxyContin sales. The consulting firm proposed a new incentive scheme that would help with "turbocharging Purdue's Sales Engine," as the consultants called it.[38] Over the following years, OxyContin would bring billions in profit while triggering probably the biggest human-caused epidemic. The painkiller became a "death trap," as a New York prosecutor would later conclude. In 2020, Purdue Pharma pleaded guilty to criminal charges, agreeing to pay substantial fines and filing for bankruptcy as part of a settlement to resolve thousands of lawsuits. McKinsey also settled the case without admitting any guilt.[39]

Purdue succeeded in reframing chronic pain as a problem that could be treated by a bottle of pills without dangerous side effects. Pain experts, regulators, doctors, journalists, and even patients themselves not only bought into this baseless claim—the frame was institutionalized and became deeply embedded in the belief system of all stakeholders involved. And the addiction problem? The many people overdosing on OxyContin? The fact that contradicted the narrative, like the spaceship that did not come? Those making money with the painkiller rationalized it away as a problem created by the morally doubtful and often criminal drug abusers themselves. We do not know whether the Sacklers and Purdue leaders believed in their own rationalization, but the framing worked for their stakeholders and kept the money flowing. And McKinsey? It acted fully aligned with its corporate "values" that are very simple and consider only two stakeholders: clients and McKinsey consultants.[40]

Festinger's spaceship story is a prime example of how people can collectively develop a distorted perception of their reality and how this can have devastating effects. Those who perceive the world in such a distorted framework tend to rationalize away the cognitive dissonance they feel. And as the Purdue/McKinsey example shows, they also manage to push away the moral consequences of their behavior.

MORAL DISENGAGEMENT

Since people find it difficult to live with moral conflicts, they usually try to distance themselves from the ethically dubious things they have done (or are doing or will continue to do). Psychologist Albert Bandura has labeled such distancing as *moral disengagement*.[41] Cognitive dissonances do not simply go away; we have to invest some energy, consciously or unconsciously, to *make them go away*.

People who are able to morally disengage from an unethical action are more likely to perform that action. Why? We all have moral norms, and we use these norms to regulate our behavior. Any behavior that violates our norms is usually recognized as such, and our self-regulatory control mechanisms ensure that we do not commit such acts. Conversely, any successful attempt to construct our own reality and narratives in such a way that the norms do not apply or the problems become invisible may just offset the self-regulatory processes that normally ensure that people behave in accordance with their moral standards.

There are several mechanisms we can use to morally disengage. The first three mechanisms are about how behavior is seen and evaluated. *Moral justification* basically means that unethical behavior is seen as morally justified, which in turn makes it socially acceptable. Examples of this would be using torture to obtain information necessary to protect others, or the justification of holy terror through religious principles. *Euphemistic labeling* can serve to make harmful behavior respectable and reduce responsibility for it. For example, military attacks are labeled "clean, surgical strikes," victims are referred to as "collateral damage," and terrorists call themselves "freedom fighters." Indeed, language plays a crucial role in the construction of reality, which we will discuss in more detail later. An *advantageous comparison* contrasts one's own harmful behavior with the clearly harmful behavior of someone else, thereby trivializing one's own immoral behavior. For example, American military interventions during the Vietnam War led to massive destruction, and these actions were portrayed as saving the local population from communist enslavement.

The next mechanism is about the detrimental effects. A bad conscience can also be assuaged by *minimizing, ignoring, or misconstruing the consequences*. It is relatively easy to harm others if the harmful consequences of one's own actions are ignored, if they are not visible, if they are not associated with one's own actions, or if they are realized at a very distant location. Psychologically, it makes a difference whether someone kills a sleeping victim with a knife or whether he uses a computer mouse and a screen to control a drone to kill that person.

The next two mechanisms of moral disengagement focus on the link between action and effect. The *displacement of responsibility* distorts the link between actions and the consequences they cause. It is easier for people to do something unethical if a legitimate authority has ordered it and takes responsibility for the consequences. In such a case, the performer of an inhumane action will no longer perceive it as their own action; they are only the functionary. They only produce the effect, but the action, the real actor, is someone else. Remember what Hannah Arendt said about the banality of evil and the Adolf Eichmann trial. Eichmann argued that he was just a loyal bureaucrat following orders. The *diffusion of responsibility* becomes particularly apparent in very large groups. If everyone is responsible, no one is responsible. Collective action provides anonymity, which allows for a weakening of moral control. In a large group, it is in fact very easy for each group member to perceive their own share and influence as minimal. So why should you be the one to do something—or refrain from doing something unethical—when so many are in the same situation as you?

The last two mechanisms of moral disengagement are related to the victim. *Blaming the victim* makes it easier to harm him or her because, after all, the victim somehow deserved it. A perpetrator can later say, for example, that the other person started the whole argument with a few provocations. This triggered justified defense reactions, and in the end the original attacker was, oops, suddenly and somehow dead. So, the victim is portrayed as the bad guy, and what happened was their own fault. The *dehumanization of the victim* means that they are no longer seen as an individual with feelings, hopes, and worries, but rather as an object or an animal. This process of animalistic dehumanization is most often achieved through the use of metaphors. For example, the Nazis regularly compared Jews to "rats," and during the genocide in Rwanda in the 1990s, the Hutu usually referred to the Tutsi as "cockroaches" in their propaganda. Killing a human being is certainly more difficult than killing a disgusting animal.

The construction of reality and the development of moral standards unfold over time. Relatedly, becoming ethically blind should be seen as a process. When managers make unethical decisions in organizations, probably all of them experience a conflict at the beginning, and some will suffer continuously. The majority, however, will presumably succeed in "resolving" the conflict. They morally disengage and over time, the inappropriate behavior is routinized. The inner conflict fades away. In this way, what begins as a conflict can turn into a thoughtless habit that is repeated without further thought.

It is not easy to navigate the complexities of modern life. Ethical and unethical behavior is a fascinating but thorny area. It is often not easy to judge the actions and omissions of others who have gone through a certain dynamic (which we have not), who act in a certain context (which we do not experience), and who therefore see the world around them from their point of view (which is not ours). People in organizations can develop a totally distorted idea of reality. We have shown how this process unfolds in their minds through framing, confabulation, and moral disengagement. As we have already highlighted, this process is driven by contextual forces. Context can be stronger than reason. We now turn to the question of what context can do and what role it plays in the processes of becoming ethically blind. What are the forces that drive good people to do bad things?

2
THE POWER OF CONTEXT

Individual decision-makers play an important role in every scandal, but that is only half the truth. It always takes two to tango. People are embedded in a context, and contexts can distort their perception of reality and render them ethically blind. This power of context can be found in all companies involved in a scandal. However, instead of starting with a discussion of context in general, we invite you to a very strange place. The following fairy tale by Hans Christian Andersen will help us to illustrate the power of context.[1]

"THE EMPEROR'S NEW CLOTHES"

Once upon a time there lived a vain emperor whose only worry in life was to dress in elegant clothes. He changed clothes almost every hour and loved to show them off to his people. Word of the emperor's refined habits spread over his kingdom and beyond. Two scoundrels who had heard of the emperor's vanity decided to take advantage of it. They introduced themselves at the gates of the palace to the guards with a scheme in mind: "We are two very good tailors, and after many years of research we have invented an extraordinary method to weave a cloth so light and fine that it looks invisible. As a matter of fact, it is invisible to anyone who is too stupid and incompetent to appreciate its quality."

The guards sent them to the chief of the guards, who heard the scoundrels' strange story and sent for the court chamberlain. The chamberlain notified the prime minister, who ran to the emperor and disclosed the incredible news. The emperor's curiosity got the better of him, and he decided to see the two scoundrels. "Besides being invisible, Your Highness, this cloth will be woven in colors and patterns created especially for you." The emperor gave the two men a bag of gold coins in exchange for their promise to begin working on the fabric immediately.

"Just tell us what you need to get started, and we'll give it to you." The two scoundrels asked for a loom, silk, and gold thread and then pretended to begin working. The emperor thought he had spent his money quite well: in addition to getting a new extraordinary suit, he would discover which of his subjects were ignorant and incompetent. A few days later, he called the old and wise prime minister, who was considered by everyone as a man with common sense. "Go and see how the work is proceeding," the emperor told him, "and come back to let me know."

The prime minister was welcomed by the two scoundrels. "We're almost finished, but we need a lot more gold thread. Here, Excellency! Admire the colors, feel the softness!" The old man bent over the loom and tried to see the fabric that was not there. He felt cold sweat on his forehead. "I can't see anything," he thought. "If I see nothing, that means I'm stupid! Or, worse, incompetent!" If the prime minister admitted that he didn't see anything, he would be discharged from his office. "What a marvelous fabric," he said then. "I'll certainly tell the emperor." The two scoundrels rubbed their hands gleefully. They had almost made it. More thread was requested to finish the work.

A few days later, the emperor sent another trusted official to observe the weavers' progress. This man was a courtier of high rank, known for his keen eye and refined taste. As he entered the room, he saw the two swindlers busy at their looms, working with all their might at empty frames. "Goodness gracious," he thought, "I see nothing at all. Is it possible that I am a fool?" he wondered in dismay. "Or perhaps unworthy of my office?" But he kept his thoughts to himself, went back, and reported to the emperor that the work was proceeding splendidly.

Finally, the emperor received the announcement that the two tailors had come to take all the measurements needed to sew his new suit. "Come in," the emperor ordered. Even as they bowed, the two scoundrels pretended to be holding a large roll of fabric. "Here it is, Your Highness, the result of our labor," the scoundrels said. "We have worked night and day, but at last, the most beautiful fabric in the world is ready for you. Look at the colors and feel how fine it is." Of course, the emperor did not see any colors and could not feel any cloth between his fingers. He panicked and felt like fainting. But luckily the throne was right behind him and he sat down. But when he realized that no one could know that he did not see the fabric, he felt better. Nobody could find out he was stupid and incompetent. And the emperor didn't know that everybody else around him thought and did the very same thing.

The farce continued as the two scoundrels had foreseen it. Once they had taken the measurements, the two began cutting the air with scissors while sewing with their needles an invisible cloth. "Your Highness, you'll have to take off your clothes to try on your new ones." The two scoundrels draped the new clothes on him and then held up a mirror. The emperor was embarrassed but since none of his bystanders were, he felt relieved. "Yes, this is a beautiful suit and it looks very good on me," the emperor said, trying to look comfortable. "You've done a fine job."

"Your Majesty," the prime minister said, "we have a request for you. The people have found out about this extraordinary fabric, and they are anxious to see you in your new suit." The emperor was doubtful about showing himself naked to the people, but then he abandoned his fears. After all, no one would know about it except the ignorant and the incompetent. "All right," he said. "I will grant the people this privilege." He summoned his carriage, and the ceremonial parade was formed. A group of dignitaries walked at the very front of the procession and anxiously scrutinized the faces of the people in the street. All the people had gathered in the main square, pushing and shoving to get a better look. An applause welcomed the regal procession. Everyone wanted to know how stupid or incompetent his or her neighbor was, but as the emperor passed, a strange murmur rose from the crowd.

Everyone said, loud enough for the others to hear: "Look at the emperor's new clothes. They're beautiful!" "What a marvelous train!" "And the colors! The colors of that beautiful fabric! I have never seen anything like it in my life!" They all tried to conceal their disappointment at not being able to see the clothes, and since nobody was willing to admit his own stupidity and incompetence, they all behaved as the two scoundrels had predicted.

A child, however, who had no important job and could only see things as his eyes showed them to him, went up to the carriage. "The emperor is naked," he said. "Fool!" his angry father reprimanded, running after him. "Don't talk nonsense!" He grabbed his child and took him away. But the boy's remark, which had been heard by the bystanders, was repeated over and over again until everyone cried: "The boy is right! The emperor is naked! It's true!" The emperor felt that the people were right but could not admit to that. He thought it better to continue the procession under the illusion that anyone who couldn't see his clothes was either stupid or incompetent. And he stood stiffly on his carriage, while behind him a page held his imaginary mantle.

ONLY IN FAIRY TALES?

Many of us have read Andersen's fairy tale of the emperor's new clothes to our children, or our parents read it to us when we were children ourselves. Most children show the same reaction to the story. They find it very funny and are astonished by the strange and ridiculous behavior of the various actors. Children easily identify with the seemingly only reasonable person in an otherwise pathological environment—the little boy. And for the rest of us, the way this story plays out may still seem far-fetched (as many fairy tales do). Nothing like this would happen in the real world. In the real world, reason would interfere, and the two tailors would have been exposed as what they really were: crooks with a stupid story. In the real world, the guards at the gate would have chased them away or even put them in prison. After all, their job was to keep the emperor safe. Or, if the guards were really that stupid, their superior would have seen through the story. In any case, the court chamberlain or, as a last resort, the wise prime minister would have revealed the lie instead of disturbing the emperor. There were many layers of gatekeeping between the crooks and the emperor. The emperor himself would not have walked the streets of his kingdom naked, or else the crowd would have laughed at this strange procession with the royal page holding an imaginary mantle.

Well, the power of reason should not be overestimated. We regularly use this fairy tale as a case study in our courses with students or in workshops with managers when we teach the concept of ethical blindness. One reaction we regularly get from practitioners is this: "The story reminds me of my own organization...." So, it might be useful to have a closer look at the dynamic of the story and the behavior of the different actors.

Fear and Defensive Decision-Making
Let us begin by looking at the fairy tale and trying to imagine how the various actors feel. In what kind of atmosphere does the story unfold? Ask yourself, what sentiment might dominate the kingdom and thus influence the behavior of the various actors? The cold sweat on the forehead of the old and wise prime minister or the panic of the little boy's father gives us a clear hint. This strange kingdom is ruled by fear. The guard, the chief of the guards, and the court chamberlain know about the predilection of the emperor for beautiful clothes. They cannot dare to chase the presumed tailors away. The emperor would certainly boil with rage if he found out about the missed opportunity. They are all terrified of making a wrong decision and being punished for it by their absolute ruler. The prime minister turns pale. He can't see the cloth and decides to lie to the emperor. So does the second official. They fear losing their office. People in the crowd certainly fear the punishment of the emperor, but also the evaluation of their neighbors left and right. You do not want to stick out as stupid if everybody else is competent! The little boy's father panics, because he fears being punished for the spontaneous shouting of his son. All of them are terribly afraid of something, and they show a very common reaction to fear: they don't dare to use their own brains and rather stick to what seems to be a shared interpretation of the

situation. They take each other as reference points for interpreting their reality. And finally, even the emperor himself is getting nervous and does not dare to admit that he can't see anything.

Fear is also one of the dominating feelings in many modern organizations. Fear of not living up to expectations of a superior, fear of being marginalized by one's peers, fear of the time pressure and complexity of the work, fear of not making that quota, fear of mistakes, fear of being aggressed, harassed, humiliated, or expelled from the system. It is not without irony that organizations harm themselves when they keep their members in a state of fear. Being accountable for one's actions and decisions has an impact on how those actions and decisions will turn out.[2] When managers are afraid of being punished if something goes wrong, they often do not choose the option that they believe is best for the organization but instead make defensive decisions and choose the option that allows them to "cover their ass."[3]

The two crooks know what to do—they play on that fear. Playing on fears is quite a common strategy for switching off reason in others. Who creates the fear? Obviously, in an autocratic system such as this once-upon-a-time kingdom, it must be the emperor himself. It is probably the only way for an absolute ruler to stabilize autocratic structures: to create or use the fears of others to reinforce his own domination over their lives. Without fear, people would use their own reason, which is probably the biggest threat to authoritarian structures in social systems of any type and size. Interestingly, fear is contagious even for those who create it in the first place: in our story the emperor is afraid as well. This is quite surprising, given that he is the one who created this terror regime under which his entourage does not dare to make a mistake. As in Mary Shelley's Gothic novel *Frankenstein*, in the end, the monster crushes his own creator.

Values and Frames
This depressed atmosphere of the kingdom makes it easy for the two crooks to push their story forward, up to the ruler himself. However, this is not the only reason why such an astonishingly silly story can unfold such a powerful dynamic. Beyond any doubt, the two crooks are good observers, and they know how to tell their story in order to catch the interest of the emperor. Why does the emperor so easily buy the story? Vanity? Well, vanity plays a role. However, if the two had come with a new powerful weapon for his army, an enchanted flower for his garden, or a training for better governmental speeches, the guards would not even have bothered going to their superior and telling the story. As we know, the emperor has one and only one interest: a passion for clothes and the desire to express his vanity by exhibiting exciting outfits in front of others. So, it is not general vanity but his special form of vanity that opens the door for the two crooks. The emperor has a particular way of perceiving the world: today we would probably describe him as a fashion victim. Clothes are his one and only interest in life. Everything else is just noise for him and is filtered out of his worldview. It does not fit into his framework and therefore no longer reaches him. The two crooks have tailored their story to him and take advantage of his tunnel vision. As we explained in the first chapter, we use frames to interpret the world and make sense of it. However, if our frames get too narrow, as in the case of the emperor, we paint an inappropriate picture of reality and thus risk making flawed decisions.

Mistrust in One's Own Judgment and Groupthink
Let us return to the prime minister for a moment. What does he actually *see*? Well, the answer seems obvious. He sees nothing. In fact, nobody in this story actually sees any cloth, because there is nothing

to be seen in the first place. The much more interesting question is, what does he think as he sees nothing—What does he *believe*? Does he see through the ruse of the two crooks but fear that the emperor will not believe him? Is he aware of the fact that there is nothing but does not dare to report this to the emperor? In this case, he would just be a coward who lies. Well, as we are told in the story, he is not a very courageous man, but look at his knee-jerk reaction when the two tailors invite him to admire the cloth. He turns pale. He gets nervous. He has cold sweat on his forehead. He is convinced that *there is something*, but he cannot see it. In his fantasy, he imagines the cloth. What makes him nervous is not that he must report to the emperor that the cloth doesn't exist, thus deeply disappointing his ruler. No, he panics because he cannot see what he believes everyone else can see, or at least what any competent person can see. The cloth must be invisible to him because he is incompetent! He buys the story of the tailors, and he mistrusts his own judgment. He does not question the story, which is imposed on him by the two crooks. Instead, he questions himself. He actually *feels* incompetent. And so does the advisor who comes after him. Both politicians try to cover up their apparent incompetence. Both of them have something to lose, and their fear makes them praise the quality of the cloth that does not exist. Pathological contexts in organizations often unfold because the actors within the system do not question the routines, opinions, and behaviors of others, whether because they manage to convince themselves that there is something wrong with their own judgment, or because they fear the consequences of defying others.

Tunnel Vision and Outside View

And what about the boy? One might argue that in contrast to the other actors in the story, he has nothing to lose and thus can tell the truth. But this does not really convince as an explanation. The little boy is not thinking in such categories. He is not making an ad hoc calculation like the other actors who try to save their position. He is simply shouting out what he thinks. He does not reflect upon it. His reaction is spontaneous. Unframed. Indeed, if he had thought in win-lose categories, he probably would not have dared to say anything, because he indeed has something to lose. His father is angry; he is grabbing him, pulling him back, harshly ordering him to shut up. In this moment, the little boy probably realizes that he made a big mistake—but only after his father had placed him into the context of this kingdom. When he spontaneously shouts out that the emperor is naked, he does so from the same position we have as readers of this fairy tale: without fear and without opportunistic calculation. And that makes him, on the face of it, the only rational actor in this otherwise-mad kingdom. But we should not forget that rationality can be understood as the appropriate use of means to achieve ends, which ties the concept of rationality to context. The adult actors in the kingdom behave perfectly rationally, after all—their behavior helps them to keep their office, their dignity, the recognition of the others, their self-assurance, and their place in a world dominated by fear. All other behavioral options might disrupt their life. From *inside* the context of this story their behavior makes sense. Only for us, with *outside* perspective, does their behavior seem irrational. This difference between the inside and outside views has been observed in numerous corporate scandals as well: what seems to be highly unethical, irrational, and inappropriate from outside (and with hindsight) might look different from inside the context—and actors inside are often not able to take the broader perspective of the outside observer.

Comfortably Numb

Under certain conditions, the context in which we make our decisions is stronger than our ability to use our own reason, our good intentions, our interests, or our values. This becomes evident if we look at the probably most underestimated element of the fairy tale. How does it end? The boy reveals the nakedness of the emperor, the crowd confirms this perspective, and the emperor suddenly *feels* naked and embarrassed. But what does he do? He continues the procession as if nothing had happened! The updated perception of reality does not trigger a change in his behavior, nor in that of his page or the other dignitaries following behind. The same can be observed in many corporate scandals. The fact that inside the organizations illegal practices get criticized does not mean that such practices are disrupted immediately. Long before illegal practices erupt in public scandals, often leading to multibillion-dollar damages, people inside the organization have realized that there is something wrong with how they do things. And yet, they might not see an alternative or perceive any alternative as worse and thus continue.

Escalation of Commitment

The context in which the protagonists of the story make their decisions and act is shaped by the powerful phenomena that we examined already: the atmosphere of fear, the narrow framing of the emperor, the mistrust of individuals in their own judgments, the pressure of the group. However, the idea of a strong context goes beyond those phenomena. Let us have a closer look at the dynamics that unfold between the prime minister, the advisor, and the emperor. On the surface, there seems to be no big difference in their reaction to the story. All of them are exposed to the same situation by the two crooks. All of them get nervous, feel incompetent, and decide to lie. However, there is one big difference between the three. They are not exposed to the *same* situation. The story escalates from the minister to the advisor to the emperor. The decision of the minister to confirm the story of the crooks makes it more difficult for the advisor not to believe the story. Put yourself in the shoes of the second official. Rumors spread across the castle that two tailors have arrived with this marvelous ability to weave an invisible cloth. Everyone in the castle has heard about it and talks about it. The advisor sees the minister going to the workshop and returning. He hears him confirming the story with his own ears. He is the next to be sent out, for a second evaluation. All those elements of the story are his context. In particular, the confirmation of the prime minister that the cloth exists becomes a key element of his own decision-making context. It is not difficult to imagine that the prime minister's example makes a huge impression on the advisor, who goes next. For him, the context is different; it has become stronger. The testimonial of the prime minister has become a limiting parameter for his own evaluation. Put differently, one actor's action becomes the next actor's context.

And the pressure keeps growing. Finally the emperor himself goes. His two probably most trusted politicians have seen the cloth— Why should he question their evaluation of the tailors' work? He does not seem to be a very reflective and self-critical person anyway. He would certainly deny that the two advisors desperately try to see the cloth because of him and his leadership style. Rather, their feedback confirms his evaluation of their competence. And again, the context is different: the testimonial of both, the prime minister and the advisor, become an even stronger limiting parameter for the emperor himself. The situation escalates from one actor to the other and becomes ever stronger. Decisions become context. Gradually reality is shifted toward the narration of the two tailors. The stronger the context, the more difficult it becomes for individual actors to behave differently and to think differently. They are trapped in an escalating commitment to the story of the crooks.

We have seen the same dynamic at the beginning of the fairy tale: What is the role of a guard at a castle? He needs to keep danger out, shut the gate, and protect the castle. However, he is afraid as well; the situation is unclear, ambiguous. He has no instructions on how to deal with such requests. He sends the crooks to the chief of the guard, who sends them to the chamberlain, who sends them to the prime minister. Another escalation of commitment, and on each step the actors following the first decision will ask themselves: Who am I to challenge the decision of all those people who checked the situation before me and identified it as important to the emperor? The more people believe in the story, the more difficult it becomes not to believe in it. The system develops a reality that is sealed off and where all the actors inside mutually reconfirm the story to each other, reinforcing it and making it increasingly difficult not to believe in it.

THE DARK PATTERN: A ROAD MAP THROUGH CORPORATE HELL

At first glance, Andersen's fairy tale appears to be a story of *stupid people*, but upon closer inspection it turns out to be a story of a *pathological context* and its potential to eliminate independent judgment. It portrays how such a context can develop and how it can make it impossible for individual actors to act reasonably. The lesson to be learned from the fairy tale is straightforward: if you put people in a pathological context, there is a high probability that they will start to behave pathologically. Contexts can be stronger than reason. This is a bitter lesson—almost an insult to those of us who hold reason up as the ideal of enlightened modernity. But it's an important lesson—after all, every therapy must begin with an accurate diagnosis.

The fairy tale shows us some of the ingredients of strong contexts: fear and authoritarian leadership, the devastating effects of unrealistic goals, the pressure of group conformity, uncertainty about our own evaluations in ambiguous decision-making situations, and escalation of behavior over time. These phenomena exist in many organizations, and they can build similar powerful constellations as the one in this far-away kingdom. As we already stated in our introduction and in our first chapter, one cannot explain illegal and immoral practices in organizations by simply examining the bad behavior of some greedy individuals with character deficiencies, the so-called bad apples. No question: the behavior of the two crooks is clearly unethical and they know exactly what they are doing. Their evil is rationally planned. However, examining their strategy or motivation does not help us understand why all the other actors in the fairy tale do what they do. These people all become victims of the psychological mechanisms within them and the pathological context they create for each other. We will see more such pathological contexts in the scandals we analyze in the coming chapters. What we won't see there, however, are crooks approaching an organization from the outside with bad intentions. But that only makes the power of pathological contexts even more frightening—and more interesting: their malignant dynamics can unfold even without external crooks. We hasten to add: and even without bad apples. As we already saw when we revisited Skilling, Gioia, and Eichmann: the problem is not the apple but the barrel.[4]

What if we could analyze a scandal in an organization as we just did with Andersen's fairy tale? Throughout this book, we do exactly this. We take a look at some of the biggest scandals of the last two decades—Theranos, Uber, Wells Fargo, France Télécom (now Orange S.A.), Boeing, Volkswagen, and Foxconn—and ask to what extent the people involved have constructed their own reality, just as the emperor and his entourage did. Relatedly, we also compare the inside and outside perspective: obviously what the people involved in these cases did was irrational, unethical, and illegal, but could it have been perfectly reasonable, appropriate, and even ethically right from the inside? How did the context in which they acted contribute to what happened?

But before we take a closer look at some specific scandals, we will, in Chapter 3, sharpen our theoretical lenses that will allow us to see more clearly the underlying pattern and hidden dynamics unfolding in these scandals. And indeed, there is such a pattern. We call it the *dark pattern*. It constitutes the toxic context for the people working in an organization. At the same time, these people also had their share in creating the context that turned their organization into a microhell—this is how we understand Jean-Paul Sartre's statement that "hell is other people."[5]

Around 1320, Florentine poet Dante Alighieri published *La Divina Commedia* (*The Divine Comedy*), which was to become one of the defining texts of Western civilization. In this poem, he takes his readers on an imagined journey to heaven and through hell. *The Divine Comedy* begins with Dante, the narrator and protagonist, lost in a dark forest and pursued by wild beasts. He has lost his path and is lonely, full of fear, in the dark, desperate, thrown into a world he tries to understand. Dante is saved by the ancient Roman poet

Virgil, who agrees to guide him through the afterlife and help him find his way back to a straight path. Dante is in his thirties in the poem, "in the midway of this our mortal life." Old enough for some deep self-reflections, young enough to give his life a new and more moral direction. His passage through hell can be seen as a metaphor for this human journey toward self-discovery and personal growth on which we hopefully all have embarked. He takes his readers with him so that they can imagine hell and change course.

Dante's hell is orderly, with a clear topography of nine circles. It has the form of a medieval city with towers, walls, and streets. It looked very familiar to his contemporary readers. They might even have known many of the people appearing in it. This familiarity might also explain why his work had such a massive impact on the collective imagination of his time. He gave a shape to a rather unstructured understanding of the underworld in the Middle Ages.

Similarly, our corporate hell will look familiar to you, our readers. It also has an orderly and clear topography with nine building blocks, and it has the familiar form of the modern corporation. You probably even know many of the people appearing in it. Our dark pattern gives a shape to your maybe-rather-unstructured understanding of corporate scandals. And with that said: let us now descend into corporate hell!

3
THE DARK PATTERN

The dark pattern, as we see it, has nine building blocks. Each of them is, per se, neutral. There is nothing inherently wrong with *ideology, leaders, language, goals, incentives, rules, fairness, groups,* and *change*. Just as there is nothing wrong with a knife or a car—as long as these are used, for instance, to cut a tomato or to drive from point A to point B. However, both can also be used to kill someone. Likewise, any of the nine building blocks that characterize an organization can be misused, thereby paving the way for potentially disastrous outcomes. Moreover, the building blocks are mutually reinforcing, and "the whole is greater than the sum of its parts."[1] Even if none of the elements alone might be able to push an organization over the moral and legal edge, together they form a dark pattern—the recipe for moral and legal disaster. And often hell for those who have to work in such a setting. It is crucial to understand each building block so we can be aware of them creeping into our own organizations.

Before we present the nine building blocks of the dark pattern in more detail, here is a brief overview:

1. *Rigid ideology* is a shared belief system that narrows the view of decision-makers at the expense of other views, risking them losing sight of ethical dimensions.
2. *Toxic leadership* can create fearful contexts when narcissistic, Machiavellian, or psychopathic leaders abuse their power and cause harm, be it through direct orders, leading by example, or a carrot-and-stick approach.
3. *Manipulative language* restricts how things are perceived and evaluated, influencing people's judgments, decisions, and behaviors in ways that contribute to evil.
4. *Corrupting goals* and unrealistic targets divert people's attention so that they lose the ability to see the bigger picture in which their decisions are embedded—and the ethical dimension of their behavior.
5. *Destructive incentives* create a tunnel vision of reality and lead to unhealthy competition and fights.
6. *Ambiguous rules* create a gray area where people at best are confused and at worst can morally disengage when they do something bad because, after all, they were just following the rules.
7. *Perceived unfairness* can lead people to engage in illegal practices while feeling that they are restoring justice.
8. *Dangerous groups* may force individuals to conform, encourage aggression against members of out-groups, or pressure those who are considering speaking up not to do so.
9. Finally, people who are on a *slippery slope* may not realize how they are straying from the right path to the point of

escalating their commitment to evil things without even realizing how they have changed.

RIGID IDEOLOGY

In September 1970, Milton Friedman published his essay "The Social Responsibility of Business Is to Increase Its Profits," in the *New York Times*. His piece struck a chord amid mounting criticism of American corporations since the late 1960s, seen as bureaucratic entities and facing pressure from agile Japanese competitors. Urgent questions arose: How to enhance corporate competitiveness and innovation while ensuring managerial decisions aligned with shareholders' interests? Friedman's answer was clear: "In a free-enterprise, private-property system, a corporate executive is an employee of the owners of the business. He has direct responsibility to his employers. That responsibility is to conduct the business in accordance with their desires, which generally will be to make as much money as possible." Friedman argued that prioritizing profit maximization would foster innovation, bolster wealth, and restore American competitiveness. This was not about denying the existence of moral obligations beyond maximizing shareholder value. Rather, Friedman highlighted that such obligations existed for managers only *in their other roles* as churchgoers, parents, or citizens. In the same vein, McDonald's founder Ray Kroc once famously explained: "I believe in God, family, and McDonald's—and in the office that order is reversed."[2] Kroc could neatly classify his decisions into separate categories. Sure, God was important to him, and so was his family. But the office had its own divine rules.

When we make our decisions, we are typically not as autonomous as we may think. After all, we are born into a particular societal order with its beliefs, habits, and values. Such shared understandings of the world are important. Like large-scale cognitive maps they structure and guide our behavior noiselessly behind our backs. We call such shared understandings *ideology*. The world is overwhelmingly complex, and such a structured simplification helps us to navigate it.[3] At the same time, ideologies also limit what we can see and blind us to moral problems that come with the mindless and rigid enactment of established beliefs, values, and routines. In his book *Thinking, Fast and Slow*, Daniel Kahneman calls this "theory-induced blindness."[4]

The theoretical framework that Friedman laid out in his article would soon leave the ivory tower of the University of Chicago and start to shape economic and political decisions in the US and the UK. Widely known as *neoliberalism*, it has gone on to conquer the world. Today, managers across the globe tend to believe in "the magic of the marketplace," as former US president Ronald Reagan famously called it.[5] According to the neoliberal ideology, human beings are, by default, egoistic. Alan Greenspan, then the chairman of the Federal Reserve, argued in the 1990s that "it is precisely the greed of the businessman...which is the unexcelled protector of the consumer."[6] Our fellow citizens are for us either an obstacle or a means to achieve our own goals. We fiercely compete with them. Free markets on which egoists engage in their transactions are the best mechanism to produce welfare for all—the magic trick. Under the pressure of competition, companies become more efficient and improve their products. Innovation occasionally disrupts markets completely, and progress results from what the economist Joseph Schumpeter in the early days of nineteenth-century industrialization called the "creative destruction" of competition through game-changing innovations. In 1995, Harvard Business School professors Joseph Bower and Clayton Christensen modernized this idea by arguing that previously successful companies can well manage incremental technological change but often utterly fail to evaluate the potential of more radical changes. "Small, hungry organizations" are better positioned to reap the advantages of disruptive changes. They move faster than their big competitors and thereby disrupt entire markets.[7] As Mark Zuckerberg once famously told his Facebook team, "Unless you are breaking stuff, you are not moving fast enough."[8] Governments should interfere as little as possible in this interplay of market forces, because regulations reduce efficiency and limit freedom. It comes as no surprise that around the 1980s, several waves of deregulation and privatization hit the shores of Western societies as a result of this creed. Deregulation has continued since then.

It is only a small step from Ronald Reagan's "Government is not the solution to our problem, government is the problem" to considering the government as the enemy and moral and legal rules as obstacles to successful business.[9] Of course, managers who are trained to reduce their decisions to morally neutral mathematical calculations on behalf of shareholders, who are convinced that markets are fair, greed is good, laws are bad, and who aggressively try to disrupt their competition will not *necessarily* end up making unethical or illegal decisions. However, a too rigid and mindless enactment of such an ideological script will almost certainly create and promote an atmosphere where rule breaking becomes more probable. That is the dark side of ideologies. The firmer their grip, the harder it is to see the warning signals or to develop alternative ideas about the world.

There is compelling research demonstrating that people who come from business schools and make decisions in companies tend to execute the neoliberal narrative they were taught during their studies, and sometimes they push the magic of the market beyond the moral and legal breaking point.[10] The Enron scandal illustrates the effect. The company operated with a culture of extreme individualism, where aggressive cleverness was praised, making deals was the only yardstick, and rule following became increasingly optional. CEO Jeff Skilling constantly pushed the limits of his young traders who were hired from Wharton and Harvard. He expected them to beat the system and to find the holes in the rules of the game while making as many deals for Enron as possible. A former employee confessed that "it was all about an atmosphere of deliberately breaking the rules."[11] As Beth Schacter, one of the producers of a TV series on the Uber scandal, observed, "Disruption is often the soil that monsters grow in."[12]

TOXIC LEADERSHIP

In the early 1940s, Erich von Holst, a founding figure in behavioral ethology (the science of animal behavior), presented his work in the presence of a high official of Adolf Hitler's National Socialist Party (the NSDAP). When the official, intrigued by the ideological implications of biology, inquired whether animals exhibited a "Führer principle," von Holst explained one of his experiments to him. He had removed the forebrain of a minnow, a small freshwater fish. Minnows easily survive this surgery, but it changes their character. They lose any fear. The minnow is a schooling fish. The school has an anonymous structure; there is no hierarchy in it and no leader. Their movements are based on simple forms of synchronization. This changed immediately when von Holst returned the operated fish to the shoal. Now, all at once, everything hesitant had disappeared from the school's movement. The forebrainless animal, without any timidity, took the lead, went the way it felt like going, and the others, as if overwhelmed by so much determination, followed it blindly. As von Holst boldly told the NSDAP official: "So you see that it only takes a brain defect to make an individual become the leader of the group."[13]

Even though there are, of course, many differences between freshwater fish and us, von Holst's story may still inspire intriguing questions regarding dark dimensions of leadership in humans. For instance, could it be that some human leaders have some deficient—or dark—personality traits, and that they became leaders not *despite* but *because* of them? Relatedly, could it be that some leaders are built not to get *along with* others but to get *ahead of* others?[14] Even more importantly: Can their behavior influence or even drive the moral collapse of an entire organization?

In an influential article published in 2002, Delroy Paulhus and Kevin Williams investigated the psychometric properties of what they called the "dark triad of personality."[15] Their dark triad consists of narcissism, Machiavellianism, and psychopathy. *Narcissists* are characterized by vanity, arrogance, feelings of superiority, dominance, a strong need for admiration and entitlement, and a lack of empathy. When they enter a room, they fill it, attract people's attention, and dominate the conversation. *Machiavellians* are excessively motivated by self-interest. They are typically highly intelligent, unemotional, and callous. They use manipulative techniques to achieve goals, including exploiting, deceiving, and tricking others. For them, moral principles are just part of the overall equation, and the ends justify the means. *Psychopathy* is typically considered to be the most malevolent of the dark triad. Psychopaths are often characterized by continuous exploitative and antisocial behavior, interpersonal coldness, low levels of empathy, high impulsivity, thrill seeking, selfishness, and remorselessness. Now imagine a leader displaying all those character traits *combined*!

Scholars have found that within any larger community, a subgroup of people with the dark triad personality exists.[16] Unfortunately, in corporations, they are not only overrepresented, but they also climb the career ladder faster than their colleagues. While the prevalence of the dark triad in the general population is estimated at only around 1 percent,[17] the proportion of *corporate* psychopaths is considerably higher.[18] Estimations vary between 10 and 21 percent, with the latter being comparable to prison populations. And the incidence of male psychopaths is higher than that of females.[19] Of course, the question arises why corporate psychopaths are hired and promoted in the first place. Typically, they are not identified as such early on. If they are also narcissists, they can be very charming. Organizations may not be aware of what is behind their facade.[20] Even more, the outside appearance may be quite appealing from a corporate perspective: many psychopathic individuals display traits that are associated with leadership and success, such as persuasiveness, charisma, and creativity.[21]

It's important to note that corporate psychopaths are typically well able to understand right from wrong. And when they engage in morally inappropriate behavior, it's because they simply don't care about the consequences that follow from their behavior. They believe that rules do not apply to them.[22]

By now, you know already that we do *not* explain scandals by zooming in on the character of toxic leaders. And yet, they do belong to our nine building blocks, because they influence their followers and shape the culture of their organizations. And indeed, leaders in organizations who score high on the dark triad may not only engage more often in unethical behavior themselves but also promote unethical behavior among their teams in various ways:[23] They sometimes directly order their subordinates to break legal or moral rules. They may serve as a role model, thereby fostering followers who imitate their unethical behavior. Aggressive and psychopathic leaders create a culture of fear or intimidation, where subordinates feel the pressure to conform to the leader's expectations, regardless of their own personal values. Entire teams might engage in unethical behavior to please the leader or to avoid punishment. And finally, if leaders reward employees for achieving results at any cost, regardless of the ethical implications, they create an environment where unethical behavior is more likely to occur.

Let's look at the Karolinska Hospital in Stockholm. When they hired surgeon Paolo Macchiarini, they had the ambition to win a Nobel Prize. They knew that Macchiarini had a problematic character. The hiring committee at Karolinska received clear warning signals from the places where he had worked before: yes, at times, he could be very charming, but his diagnostic decisions were too risky, and he had difficulties dealing with the truth, lacked collegiality, had poor consideration for patients, and had a clear lack of respect for ethical rules.[24] In 2011, Macchiarini started to perform transplantations at Karolinska, replacing cancerous or damaged tracheas with a synthetic replica coated in stem cells. When his patients at Karolinska started to die cruel and painful deaths one after another, four doctors at the hospital filed a formal complaint to the president of Karolinska. They accused Macchiarini of falsifying data in his publications on the surgeries and suppressing information that would cast a shadow on his success story. Instead of investigating the case, the hospital reported the doctors to the police. Macchiarini threatened one of them that he'd make his life miserable. Only after a Swedish TV show reported on the problems did the hospital fire him. An external investigation later concluded that the hospital leadership and Macchiarini had created a culture of silence where those who spoke up were discredited and risked their career.[25]

MANIPULATIVE LANGUAGE

Lehman Brothers was a prominent and highly successful American investment bank that traced its roots back to the mid-nineteenth century. In 2007, a journalist described the success of the bank as the result of a "consistent culture," created by its CEO, Richard Fuld, internally called "Gorilla." This culture, the journalist raved, was driven by a language of war and a climate of fear. With a mixture of horror and admiration, he described Fuld inviting his traders to "rip out the throats of their enemies," and he shared the story of Fuld visiting the trading floor and shredding the tie of the second-best trader, shouting that "second best isn't good enough."[26] Not only the CEO considered Lehman to be at war. The language was contagious. Lawrence McDonald, who was working on the trading floor at Lehman Brothers, described his colleagues as "soothsayers with an AK-47" or as a "Navy Seal." Lehman was "run by a junta of platoon officers," and people working there were "battle-hardened, iron-souled regulars."[27]

Lehman was the only large US bank that went bankrupt in the storm of the global financial crisis. It turned out that the driving force of their collapse was a too-aggressive risk culture with surprisingly inefficient limits and controls.[28] Now, suddenly, the culture of the bank was evaluated differently. An article in *New York* magazine published shortly after the collapse of the company described the same war language and climate of fear. Only this time very critically: "At the top of the organization, Fuld instilled his pugilistic, paranoid view of the world: It's us against them. 'Every day is a battle,' he told his managing directors. 'You've got to kill the enemy. They tried to kill us....' And now he urged people into battle.... He even handed out some plastic swords."[29]

In the 1970s, the philosopher John L. Austin argued that language was not just an innocent tool we use to describe the world.[30] Granted, with language we give meaning, we organize our social interaction, we construct our worlds, we make things visible and invisible. But according to Austin, there is more to it. We *affect* the world through language. Language *creates* our social world. Understanding how people speak reveals not only how they see the world but also how they might eventually act.

Imagine you participate in an experiment where you are invited to play a game. In this game, you can win by either cooperating with or fighting each other. You are told that the name of the game is Wallstreet. A second group receives the identical description of the game and its rules, but this group is told that the name of the game is Community. At this point you can safely predict what will happen. When Wallstreet is played, the participants cooperate less than in Community. Same game. Same rules. Same explanation, word for word. The only difference: the name of the game. Or imagine you ask participants in a scientific study to develop solutions for crime in a hypothetical city. You tell them that the city is "virus infected" and let them figure out solutions. In another group, you tell participants that crime is a "beast preying" on the city. And again, you let them figure out ideas about what to do. Whereas the group that seemingly had to deal with a virus infection focused more on preventive measures, solutions developed by participants of the second group rather proposed punishment.[31]

If language influences behavior, wouldn't it be plausible to also assume that a linguistic analysis can help us to *predict* how people will act in the future? Indeed, recent research has demonstrated that by analyzing the language used in a company, scandals can be predicted. An analysis of comments on the website Glassdoor (where employees anonymously go to rate their company) revealed that in companies that violate US laws, the language used by employees on the website changed long before the compliance issues surfaced! Some of the words found to signal future misconduct were obvious, such as *unethical* or *lack of integrity*. Others were not directly linked to misconduct but strongly correlated with it; namely, words that signal a lack of support from management (*difficult, unable*), words describing an aggressive management style (*push, force*), words conveying negative emotions (*miserable, hostile, discouraging*), and words signaling fairness issues or discrimination (*harass, pay, favoritism*).[32]

While such words signal ethical problems ahead (and relate to many other building blocks of the dark pattern), three types of language are especially relevant for us because they might actually *drive* unethical decisions in organizations. First, *war language*—in the case of Lehman, such language built a bridge between the practice of warfare and the practice of management. The bank was at war, and in a war, rules don't count. Second, *euphemistic language* helps managers to remove ethical concerns and disengage from problematic consequences.[33] "Creative accounting" not only sounds better than tax evasion, but it also makes it easier to engage in it. After all, what could be wrong with creativity? At Enron, traders were "exploiting the loopholes" or "beating the system," which sounds much better than breaking the law. And if you frame your activity as a game, you render it pretty harmless. Finally, there is *cultish language*, which can contribute to turning members of an organization into obedient followers who would rather question their own state of mind than challenge their (cult) leaders.[34] If your organization is "changing the world," on a "spiritual journey," or on a "mission for humankind," you know that rules do not count for you even if the outside world doesn't understand it. All those terms signal trouble ahead. The way to corporate hell is paved with words.

CORRUPTING GOALS

Goal setting is probably the most effective tool managers can use in organizations. When people are given goals that are specific and difficult instead of vague and easy, they work harder, are more focused, and are more motivated. Shared understandings of where to go make it easier to cooperate in teams and across organizations. When people achieve their goals, their self-evaluation is more positive and they are satisfied with themselves.[35] However, there is an important difference between specific goals and *too specific goals*, between demanding goals and *too demanding goals*.

Jack Welch, the former CEO of General Electric, whose "creative" ideas on leadership will play a key role in many of our scandals, defined what he called "stretch goals" for his teams. A stretch goal is one that seems impossible to achieve. Welch's argument was that this creates an uncomfortable situation. Under pressure, managers will become creative to achieve the most unrealistic goals. They will be forced to think outside of the box and disrupt and revolutionize products and processes. One of the most notorious stretch goals set by Jack Welch was his expectation that each business unit had to become the number-one or -two player in every market where GE competed. If a GE business could not achieve this ranking, it faced divestiture, restructuring, or closure.[36] Welch was inspired by Japan's development of the first high-speed train system, the Shinkansen. It achieved speeds that had previously been considered impossible. They did it by simply setting ever higher goals for the speed of the trains, and assuming it would get done, until engineers were eventually able to create the "bullet train."

Not only did the high-speed train system transform Japanese mobility, but it also changed the entire society. The fast economic growth of Japan between the 1960s and 1990s was called the "Shinkansen effect." Bullet-train thinking entered Management 101 textbooks with Jack Welch at the helm of General Electric. However, overly ambitious goals have a dark side. What if people in an organization realize that their goals do not only *seem* unrealistic, but *are* unrealistic? What if goals can only be achieved at a certain price, for instance, through reduced safety and the associated risk of a bullet train crashing at full speed? What if achieving goals comes with psychological rewards, but failure or the fear of failure comes with even higher psychological costs?

The failure to achieve very demanding and specific goals can damage a person's self-esteem and motivation.[37] Not achieving a goal can even turn into a perceived existential threat. In such situations, people will tend to engage in higher risks, including using unethical means if they fear losing something and if they consider the loss too big to bear.[38] Under such pressure, they may lie, manipulate information, and steal, just to achieve their goals, and as leaders they will show more abusive behavior toward their teams.[39] However, pressure does not necessarily lead to *selfish* unethical behavior. It might also create more *pro-organizational* unethical behavior. When Siemens was caught in a big corruption scandal, managers involved in the illegal business practices argued that bribes were paid to keep business units alive and to protect jobs.[40] When illegal and immoral practices are tolerated and promoted, people will break the rules "for the company" (bribery, cheating customers, or other types of rule breaking).[41]

When goals are unrealistic, they are very often also too narrowly defined. Unrealistic and narrow goals transform a "management by objectives" culture into a "being managed by one's objectives" culture. The chosen goal becomes a fixation since people risk being invested in the goal beyond their capacity for critical judgment. They might lose sight of their values, the side effects of their actions, and the doubtful means they use to achieve their goals.[42] In such a case, organizations suffer from "teleopathy" or "goal sickness," the "unbalanced pursuit of purpose."[43] Being fixated on, or obsessed by, one goal over any other consideration will blind decision-makers to the consequences of their decisions. They become detached from their broader (both organizational and societal) context and risk losing the ability to see the big picture in which their decisions are embedded.[44]

Fixation may even be the result of organizational or institutional design; specifically, it may result from organizational division of labor. Focusing on a certain dimension of a decision may prevent people from seeing the overall picture, thereby leading to a diffusion of responsibility, as psychologist Albert Bandura pointed out. In his words: "People shift their attention from the meaning of what they are doing to the details of their specific job."[45] When they are siloed, employees tend to focus on their goals without asking questions about their overall meaning and embeddedness. This way, a group of people may jointly produce an unethical outcome, but no one feels responsible—in the extreme case, no one may even notice that the outcome is unethical—because everyone is exclusively working on some innocent element of the chain.

Such *channelized attention* doesn't mean that people sit in their office and make some conscious decision to focus on a particular goal at any cost, regardless of morally or legally questionable means. With sufficient pressure, goals narrow down in a much more unconscious way. The problem of channelized attention was, for instance, examined by the US Air Force. Flying an airplane requires multitasking. Pilots must pay attention to many different things at the same time. Analyzing airplane accidents, the US Air Force found that most of the time, these accidents were not provoked by a lack of attention or concentration, but on the contrary by *too much attention paid to one particular aspect* of the situation. Fatal mistakes resulted from a fixation and the resulting channelized attention. The effect in organizations is comparable. When people are put under the stress of unrealistic and too narrowly defined goals, they might become emotionally and cognitively exhausted. They will pursue their goals at any price.[46] Goals thus can set an organization on a fast track to the dark side.

DESTRUCTIVE INCENTIVES

Jack Welch became CEO at General Electric in 1981. He inherited an inefficient and slow company and set out to change this by fighting the "bureaucratic tentacles," as he called them.[47] If GE wanted to be more profitable than its competitors, it had to engage in an ambitious cost-cutting program and sell underperforming businesses.[48] Each business unit had to be put under pressure to remain or become number one or two in its industry—or else be closed or sold.[49] For Welch, it was obvious that he could not achieve his goals with the same managers who had created the bureaucratic monster in the first place. To disrupt the corporate culture at GE, he established the same aggressive competition *inside* the company that he pursued in the market. During one of his first meetings with managers in 1981, he gave them an appetizer of what they had to expect. Welch invited them to "take a look around, because you won't be seeing each other anymore." Most of the managers in the room were later fired.[50]

For him, the world was divided into winners and losers, and he only wanted winners on his team. This is how he transformed the culture of GE: as the new CEO he introduced a "rank and yank" performance-evaluation process, using what he called the "vitality curve."[51] This was a simple Gaussian distribution curve with three segments: the top 15 percent of employees were the "1s," the middle 75 percent were the "2s" and the bottom 10 percent were the "3s."[52] The 3s were put on notice as low performers and kicked out if they did not improve fast.[53] Welch called them "dead wood."[54] The evaluation was based on the already discussed "stretch goals." As Welch explained in a shareholder meeting, this "essentially means using dreams to set business targets—with no idea of how to get there." With the vitality curve hanging over their heads, managers knew that if they did not achieve these lofty goals, someone else would. Within the first five years as CEO of GE, while continuously ranking and yanking the entire company, Welch fired 118,000 people—one-fourth of the total workforce.[55]

His approach was soon adapted and refined by others. The energy trading company Enron, for instance, evaluated its traders on a Gaussian curve as well. As it went from Wall Street's darling and "America's Most Innovative Company" to fraudulent bankruptcy in the early 2000s, it eagerly copied Welch's performance-evaluation system.[56] Enron traders were expected to make as many deals as possible at an ever-increasing pace, and to invent new markets for more deals. Hundreds of young and inexperienced traders in their early twenties were pushed to make decisions about trades worth up to $5 million without the formal approval of their managers. They were promised by CEO Jeff Skilling that they would "eat what they killed."[57] No prey, no compensation. In doing so, Enron created a special risk-taking culture to maximize the self-interest of its traders.

Bonus days at Enron were legendary and resembled "auto shows," as executives quickly converted their bonus checks into luxury vehicles and displayed them at headquarters.[58] For the roughly 15 percent of traders who fell into the category of underperformers, bonus day was doomsday: they were separated from the others and given a few weeks to find a new job. While at GE people were ranked and yanked once a year; Enron did it twice a year to its employees.

It does not take much to see that incentives embedded in a *zero-sum meritocracy*, where individual success is only possible at the expense of others, will lead to a fight for survival among employees and drown a corporate culture in testosterone. After all, who wants to be fired from a company like Enron that is considered the future of capitalism? How to explain this stain on your CV to future employers? There is an enormous amount of data on the relationship between incentives, competition, and ethics, and that data leads to the same conclusion: pitching people in an organization against each other results in aggressive competition. But not only that. Knowing that they can only go up if someone else goes down, many forms of individual unethical behavior are triggered, including cheating, lying, stealing, victimization, test-score manipulation, or fraud.[59] Nobody wants to be humiliated and punished as the loser in this Darwinist game.[60] In a zero-sum meritocracy, individuals are encouraged to compete. They are incentivized—and thus motivated—to place their own success and performance above the well-being of others and the organization itself. If survival is at stake, people tend to care more about their relative position within their reference group than about the well-being of the organization. They won't cooperate.[61]

Financial incentives are associated with a reduction in empathy, compassion, and self-reflection, and it thus does not even come as a surprise that aggressive competition leads the winners to develop a sense of entitlement, which again reduces their moral inhibitions even further. The combination of unrealistic "dream goals," narrow financial incentives ("to make those deals," "to achieve that quota"), pressure, and aggressive internal competition provides a toxic cocktail.[62]

And yet, despite all that knowledge about the devastating effects of a rank-and-yank system, about 30 percent of Fortune 500 companies still use it, and still others have introduced it recently. One reason might simply be that today, new technologies are enabling seemingly objective performance measurements, based on data that is automatically generated, manipulated, and processed by software, allowing for fast calculations, graphic visualizations, and simplified analyses.[63]

AMBIGUOUS RULES

In 2000, I (Guido) was invited, along with my wife, Bettina, to do an ethics training for a company. For me, this was the first time that I would teach ethics to managers. This globally operating firm had developed a new code of ethics, and we were invited to train a group of what it called their "young high potentials"—a group of young managers coming from around the world who were on a fast-track career. At that time, we both had just finished our PhDs, and we naively compiled some ideas about how to use abstract ethical theories to make good decisions. During the workshop, three of these young managers approached us, telling us bluntly that they had to pay bribes to potential clients. Their managers would push them to do so by setting sales targets they would not be able to achieve otherwise. They also told us that from their perspective, this training and this code were only meant to protect their own managers against them.

If one day their illegal business practices surfaced, their superiors would argue that they knew nothing about it and that they had done everything to sensitize their teams to do business with integrity. The situation felt very awkward, and neither of us really knew what to say at that moment. I soon forgot the episode, but the conversation with these young managers came back to my mind a few years later, when the same company was suddenly all over the news for a big corruption scandal. And as the participants of our workshop had predicted, their superiors claimed total innocence.

The young managers who approached us during the workshop had been caught in what Gregory Bateson has labeled a "double bind" situation.[64] This is how Bateson explained the basic structure of a double bind: Two people or groups of people communicate with each other. One party has power over the other—for instance, a parent over a child, or a manager in an organization over their team members. In a first step, the powerful actor formulates a *negative injunction*. It normally takes the form of "Do *not* do X or I will punish you." Then, in a second step, the powerful actor sends a second message with the *contradictory injunction* "Do X or I will punish you." Both these (contradictory) injunctions, if obeyed, will potentially threaten the survival of the person or group in their respective social system. While the first injunction is communicated directly, the second one is often transmitted on a different level of communication. The power holders might even be different actors—in our example, two different managers in the same company. There is a third element that concludes the double-bind situation: the persons exposed to the contradictory injunctions cannot escape the system—or at least firmly believe that they cannot escape it.

What sounds rather abstract becomes clear if we go back to the story of the company at which my wife and I delivered the ethics workshop. With this training and its code of ethics, the company conveyed an official message: "Do not violate our ethical rules." This is the first, negative injunction. Before and after the training, however, the young managers were confronted with a second, this time positive, injunction. Their superior might have told them: "Bring me this contract tomorrow" and "I do not want to know how you do it." In a double bind, nobody will bluntly say, "Pay this bribe." In fact, if one of these young managers had directly asked their superior whether they were supposed to pay a bribe, the latter would have rejected this idea with indignation. "Of course not!" This represents the third element of the double-bind situation: It is not possible to metacommunicate about the perceived tensions with the manager.[65]

Why not? First, in organizations with double-bind dynamics, the actor caught in contradictory orders will not be accustomed to challenging the power holder. In such organizational cultures, speaking up does not belong to their operational routines; admitting a problem might be a career-terminating move. People cannot simply put the double bind on the agenda of a meeting. Furthermore, they will be *repeatedly* exposed to the double bind. It is never just a single interaction. In a unique situation that differs from the norm, it would be comparably easier to point out the contradiction: "We don't do these things here!" In a double bind, the tensions are normalized.[66]

Furthermore, the leader exposing an employee or an entire team to a double bind might not want to be confronted with the problematic information but prefer to remain in a state of deliberate ignorance. In an organization where doubtful business practices are routinized, leaders themselves are probably embedded in the very same situation as their teams: they also must achieve goals while following the rules of the game, knowing that they can achieve them only by ignoring those rules. Managers often simply move their own double bind further down the hierarchy where others then "solve" it for themselves. Deliberate ignorance helps them create an illusion of agency and control in a situation perceived as overwhelming, unclear, and fast changing. "I don't micromanage" can "solve" many of their ethical problems.[67]

The double bind creates a moral gray zone. What is right and what is wrong is not clear because formal rules and informal practices are not aligned. The latter are never officially communicated or approved of. They just exist, are tolerated, incentivized, expected. In a double bind, it is impossible to make a good decision—one that fulfills both the negative and the positive injunction simultaneously. And yet the superior expects a decision. Deregulated markets or new industries with unclear rules even extend this zone of gray. Managers will be caught between complying with the law and "beating the system" or "finding the loopholes." In such an ambiguous situation, people will look left and right to figure out what others do, what the real rules and the real expectations are. Under pressure to decide, they remove the ambiguity themselves. On various levels of the organization, the moral double bind is thus transformed into a purely technical problem, which can be solved with clear objectives and performance measurement. Being busy with daily struggles becomes the perfect distraction from systematic moral problems created by ambiguous rules.

PERCEIVED UNFAIRNESS

When he could no longer deny that he had secured all his seven Tour de France victories with the help of EPO—a blood-thinning drug that gave him 10 to 15 percent higher performance—superstar cyclist Lance Armstrong went on *The Oprah Winfrey Show* to confess.

When Oprah asked whether it never occurred to him that what he did was wrong, he gave a surprising answer: "It didn't *feel* wrong, it didn't feel like I was cheating.... I looked up the definition of cheating in a dictionary: it says gaining an unfair advantage on a competitor. It didn't feel that way." German Tour de France winner Jan Ullrich made a similar argument in a press conference when he ended his career: "I have always tried to be fair in my career and I am proud to say that I have never cheated or harmed anyone. That is very important to me."[68]

Taking drugs to win but being convinced that taking drugs is doing the right thing? How is this possible? In 1999, less than a month before the start of the first of the seven Tours de France Lance would win, one of his helpers asked Armstrong what he planned to do. His answer: "What everybody does."[69] Recently, almost two decades after his career was abruptly ended by a positive doping test, Jan Ullrich finally confessed to the use of EPO as well. Looking back, he argued that "without help, the widespread perception at the time was that it would be like going to a shooting armed only with a knife."[70] He did it because he thought everyone else was doing it. World champion Tyler Hamilton even emphasized the strong work ethics of pro cyclists, arguing that performance-enhancing drugs did not replace hard training and suffering but rather rewarded such efforts by giving them some control over the power decline on a Grand Tour.[71] From the perspective of all those cyclists, using EPO helped to bring fairness back to the competition. It was self-defense. A little support for hardworking people.

Research demonstrates how perceived unfairness affects people's behavior. Psychologist Jerald Greenberg showed for instance that during a period when employees in a manufacturing plant faced a 15 percent pay cut, theft rates rose significantly. When the reason for the pay cut was sensitively explained, feelings of inequity were lessened, and the theft rate went down. Three years after this study, Greenberg published the results of a groundbreaking experiment where he showed that perceived unfairness leads to moral outrage, which, in turn, makes it easier to use moral arguments to break rules. In his experiment, Greenberg had students do work in a lab, promising a certain amount of money for the work. Students had to take the money out of a box at the end of their shift, unobserved by the professor. In one group, he confirmed the previously agreed amount of money, and in another group, he told students that he had made a mistake, and they would receive less than they were promised. The study was published with the title "Stealing in the Name of Justice," which spoils the outcome: students in the second group who felt that they were treated unfairly stole money when they were given the opportunity. Like the cyclists injecting EPO, they broke the rules to restore justice.[72]

Such feelings of being treated unfairly can occur within and across organizations. Greenberg's experiment shows what people are willing to do if they see their own organization (represented by the lab supervisor) treating them unfairly. The Tour de France example demonstrates what people are willing to do if they consider their competitive environment to be unfair. Similarly, sales representatives might pay bribes because they are convinced that their competitors do so and that they have the moral right to level the playing field.

The effects of perceived unfairness have been widely studied, with a consistent pattern emerging: it negatively affects employees and increases the risk of their engaging in unethical behavior. The empirical evidence suggests that people react to perceived unfairness in an escalation that moves forward in three steps. It starts with *feelings*: if organizational decisions and actions are perceived to be unfair, affected employees may experience anger, outrage, and resentments, developing a desire for retribution and a felt need to punish those whom they blame for the problem.[73]

The escalating response continues with subtle reactions bordering on rule breaking.[74] Why subtle? Perceptions of unfairness are only possible with a functioning moral compass, and it may be precisely this compass that prevents those who have such perceptions from reacting to their negative emotions immediately. Also, fear can keep people in check for a while. Employees who feel unfairly treated and take some first and cautious measures to balance things in their own favor may not even realize that they are retaliating. They may just feel frustrated, be demotivated, and simply disengage. It is only later in the process that their feelings may lead to the articulated argument that an employer who treats them unfairly does not deserve greater engagement on their part. And presumably only a small minority would go even further and intentionally harm the organization to restore fairness and to "get even."

Ultimately, in some cases, employees are willing to engage in more extreme—and even illegal—behaviors, such as corruption, cheating, theft, sabotage, vandalism, and even workplace violence.[75] Such behaviors can be seen as the tip of the iceberg and are generally rare, but nonetheless, the statistics and empirical evidence from experimental work consistently show that perceived unfairness facilitates such behavior—and is often even its best predictor. It numbs people's moral sentiments and can expose organizations to tremendous compliance risks.

DANGEROUS GROUPS

On the dawn of July 13, 1942, about 500 armed men in uniforms arrive at Józefów—a small Polish village with a then large Jewish community. They enter houses. Shots and desperate cries fill the air. They separate families. Male Jews of working age are loaded onto trucks and brought to a work camp. All others—women, children, and elderly—are taken to the nearby forest to be executed. As shocking as it is to hear about these atrocities, it is as astonishing to read the report of historian Christopher Browning on what had happened right before the attack on Józefów: Major Wilhelm Trapp, a fifty-three-year-old career policeman affectionately known by his men as "Papa Trapp," had called upon the members of the German Reserve Police Battalion 101, who "assembled in a half-circle around" him. "Pale and nervous, with choking voice and tears in his eyes," Trapp announced that the battalion had to execute a "frightfully unpleasant task." That task "was not to his liking... but the orders came from the highest authorities.... Having explained what awaited his men, Trapp then made an extraordinary offer: if any of them did not feel up to the task that lay before him, he could *step out*."[76] Browning continues: "Trapp paused, and after some moments.... Otto-Julius Schimke stepped forward. Captain Hoffmann... was furious that one of his men had been the first to break ranks. Hoffmann began to berate Schimke, but Trapp cut him off. After he had taken Schimke under his protection, some ten or twelve other men stepped forward as well. They turned in their rifles and were told to await a further assignment."[77] Shortly after, the shooting began. On that morning, 1,500 Jewish inhabitants of the village were killed: women, children, and the elderly.

Only twelve soldiers stepped forward! Twelve out of 500! Why not more? It seems that these men followed a simple heuristic—don't break ranks![78] When formulating his offer, Trapp set a *default*. A default is what happens if one does not do anything in a given situation.[79] That morning, when Trapp made the offer, doing nothing—not stepping out—meant taking part in the killings. In order to not kill, one had to do something—break ranks. Soldiers had to move away from their comrades; they had to separate from the group. Now, belonging to a group fulfills important psychological needs and often also offers administrative and logistic advantages. Leaving one's group typically comes at a price. Particularly during wartime, group coherence is of utmost importance. Even though Trapp took dissenters under his protection, he could neither protect their reputation among their comrades nor restore their self-esteem damaged for refusing to take part. After all, in that situation, keeping one's hands clean meant putting even more blood on the hands of one's peers. Whereas group conformity, coupled with the power of defaults, could be considered as nothing more than a post hoc explanation for what happened at Józefów, we can easily imagine a less extreme situation from a corporate context with the same psychological dynamics: suppose someone joins a company where most employees routinely pay bribes to secure contracts and favorable deals. Would they say something? Try to stop the practice? Break ranks? As a new hire, they will fear exclusion or negative repercussions and with a high probability, many people will quickly adopt the same unethical practice, thus reinforcing and perpetuating the culture of corruption within the organization.

There has been no scarcity of rigorous experimental work on group conformity. In his classic experiments, psychologist Solomon Asch had participants—who had been led to believe they were taking part in an eye test—say out loud, in a group of eight and one after another, which of three unequal lines (A, B, or C) matched the length of a given line. What participants did not know: they were the only "real" participant in their group—the others were confederates of the experimenter. Asch wanted to find out what would happen if the unanimous decision of the group was clearly wrong. Would the real participant follow the group or their own judgment? Asch found that 74 percent of the participants gave an incorrect answer on at least one of the trials and 30 percent answered incorrectly in more than half of the rounds. They followed the group. The interviews after the experiment revealed the reasons of those who gave an incorrect answer at least once. Asch distinguished two explanations for their seemingly irrational behavior: a *distortion of judgment*, which makes people look for the problem in themselves instead of challenging a majority of peers, and a *distortion of action*, which drives people to follow the group simply to avoid appearing different or inferior in the eyes of others.[80]

Can people's reluctance to leave the flock also be observed if they do not form a group but they simply happen to be at the same place at the same time, without interacting with each other? Yes. This has been called the *bystander effect*. When people face a critical incident alone, such as observing a person in need of help, they will tend to interfere, while they will tend to do nothing if other people are observing the incident as well. They will wait for someone else to act.[81] Three main reasons were proposed for not helping: *diffusion of responsibility* (the more bystanders there are, the less personally responsible any individual will feel), *evaluation apprehension* (fear of being judged by others when acting publicly), and *pluralistic ignorance* (the tendency to rely on the overt reactions of others in an ambiguous situation).[82] This list makes it obvious why the bystander effect has also been linked to speaking up within organizations. Why would I help or why would I speak up if others are present who could do so as well?[83]

Strong group coherence can make it even more difficult to dissent and speak up. Such groups can promote an us-versus-them mentality, which comes with in-group favoritism and out-group discrimination.[84] Preferential treatment of others who are members of our in-group serves the need to belong and the need for positive distinctiveness.[85] Group coherence can in extreme cases lead to what social psychologist Irving Janis dubbed *groupthink*. In the worst case, group members let "striving for unanimity override their motivation to realistically appraise alternative courses of action."[86] Symptoms of groupthink include the illusion of invulnerability, belief in the inherent morality of the group, collective rationalization and ignoring of warnings that may challenge the group's assumptions about the world, stereotyping of out-groups, self-censorship, illusion of unanimity (silence is interpreted as agreement), direct pressure on dissenters, and self-appointed mind guards.[87] Groupthink can in some cases lead to *collective hubris* and *narcissism*, driving entire organizations to believe that "rules do not count for us."[88] In this case, groups jointly create their own (distorted) reality, which all too often leads to problems not only for themselves but also for others.

SLIPPERY SLOPE

Former professional cyclists describe their decision to use the already mentioned performance-enhancing drug EPO as a slow "descent."[89] Young and promising cyclists were not immediately pushed to use it when they joined a team. Former pro cyclist Tyler Hamilton describes it as 1,000 days of clean riding before they stood at a "fork in the road" and had to make a decision.[90] Before then, however, they had already gained ample experience with injections—legal injections like iron or vitamin B. These injections were always framed by the team doctor as being done for their health and to help them recover faster.[91] At a later stage, they would use the same argument for

EPO. Doping came in "baby steps," as another former pro cyclist describes it, and it often started with a comparably harmless (but still illegal) cortisone injection.[92] The decision to eventually use illegal drugs was often perceived as easy, after years of getting used to injections. David Millar, the former time-trial world champion, describes the moment when he lost his innocence: "I went from thinking one hundred percent that I would never dope to making a decision in ten minutes that I was going to do it."[93] Others felt that their sense of morality was "steadily eroded, twisted, and darkened" so that they could even feel a sense of relief when finally taking the last step toward performance-enhancing drugs.[94]

This effect of a slow descent—and the experience of those cyclists is just one example of this—was investigated by maritime biologist Daniel Pauly about thirty years ago. Pauly wanted to find out how fish species populations changed over time and how this was affected by commercial fishing.[95] When he interviewed fishermen, he found that each generation used the stock size and species composition at the beginning of their careers as a reference point for assessing changes. Each fisherman reported a slight decrease in fish populations relative to what they considered normal, but almost nobody (except for a few very old fishermen) had a perspective spanning more than a single generation. Almost everyone suffered from what has been called "environmental generational amnesia."[96] In the absence of this cross-generational perspective, no one recognized the dramatic changes that occurred over time, and no one realized that perhaps the practices of the previous generation had reduced the fish population they encountered.

When researchers supplemented Pauly's anecdotal evidence with a large survey covering three generations of fishermen from Mexico's Gulf of California, the following picture emerged.[97] Fish populations had declined sharply over the past sixty years: compared to the young fishermen, the old fishermen named five times as many species, named four times as many fishing sites, and caught up to twenty-five times as much Gulf grouper as the young fishermen. At the same time, each generation perceived the status quo in their environment as natural—which helps explain why society tolerates the creeping loss of biodiversity.

People perceive changes in their environment relative to their own experience, which serves as a baseline when determining what is normal and natural. With gradually and slowly shifting baselines, the severity of change is grossly underestimated.[98] What is shifting in this process is what people consider normal, appropriate, and objective. The fishermen were not alerted by the annual changes of fish stock because these changes over time were small and below what psychophysicists call the *just-noticeable difference*: the smallest difference between two stimuli that a person is able to notice. Such small differences can add up to a dramatic transformation that barely anyone will notice.

Unfortunately, the same effect can be observed with regard to (un)ethical behavior. Small steps lead to little changes that over time shift moral standards. Such a slow decay of morality happens even in professional domains where we would least expect it, such as in hospitals: Most nurses enter the profession with the best of intentions. They value maintaining high standards of care and doing what is best for patients, without compromises due to budgets or the constraints of length-of-stay targets.[99] But then they are "often required to carry out policies they deplore, orders they believe wrong, and treatments they believe cruel."[100] The nurses' ideals are confronted with a reality that presents them with major challenges. They must not only make compromises on their own standards but also observe various unethical but tolerated practices from physicians and other nurses.[101] How did these unethical practices come about? According to Carol Kleinman, chair of a nursing department, the young nurses with high ideals are thrown into an "environment where ethical drift is encouraged, if not mandated." *Ethical drift* is, in her words, "an incremental deviation from ethical practice that goes unnoticed by individuals who justify the deviations as acceptable and who believe themselves to be maintaining their ethical boundaries." It usually occurs "imperceptibly, below the level of consciousness" and can be hard to detect because self-serving needs are not overt in clinical and administrative practice and can be easily rationalized.[102]

If one takes small steps and compares the next only to the previous, rather than to an (imaginary) objective moral standpoint, it is easier to move forward. This dynamic creates an *escalation of commitment*: the further someone advances down the slippery slope, the more difficult it becomes to stop. Not only can the slippery slope and escalation of commitment be identified, in post hoc analysis, as playing an important role in many scandals (other examples we could have picked include academic fraud, corruption, and accounting), but rigorous experimental research was also able to demonstrate that they lead to unethical decisions.[103] Central to this process is that it involves pressuring individuals to make incremental decisions that ultimately lead to unethical actions. Each decision is minor and nearly indistinguishable from the previous one; once one step is taken, the person is naturally set up for the next. This progression causes their ethical judgment to adapt along the way rather than guide their actions from the outset.[104]

Imagine you are sitting on a train waiting for its departure. At a certain point in time, while you are looking at the passengers in the train at the opposed platform, *your* train starts moving—or so you think. But suddenly you realize that it was the *other* train, while your train is still at the platform (but it could also be the other way around). A rare—but still possible—scenario would be that both trains start moving at the same time, at the same speed and in the same direction. If you had the other train as a reference point, you might not even notice that both are moving. As this example shows, changes are observed relative to a reference point. Now imagine the other train is your *moral* reference point—the taken-for-granted rules and accepted behavior in your organization. Your train represents your own behavior. If both move in parallel toward increasingly unethical decisions, you will not even see it happening. "You do it once and it smells. You do it again, it already smells less," as a former Enron manager has argued.[105] And we would add: you keep doing it and it stops smelling. Over time, an initially maybe-reluctant commitment to doubtful business practices escalates into unconscious habits. You start with a seemingly harmless or somehow-still-acceptable transgression and end up ethically blind.

WELCOME TO CORPORATE HELL

Like Dante, we now invite you on an imagined journey into specific infernos, created by leaders in certain organizations. Sit down, relax, and watch as the dramas unfold. You might, here and there, feel the urge to warn the protagonists of the fall to come. But it's too late. They will not hear you, and they wouldn't listen even if they could hear you. Just sit back and watch. Put yourself into the shoes of the protagonists in our little dramas and just imagine that it could have been you instead. Go there with us so that you don't have to end up there in reality. Our dark pattern will be your guide. And don't worry: as Virgil led Dante back to the light, to "see the stars again," we will not abandon you in these corporate hellscapes. We will lead you back to the light and show you, in Chapter 11, the bright pattern that you can use to beat the dark one.

4
THERANOS—THE EMPRESS'S NEW CLOTHES

HIGH HOPES

Silicon Valley, the mecca of innovation and technology, continues to astound the world with its groundbreaking advancements and entrepreneurial spirit. Investors are constantly searching for the next Steve Jobs or Mark Zuckerberg while those who pitch their ideas dream of *becoming* the next Steve Jobs or Mark Zuckerberg.[1]

One of those dreamers was Elizabeth Holmes. She was studying chemical and electrical engineering at Stanford when, in 2003, at the age of nineteen she dropped out and founded her own startup. She named it Theranos, a combination of *therapy* and *diagnosis*.[2] Theranos aimed to revolutionize medical diagnostics by developing a technology that could conduct comprehensive blood tests using just a few drops of blood. The company's mission was to make blood testing faster, more accessible, and less expensive, thereby transforming the health-care industry. The young founder set out to change the world.[3]

Holmes compiled a supervisory board that *Fortune* hailed as "the most illustrious board in US corporate history."[4] It included retired four-star general James Mattis, former Wells Fargo CEO Richard Kovacevich, former senators Sam Nunn and Bill Frist, and two former secretaries of state, George Shultz and Henry Kissinger.[5] Aside from the obvious, this phalanx of old, and very old, men also underrepresented one decisive type of knowledge: only three members of the board had some expertise in medicine, former director of the Centers for Disease Control and Prevention William Foege, senator and heart-transplant surgeon Bill Frist, and later Fabrizio Bonanni, a one-time pharma and biotech executive.[6] In hindsight, it should have been telling when she pitched her vision to medtech investors in 2004 and none of them found her ideas convincing.[7] For many years, money mainly came from the circle of rich friends of her family.

After operating in secret for a decade, Theranos went public in 2013 with a website and press release. Holmes and her team informed the world that they had invented a technology that would make a broad range of blood tests easier, cheaper, faster, and more accurate. For their laboratory tests, they would simply need the blood one gets by pricking the tip of a finger.[8] Why was this so groundbreaking? Normally, blood tests are very cumbersome. A needle is inserted into a vein, typically in the arm, to collect a sample of blood. This process can be painful and stressful for some patients. And it is costly, because it needs to be performed by a health-care professional. Since roughly 70 percent of medical decisions are based on expensive traditional blood tests, this innovation carried the potential to disrupt the health-care industry.[9]

In September 2013, after Theranos had gone public, the *Wall Street Journal* published an article, "Elizabeth Holmes: The Breakthrough of Instant Diagnosis," describing the potential of Theranos to "upend the industry of laboratory testing" and "change the way we detect and treat disease."[10] Theranos was the first unicorn (a private company valued at a billion dollars or more) to be founded by a woman. The article triggered an avalanche of media hype. Silicon Valley had been waiting for the next Steve Jobs, and here she was! She called her blood-testing device "the iPod of healthcare," and claimed it would find its way into every household.[11] Her long-term vision, meanwhile, was even more ambitious: Holmes wanted to ultimately build individual disease maps for patients that would predict and even prevent cancer and other diseases.[12]

In July 2015, the value of Theranos stood at $10 billion, and the company's number of employees peaked at 800.[13] At this point, "investors were falling over themselves to give her money."[14]

> Here we see **rigid ideology** at work: capitalism produces people and institutions that sit on millions and billions of dollars looking for high-yield investment opportunities. Who among them likes to miss out on a unicorn—that is, a company worth over $1 billion and not (yet) listed on the stock market—that has the potential to turn an entire industry around? Celebrating the single entrepreneur who appears out of nowhere and changes the world is deeply embedded in capitalist ideology. The very term "capitalism" comes from the Latin *caput*: the head as the part of our body that is considered the origin of ideas. Visionary, fearless, charismatic, and self-interested entrepreneurs, in turn, operate in markets that are celebrated by the neoliberal ideology

> as the engine of innovation and progress. Venture capitalism is the soil in which Holmes—with her promise to disrupt an industry and to enrich investors—was able to grow and blossom.

FAKE IT TILL YOU MAKE IT

Back in 2003, Holmes hired the engineer Edmond Ku to develop the miniature blood-testing technologies she had envisioned. When Ku and his team did not progress fast enough, Holmes hired a second team of engineers to work on alternative concepts and pitted both groups against each other. In September 2007, the second group of engineers developed a prototype that delivered reliable results for some blood tests. Holmes fired Ku and his entire team.[15] The first functional prototype was called "Edison," named after the renowned inventor Thomas Edison.

In 2010, the company developed the so-called miniLab, which was supposed to supersede the Edison by performing a more extensive variety of blood tests.[16] A representative of Theranos explained to *Business Insider*, "We can perform hundreds of tests, from standard to sophisticated, from a pinprick and tiny sample of blood, and we have performed more than 70 tests from a single tiny sample."[17]

How exactly did the Theranos devices work? Nobody knew. Scientists struggled to get answers from Theranos with regard to these challenges. As *Business Insider* wrote at the time, "The specifics of how those Edison machines work is a mystery."[18] In a similar vein, the *New Yorker* wrote in late 2014 that Theranos treats its technology like a "state secret," explaining only in a "comically vague" way how it functions.[19]

Eight years earlier, Holmes had tried convincing pharmaceutical companies to work with Theranos, pitching her innovation as a potential component in their clinical testing. However, discussions with Novartis and Schering-Plough led nowhere.[20] Holmes changed her strategy and decided to target retail companies. Theranos looked to Walgreens, one of the largest retail pharmacy chains in the United States. The idea was to install blood-testing services in their stores, with blood samples being sent for analysis to the Theranos lab.[21] Before signing the deal, Walgreens never validated the Theranos technology or capability for mass blood testing. It committed to a rollout of blood-testing centers in thousands of drugstores across the United States. The rollout began in 2013.[22]

If Walgreens had tried to validate the technology, it might have realized it was not able to conduct many of the blood tests Theranos had promised. The blood sample was too small to run all the different tests, and the miniaturization of the analyzer created insurmountable problems. Former Theranos software engineer Del Barnwell recalled, "The machine did not work at all. When Walgreens signed.... I was looking at my two buddies, 'I'm like dude what the hell are these people thinking?' It doesn't do anything."[23]

In Silicon Valley, "fake it till you make it" is a well-established—and sometimes successful—practice.[24] As corporate-fraud expert Freya Berry wrote, "We live in the age of the corporate fairy-tale: a magical land of unicorns and eternal growth. 'What's the story?' investors like to ask about the latest hot startup, willing the narrative to be true even as they live the myth of their own absolute rationality."[25]

About two decades before Holmes developed her vision, scientists were already at work on microfluidic technologies and miniaturized fluid manipulation. The potential to revolutionize biology and diagnostics was clearly there. Theranos's task was to make the tests more reliable. This was not an unrealistic goal. Alas, it didn't work out, despite the best efforts of those who toiled day and night. Miniaturizing the technology and squeezing too many different blood-test procedures into one small machine was simply not possible.

While the authors of the *Fortune* article praised the disruptive power of the innovation, they also noted that normally a new med-tech solution would require validation from independent scientists. They assured their readers that this was not necessary for Theranos, since the company was using well-known "basic fundamental chemical methods." Because scientific research existed already, the Theranos analyzers were following peer-reviewed standards.[26] But that was only an assumption.

There is another mechanism that could have evaluated the claims made by Theranos: the certification process that the US Food and Drug Administration had put in place for blood analyzers. However, the FDA certification process was only imposed on companies that produce *and sell* analyzers—companies like Siemens or Beckman Coulter. Companies *using* analyzers in their own labs did not have to go through certification. Laboratories had a different certification process, which was not performed by the FDA but by another regulatory body, the Centers for Medicare & Medicaid Services (CMS). But the CMS only certified laboratories that were *buying* analyzers. Theranos was producing and using analyzers, but not selling or buying them. Therefore, it belonged to neither group. A regulatory gap.[27]

Here we see three more elements of the dark pattern at work.

Ambiguous rules: Not only did the company operate in a regulatory gap, with its fake-it-till-you-make-it strategy, it was operating in an ethical no-man's-land between right and wrong as well. Thinking wishfully that problems would turn into solutions, but also not wanting to lose their jobs, employees falsified data and distorted progress. No one was reprimanded, and failure was unacceptable. Faking became the unwritten rule. Some could easily rationalize their misconduct to themselves by arguing that they wanted to change the world and make health care affordable. Venture capitalists expect startups to tell them exciting and disruptive stories. Overselling and overpromising is how Silicon Valley works.

Dangerous groups: Those who disagreed with the practices of faking left the company. Those who remained engaged in groupthink and reinforced each other's belief that the end justifies the means. Or at least: they kept believing that sooner or later they would stop faking and start making it.

Perceived unfairness: How does it feel to be penalized for not achieving goals that cannot be achieved? Conversely, those who believed in Theranos's mission tried to prove the skeptics wrong, who they felt were unjustly harsh on the company. When people are on a righteous mission, they can overlook the small missteps they take to achieve that honorable goal. Criticism from scientists felt unfair, as did the pressure to be more transparent. After all, their inventions had to be protected.

Theranos technology remained a black box not only to investors, scientists, business partners, and regulators, but also to most employees. From the very beginning, the culture at Theranos was characterized by "secrecy and paranoia."[28] Theranos was about to disrupt an entire industry, and its leadership was rightly concerned that competitors would find out about its technology. To better protect their knowledge, Theranos siloed the different development activities and prevented teams from communicating with each other. For example, the engineering team working on the machine and the chemistry group working on the blood analyses had no line of communication, by design. Consequently, no group tested the entire system.[29]

A culture of suspicion and secrecy, underpinned by nondisclosure agreements, is nothing unusual for Silicon Valley tech startups.[30] However, at Theranos this was pushed to such an extreme that "people started forgoing simple courtesies like saying hi and it became increasingly difficult to communicate, even important matters."[31]

> Here we again find a **dangerous groups** effect: to prevent bad news from spreading—and to prevent industrial espionage—Theranos cultivated a culture of secrecy and paranoia, compartmentalizing various activities and creating bubbles that had no view of the entire system. Different teams were pitted against each other, creating an atmosphere where employees were afraid to collaborate and colleagues were viewed as potential enemies.
>
> In addition to these structural measures, Theranos used the stick on those who doubted the vision, firing them for speaking up. Opinions, criticism, and negative feedback were considered attacks and led to reprisals and terminations. The employees of Theranos—with a few notable exceptions—doubted their own

> abilities and deferred to the decisions of their managers or the approval of their colleagues. This created group conformity and the diffusion of responsibility. Groupthink ran wild.

Theranos established 24/7 working hours in the engineering department. When the department head complained that the pace of work would burn his people out, Holmes reacted coldly: "I don't care. We can change people in and out.... The company is all that matters." Employees were expected to be "married to Theranos."[32] They were driven by their bosses above them, their peers surrounding them, and their own ambitions within them.

Ramesh "Sunny" Balwani joined Theranos and became the COO in 2009. Like Holmes, he would pit different teams against each other. When he sensed that people were not working hard enough, he sent them aggressive emails. On one occasion, he criticized a team for not working long enough, explaining that their colleagues had worked until 3:00 a.m. and returned to work at 10:00 a.m. the same morning.[33]

Zack Morrison worked for Theranos as an automation engineer. His responsibility was to build a robotic assembly line to produce blood-testing kits. He had been with the company for three months when he had his first clash with Balwani. His team had been given the goal of creating a 40,000-kits-per-day production capacity within two months. They were far from achieving this. "We were struggling to make 100 kits per day by hand and hadn't even finished the design for the automated assembly line required for such throughput. It was an impossible challenge." Balwani angrily criticized the team: "I didn't see you in the lab when I went down there at midnight last night. If you're not willing to put in the work that's necessary, then just say the word and you're gone!" As Morrison remembered, "Trembling in fear, we looked at each other and reluctantly agreed. 'We'll make it happen Sunny.'"[34]

> **Corrupting goals** are clearly visible here: people were always running behind schedule, failing, arguing, and accumulating evidence that proved their goals could not be reached. The milestones were too demanding and too specific. In the lab, engineers worked day and night and failed again and again, simply because the miniaturized blood analyzer that would do all the promised tests was impossible to build.
>
> They toiled hard under the pressure of **toxic leadership**: neither Holmes nor Balwani cared about their employees, who either obeyed and performed or were kicked out. Lies and deceit were an easy way to survive in this toxic culture, at least for a while. Moreover, Holmes and Balwani were perfect role models for their employees: watching their bosses lie to investors made it easier in turn to lie to them.

To keep the pressure high, Theranos constantly fired people. It called this practice to "disappear someone."[35] The constant firing took a toll on the employees. Everyone feared becoming the next one to get disappeared.[36] Starting in 2011, Theranos systematically hired foreign workers on H-1B visas, many of them from India. Some were even hired for key leadership positions. Being on an H-1B visa meant that their ability to stay in the US depended on their working contract. When they were fired, they had sixty days to find another one; otherwise their visas were revoked. This turned many of them into yes-men.[37]

> **Destructive incentives** come into play here: contribute to the revolution or lose your job—and for some, your right to work in this country. At first glance, it should be easy to choose between the carrot and the stick, but in fact both were used as instruments to manipulate people and to exert pressure.

In July 2015, Theranos received FDA approval for one of the minor tests Edison could perform: a herpes test.[38] In a subsequent public communication, Theranos stated that the FDA examination was performed at their own request and that the approval included all aspects of the Edison: the device, the software used for the analysis, and the test tubes.[39] The Theranos herpes test was much cheaper than the traditional herpes blood test ($9.07 compared to $175) and already gave a taste of the disruptive power of the Theranos technology.[40]

A herpes test is a simple yes/no analysis, while most other blood tests require a much more complicated quantitative analysis. The FDA approval gave a misleading impression about the performance of Theranos blood analyzers. While Theranos was celebrated, in truth, their technology was not working properly. It could only do a fraction of the blood tests it promised, and it generated too many false positive and false negative results.

PROMISES MEET PATIENTS

The Walgreens deal changed Theranos's situation dramatically. It was not just another tech company making airy promises. It was a medtech company using its products on real patients. False positive or false negative test results would lead doctors to draw wrong conclusions for the treatment of their patients. A wrong diagnosis, and a patient could die.

Blood tests started to come in from Walgreens customers. Theranos had to find a solution to their faulty technology. It decided to swap out its analyzer with a traditional analyzer—namely, the Siemens ADVIA 1800. Consequently, Theranos had two different laboratories running in parallel. It used its own blood analyzers in the "Normandy" lab, nicknamed to equate its product development to the World War II D-day landings. The conventional blood testing was done in the "Jurassic Park" lab, named because it viewed these conventional machines "as dinosaurs that would soon be rendered extinct by Theranos's revolutionary technology."[41] Under the pressure of the Walgreens partnership, blood tests had to be made in Jurassic Park.

> Here we see the use of **manipulative language**: the lab names, as well as many other terms, were carefully chosen, but the power of language became even more apparent when listening to Holmes. She used her charisma to motivate—and seduce—people, turning them into committed followers. She made grandiose statements celebrating the Edison blood analyzer as the most important invention ever made by humankind, one that would revolutionize preventive care and make good health care affordable to everybody on this planet. It was that visionary language that persuaded illustrious rich people to invest in, and top engineers to join, the small, unknown startup. It feels exciting and important to be part of a revolution.

Around 2015, Theranos sold more than 1.5 million blood tests, analyzing the blood of almost 176,000 patients. At least one in ten tests came back with inaccurate results.[42] The Siemens machines solved one of their problems. As promised, they could perform different classes of blood tests. However, another problem remained: the high number of false results. Theranos found a solution for this as well: it simply faked data.

Tyler Shultz was a research engineer working on the assay-validation team. He described how in the lab, they "would delete sections of an experiment and replace it with new data. At first it seemed kind of weird but then eventually you kind of fall into the habit of doing that and it's a very bad habit."[43] When his team performed a syphilis test using the Edison machine, they received strange results: "A ton of us tested positive for syphilis. I remember the manager of our lab just going: 'Guys, it's not impossible.'... Obviously, no one took that seriously."[44] Shultz reached out to Holmes via email and received an answer from Balwani. Shultz was told that he was "arrogant, ignorant, patronizing, reckless, with no basic understanding of math, science, or statistics." Shultz eventually left the company.[45]

Erika Cheung was a lab assistant in the validation team of Theranos's R&D lab. She started to doubt the Edison technology when she observed that "executives [were]... encourag[ing] scientists to 'cherry-pick' and manipulate data to make the results seem more accurate than they were." When she raised her concerns, Balwani asked her, "What makes you think you're qualified to say that? You need to do the job I'm paying you to do and process patient samples."[46] Cheung saw her more experienced colleagues performing the tasks that she found problematic, and despite her doubts she ended up doing the same. Initially, she challenged herself rather than the practice. "In a context where everyone seems to agree, they automatically make you believe you are the crazy one," she argued.[47] However, like many of her colleagues before her, she eventually decided to leave the company.[48]

Adam Rosendorff joined Theranos as a lab director in 2013. He felt "tremendous pressure at the company to show that this technology was successful," because Holmes "wanted to rapidly expand the use of the Edison from the time of rollout through the rest of the time [he] was at the company." He quickly came to realize that the technology was not working well, but he had to convince others of the contrary.[49] Rosendorff repeatedly clashed with Balwani, whom he experienced as very demanding, brutal, and uncompromising. Balwani was considered the "fearsome enforcer who would terrorize company employees with a corporate culture ruled by paranoia, subterfuge, bullying, and threats."[50] Rosendorff was instructed to explain to doctors that wrong test results could be explained by other factors, such as the drugs a patient was taking, and that in no way was it the result of a problem with the Edison machine. Rosendorff quit the company in 2014.[51]

Micah Nies, a customer service manager, recalled, "The atmosphere was so toxic you would hear the stories of people being disappeared. There was always this fear of retribution and afterward you carry it with you." At the same time, Holmes could be charming and persuasive, as Nies indicated: "We would get bad news and the next day she would hold a town hall and everybody's eyes would glaze over. She's very charismatic in the sense that she knows how to talk to people."[52]

Erika Cheung joined Theranos because this idea of changing the world by making health care more accessible and affordable appealed to her.[53] And she found that Theranos carried a "strong team identity and sense of purpose."[54] Ana Arriola, a designer who came from Apple, was convinced by Holmes's ambition to work for the "betterment of humanity."[55] For Rosendorff, the company was "poised to be the next Apple," and he wanted to be part of it.[56] For Tyler Shultz, "Elizabeth is a very, very charismatic person. When she speaks to you, she makes you feel like you are the most important person in her world in that moment. She almost has this 'reality distortion field' around her that people can just get sucked into. Even I, when I was working with the product every single day seeing it fail time after time after time, I could go have a five-minute conversation with Elizabeth and feel like I was saving the world again."[57] He remembered that he saw "tons of red flags," but he wanted to be part of this vision and the company.[58] Such a reality-distortion field had been previously ascribed to Steve Jobs—Holmes's role model.

In December 2011, during the company's Christmas party, Holmes told about a hundred employees that "the miniLab is the most important thing humanity has ever built. If you do not believe this is the case, you should leave now." Holmes declared that she was building a religion. Those who had no intention of being part of the Theranos religion should just leave.[59] Of this toxic mix of preaching the gospel and instilling fear, a former employee said, "I think a lot of us were in denial."[60]

What we see here is again the strong impact of **toxic leadership** on people at Theranos: while their styles differed, Holmes and Balwani were clearly displaying characteristics of the dark triad. Holmes was temperamental, exuding charisma and inspiration and then becoming ice-cold when things did not go as she expected. Balwani was more straightforward yet volatile. He would lead with an iron fist and yell at people. Micromanaging everybody, Holmes and Balwani threatened engineers who did not advance fast enough or did not spend day and night in the lab. Those who spoke up were fired, and if necessary, they were destroyed by the company's ruthless lawyers. While, of course, we cannot make any clinical claims here, Holmes's and Balwani's behavior points at what we have described as the dark triad, the mix of narcissism, Machiavellianism, and psychopathy.

Testimonials like the one of Tyler Shultz also demonstrate the dangerous **slippery slope** on which engineers moved forward. Falsifying data first feels weird, then it becomes a habit.

THE DOWNFALL

The *Wall Street Journal* had been the first to praise Theranos, and it was the one to initiate its downfall. On October 15, 2015, investigative journalist John Carreyrou published his article "Hot Startup Theranos Has Struggled with Its Blood-Test Technology," where he raised concerns about the technology, arguing that instead of the promised 240 tests, only 15 were really performed on their own device—the company was using Siemens devices for most of its tests.[61] His article was based on information given to him by courageous whistleblowers like Erika Cheung and Tyler Shultz. After further articles in the *Wall Street Journal* it became clear that something was profoundly wrong with the Theranos story. To hit back at Carreyrou, Holmes went on Jim Cramer's *Mad Money* program on CNBC and complained: "This is what happens when you work to change things, and first they think you're crazy, then they fight you, and then, all of a sudden, you change the world."[62]

Before the *Wall Street Journal* published its critical articles on Theranos, US authorities had already launched an investigation into the startup. The FDA performed a surprise inspection at their labs and issued a report where they criticized the company for "failing to document quality audits . . . [and] selling an unregulated medical device—the 'Nanotainer.'" Another inspection by the Centers for Medicare & Medicaid Services found "deficient practices" in the lab that would "pose immediate jeopardy to patient health and safety."[63] On January 27, 2016, the devastating CMS report was published. The next day, Walgreens closed all their Theranos Wellness Centers and suspended the deal.[64] The pharmacy chain filed a $140 million lawsuit against Theranos, terminating the partnership in June 2016.[65]

On March 14, 2018, the US Securities and Exchange Commission charged Theranos and its two top managers, Holmes and Balwani, with yearslong fraud.[66] In September, Theranos shut down all operations.[67] Holmes had burned $945 million.[68] On January 3, 2022, Holmes was found guilty by a jury on multiple fraud charges and sentenced to eleven years in prison. Balwani's thirteen-year sentence followed on July 7.[69]

We can see how the company moved forward on a **slippery slope**: Theranos began with a cloudy vision presented to rich individuals. It continued with bold promises to pharma companies, putting pharma logos on their PowerPoints to make potential investors believe that Theranos was working with those companies, and using Siemens machines for lab analyses. It ended with testing unreliable technology on real patients. The initial exaggerations and deceptions escalated into a full-blown and extensive fraud. Some of the best engineers in Silicon Valley worked day and night to prop up Theranos. When should they have given up hope? When should they have abandoned the "We're not there yet" call to action and accepted the discouraging conclusion "It's impossible to get there"? Once you are slipping down the slope, it is hard to stop.

Evolutionary biologist Robert Trivers explained that the best way to lie to others is to lie to yourself first, because then—when you believe your own lies—you are, by definition and psychology, no longer lying.[70] Even more importantly, you can then convince others all the better. When one is a visionary with dreams, hopes, and beliefs, reality is blurred. Observations that do not fit our reality are simply bent into shape. Holmes developed a vision, but she could not deliver. As the stakes rose, she bent the reality of her company in order to survive. She kept bending—and her employees bent with her—until Theranos was no longer a unicorn but looked like a modern version of Andersen's fairy tale.

• • •

Theranos has been portrayed as the scandal of Elizabeth Holmes, often with a few references to her sidekick, Ramesh Balwani. But Theranos is not the story of a fraudulent entrepreneur—a bad apple. Granted, Holmes had tremendous willpower, ambition, charisma, and persuasion, but she only became the dazzling person she was because of her followers and the environment that developed around her. Investors are waiting for the next Steve Jobs, the next visionary entrepreneur to come and disrupt markets, or better: directly change the course of history while making rich those who understand early enough the potential of their idea. Elizabeth Holmes did what entrepreneurs are supposed to do: oversell and overpromise. The company turned into a cult, as reflected in the language: they were on a mission for humanity. And then, slowly over time, she and her team started to struggle. They all operated under uncertainty, presumably with the best of intentions, and then, slowly over time, she and her team started to struggle. Goals were too ambitious and engineering teams always behind schedule, despite 24/7 work shifts. In small steps, they started to bend reality for their stakeholders until telling the truth was no option anymore because the consequences would have been devastating. Some simply did what they did out of fear and in order to survive. When they were stuck, Theranos leaders increased the pressure on their teams. Driven by their mission, their hopes, their pursuit of profit, and their fear, they lost the ability to see that what they were doing was wrong. They became ethically blind. The faking was easy to rationalize: it wasn't only people at the top who were convinced that they just needed to work harder. Many believed that one day they would no longer fake it but really make it. Those who developed doubts and spoke up were crushed aggressively. With growing doubts in the media and among scientists, Theranos increasingly turned into a besieged medieval castle. Theranos is a frightening example of how organizations can bend reality under the spell of the dark pattern.

5
UBER—AN EMBATTLED UNICORN

THE INVENTION OF THE GIG ECONOMY

The taxi business is a heavily regulated, stable, protected, conservative, boring—and very profitable—industry.[1] Since Friedrich Greiner founded the first taxi company in 1897, not much has changed.[2] Until 2009, when Garrett Camp and Travis Kalanick, two tech entrepreneurs, turned it upside down. They developed a mobile app that could be used to rent a driver. Annoyed by the unreliable cabs in San Francisco, they wanted something better than a cab—an *über*-cab.[3] If you called a cab, you would not know when (sometimes even whether) it would arrive, how much it would cost, and how long the trip would take. On their app, clients had total transparency on all these parameters, they paid in advance with their credit card, and the driver would already know the destination.[4]

In December 2010, Kalanick became CEO of UberCab, and in 2011, he launched the beta version in San Francisco. The first idea was to create a luxury product. The two entrepreneurs convinced some of the limo-service operators in San Francisco to use their app. They gave a cash bonus and a preprogrammed iPhone to each driver. Customers who downloaded the app also received a bonus for their first ride and additional discounts for using the app again. A win-win situation. After fast success in San Francisco, UberCab rolled out their services across the US with the same method.[5]

The real success, however, came when Uber (the name was changed in 2011) gave up the idea of being a luxury limo service. Startups like Sidecar and Lyft had started to offer a ride-sharing service, where *anybody* with a car could pick up anybody for any destination. Uber decided to attack them with a new low-cost strategy and in July 2012 created UberX as their own ride-sharing service. Now everybody could become an Uber driver with their private car after a security check by the company.[6] Celebrated by *USA Today* as the "tech company of the year," Uber conquered city after city in the US and then spread globally.[7]

Yet the idea of using the smartphone to help customers and service providers find each other had much more potential. As it later turned out, Kalanick, almost single-handedly, created what today is called the "gig economy."[8] Uber's business model relied on hiring drivers as self-employed contractors, who were paid per "gig" on demand. Uber drivers thus did not have the advantages that come with fixed-term contracts, such as paid holidays, health-care insurance, or pension provisions. When they were sick, they had no income. Because the drivers were self-employed, Uber was not liable for what they did.[9] The company saved a lot of money.[10] When they wanted to get rid of a driver, it was enough to simply delete their account. Gig-economy platforms that followed the Uber model started to provide income to households in 2012. One decade later they gave income to about 15 million Americans, which corresponds to about 2 percent of the working population.[11] Today, *The Cambridge Dictionary* even includes a new word: *uberization*.[12]

The fast success of the company impressed investors. Everybody wanted to invest in them, fascinated by what the *Wall Street Journal* called "the genius tech founder mythology."[13] "Many believed the founders were remaking the world, making it smarter, more logical, meritocratic, efficient, and beautiful."[14] And maybe Kalanick was one of them. One of those who would make billions for his investors.

Like many tech entrepreneurs in Silicon Valley, Kalanick was a fan of the writer Ayn Rand, especially of her novel *The Fountainhead*.[15] The book tells the story of Howard Roark, who rebels against the rules and norms of society. Born in Russia and deeply affected by the absence of freedom in communist regimes, Rand considered the unfettered self-interest of individuals as the most important characteristic of human nature, and altruism as a destructive weakness. The protagonist of her novel does not follow the rules; he makes them. He demonstrates how the selfish individual drives the progress of a free society where life is about winning against others. Whatever stands in the way of individual freedom needs to be removed.[16] And that was precisely the motto of Kalanick.

> The atmosphere at Uber clearly displayed the impact of **rigid ideology**: Uber's corporate strategy—disrupting traditional taxi regulations and aggressively expanding its market—was driven by a strong belief in the principles of free markets, deregulation, and individualism. The gig economy turns employees into small entrepreneurs who fight for themselves and whose economic

> existence can be switched off by Uber's decision to disconnect their access to the app. It is a daily struggle for survival where the strong will win and the weak will lose. As Beth Schacter, one of the producers of a TV series on Uber, concluded: "Disruption is often the soil that monsters grow in."[17]

US AND THEM

Uber found itself in a fight for survival right from the start. First of all, there were the cities. In October 2010, the San Francisco Municipal Transportation Agency announced a fine of up to $5,000 per trip if they continued their operation in the city. According to them, Uber was breaking the law by operating taxi services without having the license to do so. This cease-and-desist order would have killed the young startup company immediately. As a reaction, Kalanick dropped the "cab" from the company's name, called it Uber instead of UberCab, and just continued.[18] The transportation agency did not follow up on their threat.

With its services, Uber was operating in a gray zone, and they were convinced that existing rules on transportation did not cover their ride-sharing services. As a manager of the company argued, "Often regulations fail to keep pace with innovation.... When Uber launched, no regulation existed for ride-sharing." And on top of that, as another representative of the company highlighted, "the law isn't what is written. It's what is enforced." And what is unclear is not necessarily enforced. After San Francisco, Uber wanted to enter Portland, but again, the city fought back aggressively.[19] As in San Francisco, Uber just ignored them. The German *Manager Magazin* described Kalanick's dealings with authorities very aptly: "Kalanick behaved like a cowboy who first kicks in the doors to the saloon, then shoots his way to the counter and finally expects friendly service."[20]

To conquer any new city, Uber would apply the strategy that had worked so well in San Francisco. They would fly in a general manager who would flood the city with advertising, trying to hire drivers and incentivizing them with sign-up bonuses and inducements to hit some milestones. These local managers and their teams would play cat and mouse with the local police. Cities like Portland would then try to catch the drivers by ordering Uber services via the app and then fining the drivers for violation of safety rules, missing permits, lack of insurance, or other reasons. When transportation authorities started to fine drivers, Uber would send messages to all drivers in the place, telling them that they would cover the costs and protect them. To avoid these costs, Uber developed an analytical tool that would figure out whether an Uber was called by a real client or by a police officer or another representative of the city, and it would then make certain that Uber cars were invisible to the authorities through this special app (a tool named "Greyball").[21] Uber called attempts of law enforcement representatives to fine the driver a "violation of terms of service," thus turning the tables and framing the attempts of cities to enforce the law as a violation of their own corporate legal terms.[22]

> Here we see the use of **manipulative language** to neutralize legal problems: Uber accused those trying to enforce the law of violating the terms, signaling that it was not Uber but the local authorities who were breaking the rules.

Greyball helped Uber push the service into a city to a point where it became difficult for local authorities to stop them without making citizens angry. Uber counted on this effect: once people started to use their services en masse, cities would drop their resistance. If local politicians created too many problems for Uber, the company pulled out of the market. Citizens who were now used to the service complained to the company and were told to rather direct their anger at their local politicians. Uber even created special functions on its app through which customers could directly send an email to local lawmakers, spamming them with protest messages.[23]

Uber managers considered all these tactics as legitimate, for several reasons. First, as a former top manager of the company remembered, "We were convinced that we were creating opportunities for hundreds of thousands of people.... We felt that there was a place for us."[24] Then, there was the conviction that local regulators used outdated regulation against Uber to protect the (according to Uber, corrupt) taxi industry.[25] Again, the inside perspective of Uber differed from the one taken by local regulators: "Transportation laws are complicated.... We interpreted the law, and the authorities interpreted the law. We were convinced that there was a legal space for our operations and that their interpretation was wrong not ours."[26] According to Kalanick, "There's been so much corruption and so much cronyism in the taxi industry and so much regulatory capture that if you ask permission upfront for something that's already legal, you'll never get it." He fought, arguing that you need to stand by your principles and be okay with confrontation.[27] Managers at Uber did not have the impression of doing something wrong. On the contrary, they considered the moves of the authorities as legally problematic. As a former Uber manager told us: "The authorities were under the pressure of the taxi lobby to not allow our operations and in some cases, when they realized that our interpretation of the law was correct, they would go so far as to change the law to make our operations illegal. Sometimes, local authorities even engaged in what we would consider illegal behavior to prevent Uber from operating."[28]

> We see how managers at Uber were caught in a dynamic of **ambiguous rules**: right from the start, Uber operated under the assumption that their own operations took place in a regulatory vacuum. For them, rules were—at least—unclear, but increasingly they were convinced that their business was so different from the traditional taxi business that whatever rules did exist did not apply to them. Since most of the time, local regulators did not insist, the conviction that they operated in a gray zone where they could bend and interpret rules grew stronger up to the point that they even considered the behaviors of the authorities illegal.

Uber was not following transportation laws as they were interpreted by local authorities and taxi lobbies. The company saw itself as a disrupter, reshaping these rules around its own product. What regulators saw as rule breaking, Uber considered acts of "bold disruption."[29] Taxi drivers, however, did not want to be disrupted and started to fight back aggressively wherever Uber started their business. Huge demonstrations took place, and in some cities taxi drivers were even burning tires and destroying cars.[30] Uber managers and drivers felt threatened: "As a challenger of the taxi industry, we were under attack by the incumbents. They would fight back aggressively to the point where we had to fear for our safety. In some places, our local managers only moved with bodyguards. Taxi drivers would threaten them and their families. Before working for Uber, I never thought that this would be possible. This certainly added to the intensity of how we perceived our situation. We were fighting to stay alive every day."[31]

> **Perceived unfairness** dominated the worldview of decision-makers at Uber: For Kalanick, those who protected the taxi drivers—unions, legislators, local police officers—were just supporting an old, inefficient, and corrupt industry, while he wanted to innovate transportation for the twenty-first century.[32] He felt that the fight against him was not fair. He was on a crusade for a good cause, a successful entrepreneur, celebrated by investors and clients, and the authorities were putting obstacles in the way of progress. Uber considered it legitimate to aggressively fight back; after all, it was fighting public corruption.
>
> Uber succeeded in neutralizing doubtful business practices through **manipulative language**: breaking the law is described in the language of entrepreneurial progress. Who can be against "bold disruptions" that bring so many advantages to clients?

Soon after Uber, other startups offered similar services. One of them, Lyft, was considered the biggest threat to Uber's success. Competition in Silicon Valley is often described as a winner-takes-it-all fight, where only a monopolist can be profitable in the long run.[33] This can easily be explained with the so-called network effect: for most tech platforms, the value of a service goes up with the number of people joining, and this was also true for Uber. To catch an Uber everywhere fast required the presence of many drivers, which in turn would only occur if many people used the service. That is why

Uber burned enormous amounts of cash to pay incentives to both drivers and riders, hoping that once they had crushed the competition and become a monopolist, they could raise prices without worrying anymore about competitors. And they succeeded. As Kalanick proudly told a reporter who asked about numbers: "The best metric I can give you is that Uber is killing in San Francisco and we're crushing in New York." They were killing and crushing the competition like in a war, and in a war, you need to make aggressive moves. And aggressive, Kalanick was. "It is war time," as he told his people. The space in the headquarters where Kalanick and his team met for strategic discussions was called the "war room."[34]

At this point we can see two additional building blocks of the dark pattern.

Corrupting goals: Uber was convinced that they were operating in a market where the winner takes it all. The goal was not just to be number one. The goal was to be the only one—nothing else mattered. There was no room for ethics or compromise.

Dangerous groups: If you fight to stay alive, if you are surrounded by enemies who want to destroy your success or even threaten your physical integrity while you are convinced you belong to the good guys, the disrupter of a bad service, you start to develop a strong "us" versus "them" mindset. "Us" was everybody inside Uber, and "them" was all those who created trouble for the good guys: regulators, competitors, taxi drivers, and—as we will see below—even their own Uber drivers.

THE DARK PATTERN

At one point, Uber started a driver-recruitment program that targeted Lyft drivers. They called it "Operation Slog." Driving through their cities, drivers would see aggressive advertising posters against Lyft. Then, the company hired what they called "brand ambassadors," who would call Lyft drivers during their rides. Ambassadors had "driver kits" including iPhones ready for the drivers who would be willing to switch to Uber. These ambassadors would receive up to $750 for recruiting a new driver for Uber.[35] Uber also created a program that they called "hell." Using hell, Uber employees would open fake Lyft driver accounts, which would then be used to track other Lyft drivers and to see the competitor's prices. Since many drivers were working both for Lyft and Uber, they could use the information to always go below the price of Lyft so that customers would choose Uber.[36]

> The use of **manipulative language** continues: unleashing "hell" on competitors who must be killed and crushed. Uber was fighting a war controlled from a war room. And in a war, rules do not count. Hyperaggressive language is combined with euphemistic language that frames doubtful practices as entrepreneurial disruption and societal progress.
>
> And the company slowly moves forward on a **slippery slope**: with Uber's rise from a little startup facilitating limousine renting to a global player, the stakes became higher and higher, the company had more to lose, and the battles on the various fronts became more and more intense. Moreover, with each conquest of a new city, the company learned that aggression pays off and how to fight even better. More and more illegal tools

> and methods were developed and used against regulators and competitors.

Uber was in a war not only with regulators, competitors, and professional taxi drivers. They soon realized that some of their own drivers had turned into fraudsters. With fake accounts, such drivers would harvest those incentives that Uber had established for new drivers and customers—and then disappear. Uber was losing millions and had to invest massively in a fraud-investigation team to catch up with ever-more-sophisticated fraudulent schemes and fight back.[37]

SUPER PUMPED

In September 2015, Uber threw a multimillion-dollar all-inclusive party across multiple five-star hotels in Las Vegas. For several days, more than 4,800 employees from around the world celebrated the company's achievements.[38] Kalanick used this event to present the fourteen Uber principles, the new "philosophy of work," which he had developed with former Amazon manager Jeff Holden.[39] The timing was perfect: during these celebrations, it was easy to link these principles with success. In Las Vegas, Kalanick made it very clear what he expected from his people to continue the success story. They had to be "super pumped." As an employee would later explain, "Super pumpedness is all about moving the team forward, working long hours—pretty much a do-whatever-it-takes attitude to move the company in the right direction."[40] Other principles invited Uber employees to be "always hustling" and search for "principled confrontation with others." They had to "make magic," "be an owner, not a renter," and, echoing Amazon, show "customer obsession."[41] If successful, they would be rewarded, since "meritocracy" was another one of the principles.[42]

What is a meritocracy? Enron CEO Jeff Skilling used to explain to his traders that they were entitled to "eat what they killed."[43] Conversely, if their hunt yielded no results, then they had nothing to eat. Uber's meritocracy was based on the pressure to constantly bring results that were superior to those of fellow Uber colleagues. Only when constantly hustling and being super pumped could employees at Uber keep up with expectations. This was a soul-flattening "zero-sum meritocracy," where "for one employee to get ahead, another must fail."[44] Actually, it was only logical: the same conviction that guided Uber's behavior outside on the markets—namely, that the strong must constantly crush the weak to survive themselves—was now also explicitly installed within its own organization.[45]

A key driving force of Uber's meritocracy was its performance-evaluation system. At Uber, twice per year, managers assigned a numeric rating to their team members. Given that low performers in their team threatened their own evaluation, managers pushed their teams to be more super pumped, and low performers suffered all kinds of humiliations. Managers called low performers "faggots," bullied and demoted them, threw coffee mugs at them, or threatened them with baseball bats.[46]

The consequence of Uber's meritocracy? Super-pumped employees were fighting "a game-of-thrones political war" against each other at all levels.[47] Within their teams, they fought to not be humiliated or fired as a low performer. Between local offices, they fought to outperform each other. Finally, employees were even fighting their own superiors, engaging in political games behind their back with the intention to undermine and replace them.[48] "Being cutthroat and competitive was considered an asset, not a liability.... 'Kill or be killed' was the unofficial motto at Uber."[49] According to a former Uber engineer, "It was generally understood that the entire mess came from the very top; it seemed that Travis Kalanick...liked watching...employees fight against each other."[50]

> Here we see how the dark pattern plays out in two additional dimensions.
>
> **Destructive incentives:** The application of a Darwinian appraisal system created a competitive and ruthless working environment where immense pressure, suffering, and, all too often, unethical practices prevailed.
>
> **Toxic leadership:** Leaders at Uber enforced a zero-sum meritocracy, humiliated the losers, and created an aggressive and highly toxic work environment. The aggressive leadership style permeated the organization from the top down.

Uber's hyperalpha culture made it a difficult place to work for women.[51] Former Uber employees have described Uber as a frat house. The environment was one where achievements were frequently marked by chest bumps, and men regularly engaged in push-up contests.[52] In 2014, when Uber was conquering city after city, Kalanick explained in an interview with *GQ* that since he had become a rich Silicon Valley celebrity, it was much easier to attract women. At Uber, he joked, he could have women on demand. As he told the journalist, who was teasing him about his "skyrocketing desirability," "We call that boob-er."[53] Gabi Holzwarth, who dated Kalanick for three years, remembered that the Uber parties were special: "You go to an event and there's just a bunch of models they've flown in. That's what they like to play with. That's pretty much it."[54] Yet, some took it a step further.

On February 19, 2017, Susan Fowler, who had worked as an engineer at Uber, published a blog post, "Reflecting on One Very, Very Strange Year at Uber," where she shared her exposure to Uber's toxic culture and the harassment she experienced from her superiors. This post was read by millions of people.[55] As Fowler would later write in her book, *Whistleblower*, "I was sexually harassed and bullied at Uber, and I fought until I had exhausted all options except one—to leave the company and go public with my story."[56]

Only a few days after she started at Uber, her new manager wrote her a chat message, asking her about her onboarding tasks and whether she would need help. But then, the conversation quickly became awkward. He started to talk about his upcoming trip to Hawaii, explaining to her that "vacations have some special rules attached to them in my relationship. It is an open relationship but it's a little more open on vacations haha." She tried to bring the conversation back to work issues, but her superior continued to explain to her that he and his wife would have sex with other people. She took screenshots of the messages and contacted the HR department.[57] Fowler was invited to a meeting with an HR representative, who explained to her that her superior was a high performer and that this was his first offense. She was given the choice of either staying on his team or changing teams. Fowler decided to change teams, and in the weeks following the incident, she befriended other female engineers. They all had stories to share about harassment and discrimination.

However, they had given up reaching out to HR after realizing that HR managers would rather retaliate against them than take measures against the harassers. Some colleagues and even managers at Uber who supported Fowler when she spoke up were attacked for not being team players and in some cases even fired by the company. One of the HR managers she met warned her: "The way I see it, all the complaints you've made to HR have one thing in common, and that is you." Then she urged Fowler to ask herself what she "had done to make these terrible things happen at Uber."[58]

Other former Uber employees confirmed Fowler's experience. One of them described Uber as a company "where a blind eye is turned to infractions from top performers."[59] When Fowler transferred to a new team, she got another taste of the aggressive Uber culture. While she was working day and night, her new manager would attack her and yell at her in meetings, telling her that she was not doing her job and not working hard enough. When she shared her experience with colleagues in other teams, she was told that they had similar problems with their own managers. "Almost every single one of them had started seeing a therapist for anxiety or depression related to the culture of work at Uber; the engineers who've been at Uber the longest all seemed to have suicidal thoughts."[60] According to Fowler, when she joined Uber, 25 percent of her engineering colleagues were women.[61] When she finally left Uber, it had dropped to 3 percent.[62]

When the first stories of sexism and misogyny at Uber surfaced, journalist Sarah Lacy criticized the "horrific trickle down of asshole culture." But she also described an interesting reaction that she received from investors. She was told that "his same bad-boy behavior and arrogance is the only reason he was able to run headlong into the buzzsaw of dozens of powerful taxi lobbies."[63] The widely shared assumption in Silicon Valley was that only with such a character could you cut through the resistance of corrupt and inefficient institutions. One of Kalanick's acquaintances put it in a nutshell: "Assholes create great businesses."[64]

> Three building blocks of the dark pattern can be observed here.
>
> **Dangerous groups:** Notwithstanding the fact that there was fierce competition between employees due to Uber's performance-evaluation system, the company established a high-testosterone culture where (male) group members used each other as a benchmark for what was considered acceptable.
>
> **Ambiguous rules:** On many occasions, the morally doubtful and sometimes illegal behavior of managers was tolerated as long as the perpetrators were high performers.
>
> **Toxic leadership:** The hyperaggressive behavior Uber showed in the market was duplicated internally. Alpha males "crushed" not only the competition but also women, low performers, and people speaking up. It burned out its people and pushed many into suicidal thoughts. Asshole culture was the assumed driver of business success.

THE FALL AND FUTURE OF THE FOUNDER

"By the end of 2016, life was good for Travis Kalanick. He was rich and powerful, and his empire was growing further by the day."[65]

Then, one blow after another hit the company and its founder. On February 19, 2017, Susan Fowler published her explosive post. Then, the *New York Times* published an article confirming that Fowler was not an isolated case at Uber. A few days later, Google filed a lawsuit against Uber for stealing trade secrets about self-driving cars.[66] Then, at the end of February, *Bloomberg* published a video showing Kalanick in an aggressive dispute with an Uber driver.[67] Only a few days later, the *New York Times* published an article about the Greyball tool that Uber had used to make their cars invisible to law enforcement officers.[68]

Kalanick decided to hire former attorney general Eric Holder to investigate some 215 complaints of Uber employees. When Holder published his report on June 13, 2017, he confirmed the experience of Fowler and many others. As a result of the investigation, Uber fired twenty employees.[69] Holder published a list of thirteen recommendations, including that the fourteen principles should be reformulated and HR processes improved.[70] However, point one on his list was "Review and Reallocate the Responsibilities of Travis Kalanick." One day after the report was published, Kalanick announced that he would go on indefinite leave, and only one week later, on June 21, he resigned.[71] Within six weeks following his resignation, Kalanick sold 90 percent of his Uber stock for more than $2.5 billion.[72] Arianna Huffington, a member of the Uber board, announced that from now on, Uber would no longer hire "brilliant jerks."[73] Kalanick's "war room" was officially rebranded into "peace room."[74]

And Kalanick? He invested some of the money he made with Uber into a new business idea. He bought a majority stake in a company that operates a startup called CloudKitchens. With his new company, Kalanick is buying cheap property in the US, China, and Europe, transforming the spaces into kitchens, and renting them out to people who cook for food-delivery services such as Uber Eats.[75] *Business Insider* recently reported that Kalanick's new startup is again "ruled by a temple of bros." On a retreat in a resort in Southern California in 2019, Kalanick presented the values of his new venture: people must be "super pumped" and "always be hustling." Employees are evaluated and ranked with a method that differentiates ten performance levels. Like Uber, CloudKitchens is already starting to clash with local politicians in some of the cities where they invest. The meeting room of the leader of the real-estate team is called the "snake pit."[76]

• • •

While for some the story of Kalanick and Uber looks like a prime example of the American dream, for others it has become a nightmare. A young entrepreneur appears out of nowhere with a brilliant idea that makes him a billionaire in no time at all. Driven by a mixture of the pursuit of profit and an iron will to stand up for a world without protectionism and corruption, this knight of deregulation fights an unwavering battle in the land of the free against all who stand in his way. And there are quite a few of them—for example, countless cab drivers who have a lot to lose from his easy-to-use app. From the perspective of Darwin's ideas about survival of the fittest, it seems perfectly normal and justified to be aggressive and "shoot your way to the counter" as Kalanick had done. So, this fight for a better world has losers, but that's their own fault, because why are they still clinging to an old, rotten system and standing in the way of a new, better transportation system? Moral disengagement could hardly be easier. Uber is breaking new ground with its business idea, and so there is a lot of confusion about how existing laws apply to the new reality created by Uber. It is not surprising that it starts interpreting the rules to its own advantage. Nor is it surprising when Uber supports its fight with an appropriate choice of words that portrays the company's aggressive actions as those of righteous freedom fighters. Nor is it surprising when Uber's fighting spirit, which it unleashes against external opposition, is also unleashed within the company. This is how we find toxic leadership, corrupting goals, and destructive incentives that cause people grief and pain—not only outside but also inside the company. And the ethics? Well, the old has to go, and you have to crack an egg to make an omelet. Typically, dreams unfold at night, when things are in the dark and some dimensions are no longer visible. The Uber version of the American dream seems to be no exception.

6
WELLS FARGO—SELL LIKE HELL

FROM A FIRM FOOTING TO A FAST FALL

The financial crisis of 2007–2008 devastated economies on a planetary scale, comparable in magnitude to the Great Depression of the early 1930s. Only one of the big US banks made it through the storm mostly unharmed: Wells Fargo. Founded in 1852 by Henry Wells and William Fargo, the venerable bank never played with fire like their competitors did. In 2015, the *Financial Times* wrote in admiration that "the people running Wells have grown rich and powerful by keeping their heads down and avoiding unnecessary drama," and *Barron's* ranked them the seventh most respected company in the world.[1]

During the financial crisis in 2007, John Stumpf, who had been the chief operating officer of the bank, became its CEO, and in 2010 also the chairman of the board. Under his leadership, between 2006 and 2015, the stock value of the bank rose by 67 percent.[2] By 2015, Wells Fargo had become the world's largest bank in terms of market capitalization. In contrast to other banks, they made their profits mainly in the low-risk areas of retail and community banking.[3] Relatedly, Stumpf did not fit the stereotype of those arrogant bankers sitting in designer offices on the top floor of a high tower. He was down-to-earth and developed an image that stood in stark contrast to the stereotype of the greedy Wall Street banker.[4] He called the bank's 270,000 employees "team members" and the more than 6,200 branches of the bank "stores." The bank was proud of its "culture of caring" for both customers and employees, and it was awarded the Gallup Great Workplace Award in 2014 and 2015.[5]

With all the praise and glorifying self-assessment, the fall could hardly have been greater. Only two years later, in September 2016, the former "banker of the year" found himself sitting in a US Congressional hearing, in front of Senator Elizabeth Warren, who, visibly agitated, denounced his "gutless leadership" in pretty strong terms, accusing him of squeezing "employees to the breaking point" while putting hundreds of millions of dollars in his own pocket.[6] Stumpf resigned a few weeks later. What had happened at Wells Fargo?

EIGHT IS GREAT

In 1998, incoming CEO Richard Kovacevich brought a new strategy to Wells Fargo. Called "cross-selling," it was based on a simple idea: spinning a net of multiple contracts around existing customers is much more profitable than winning new customers. Moreover, it makes it less likely that they will change banks. As of 1998, when

Kovacevich took over, Wells Fargo had sold an average of 3.2 products to each customer. He wanted to get this number up to 8. In 1999, the strategy was baptized "Gr-Eight." By 2007, when Kovacevich handed over the CEO baton to Stumpf, the average had increased to 5.5.[7] Salespeople were constantly reminded that "Eight Is Great." Wells Fargo aggressively pushed the cross-selling and imposed double-digit annual sales-growth targets on its branch managers.[8] In internal emails, Stumpf would state that the company "fight[s] like cats and dogs for those numbers!"[9] By 2016, each customer had accumulated an average of 6.15 products with the bank, which was almost four times the industry average.[10] Wells Fargo became the "king of cross-sell."[11]

In fact, the bank never reached its goal of selling eight products to every customer, but that number was partly arbitrary anyway. Even if they had achieved it, eight would not have been enough, as Stumpf made clear in the 2010 annual report: "I'm often asked why we set a cross-sell goal of eight. The answer is, it rhymed with 'great.' Perhaps our new cheer should be: 'Let's go again, for ten!'"[12] There was no end in sight.

Stumpf had selected Carrie Tolstedt to lead the community banking division of the business, which she did from 2007 to 2016. She was responsible for the sales strategy and its acceleration. Under her leadership, sales grew by more than 10 percent, year after year.[13] *Fortune* magazine ranked Tolstedt one of the fifty most powerful women in business for several years in a row, and Stumpf considered her the most brilliant community banker he ever met.[14] The cross-selling ratio was the key driving force of his and her bonuses. In September 2016, she retired, taking with her a package worth $124 million.[15]

> Here we see how the thinking at Wells Fargo was dominated by **rigid ideology**. Inspired by Milton Friedman's shareholder value theory, cross-selling was pushed with one single objective in mind: to keep the success story going by increasing the value of the stock year after year after year.

It's not that there were no early warnings. But they were gone with the wind. In October 2013, the *Los Angeles Times* published an article, "Wells Fargo Fires Workers Accused of Cheating on Sales Goals." Based on interviews with more than thirty former or current employees of the bank, the article accused the bank, in an attempt to meet unrealistic targets, of opening fake accounts for customers.[16] Wells Fargo responded by saying that the problems described in the article had been caused by isolated rogue employees. After all, the bank had "security procedures to *root out employees* who violate laws or bank ethics policy," a spokesperson for the bank confirmed.[17] At no point did the top management of the bank see a need to investigate what might be driving these fraudulent practices, beyond the attribution of the problem to individual salespeople. Stumpf always highlighted that "the one percent that did it wrong, who we fired, terminated, in no way reflects our culture nor reflects the great work the other vast majority of the people do."[18] A few bad apples? Nothing could be further from the truth.

It turns out that for the salespeople at Wells Fargo, the Gr-Eight strategy meant they had to meet ambitious sales goals under extremely high pressure. They were measured in daily quotas. If they did not reach their targets, they were threatened, mocked, and embarrassed in front of their peers. A former Wells Fargo employee remembered, "At the end of the day, the manager would call out each teller in front of everybody and share their results. It was a frightening experience.... The last three months were hell. Even though I was reaching my sales goals, it was not enough for them.... I was so stressed out, I developed shingles."[19] Another former salesperson recalled that his superior would simply say, "I don't care how you do it—but do it, or else you're not going home."[20]

Former employees remember that they had to sell six products per day, then later, eight. If they overfulfilled their quota, it did not reduce the quota for the next day.[21] In the first quarter of the year, salespeople were even expected to sell twenty products a day—boosting the numbers in the first quarter of the year was supposed to impress shareholders. As internal investigations later acknowledged, this so-called jump into January became "a breeding ground for bad behavior."[22] If selling six or eight products was already very demanding, twenty was borderline impossible. Many workers felt miserable just walking into work every day.[23] Those who were falling short risked being fired: "We were constantly told we would end up working for McDonald's... if we did not make the sales quotas."[24]

This presented a dilemma: the salespeople could either decide to engage in illegal sales practices and achieve their targets, which were incentivized by bonuses and high-speed promotions, or they could struggle every day and eventually lose the job.[25] While it should take someone at least ten years of time and experience to make it to a branch-manager position, a successful bank teller with an extraordinary sales track record could get there in under three years. Numerous Wells Fargo employees in their early twenties moved up to the position of branch manager during this time.[26] The illegal practices spread with such promotions.[27]

Tolstedt and her team called the goals they set "50/50 plans," knowing that only half of the regions would achieve them. She set the targets and handed them down to the regions. From there they went to the districts, branches, and individual employees. Branch managers had to report to their district managers. The performance of each branch was discussed four times a day, at 11:00 a.m., 1:00 p.m., 3:00 p.m., and 5:00 p.m.[28] Employees at every level were ranked against each other, with the results published daily in so-called Motivator reports. These reports increased the pressure on managers and promoted a culture of shaming.[29]

While Tolstedt and her team supposed that not more than 50 percent of the teams would achieve their goals, they pressured everybody not just to achieve 100 percent, but 120 percent. With the 120 percent goal, managers were even ready to terminate team members who only achieved 105 percent.[30] Wells Fargo had an employee turnover of about 35 percent annually (up to 41 percent in 2012), significantly higher than the industry average.[31] As a result, many of the employees who stayed were inexperienced in sales. And when they were promoted, they were inexperienced in leadership.

The bank increased its sales goals based on the results of the previous year. Given that the results were inflated by the fake accounts salespeople had created, employees found themselves caught in a vicious circle. More fake accounts required even more fake accounts the following year. Sales goals became increasingly unrealistic over time, but top management ignored complaints from regional leaders.[32]

There are a few building blocks of the dark pattern at work here.

Toxic leadership: Central management exerted pressure on the sales managers, which they passed on to their sales staff, creating a culture of competition and fear. Management was aware of the unethical practices but turned a blind eye or even encouraged this behavior. Successful fraudsters were promoted. Targets became more important than ethical principles, and aggressive sales tactics were normalized and even encouraged.

Corrupting goals: The active pursuit of unrealistic "Gr-Eight" sales targets put extreme pressure on managers and employees. This led to enormous suffering and stress but also to them gaming and manipulating the system to meet their quotas.

Destructive incentives: Achieving or exceeding sales targets was rewarded with bonuses and promotions, while failure to meet these targets led to public humiliation, pressure, and often even dismissal.

The loans, bank accounts, insurances, or credit cards that they were supposed to sell to their customers were called "solutions." In the morning, a shift would normally start with the manager telling their teams that they had to meet their "solution goals." Those who did not meet their goals were "pulled into the back room having one-on-ones for coaching sessions." Another former employee described one of her coachings: "It's like being called into the principal's office… They shut the door, lock the door." Then she says her manager would give her a "formal warning": "If you don't meet your solutions, you're not a team player. If you're bringing down the team then you will be fired, and it will be on your permanent record." After such coaching sessions, she often vomited into the wastebasket under her desk.[33]

> **Manipulative language** supported and facilitated unethical practices: the use of competitive metaphors, such as Stumpf's statement that the company was "fighting like cats and dogs" to reach the magic Gr-Eight, fostered an aggressive atmosphere. Referring to unattainable sales quotas as "solutions" had a positive connotation and facilitated moral disengagement. Similarly, humiliating sessions featuring accusations of incompetence, to the point of threatening dismissal, were labeled "coaching sessions," and disastrous feedback was dubbed "motivator reports," masking the toxic culture. The height of cynicism was probably reached when the fraudulent opening of new accounts for an existing customer was euphemistically described as "developing further relationships." Salespeople developed an entire euphemistic vocabulary around their fraudulent practices.[34]

One of the disciplinary actions taken against underperforming employees was to deny them bathroom breaks.[35] Rebecca, a former employee, said that people felt dehumanized and treated unfairly: "Wells Fargo can give $120 million to a crooked CEO—but won't allow us to pee."[36] The stress took its toll. Angie Payden, who worked as a saleswoman, described her ordeal: "I started to have extreme physical stress-related symptoms, as well as random panic attacks.... One morning, before meeting with a customer, in which I knew I was going to have to sell unneeded services, I...went to the bathroom and took a drink of some hand sanitizer. This immediately reduced my anxiety. From that point, I began drinking the hand sanitizer all over the bank. In late November 2012, I was completely addicted...and drinking at least a bottle a day."[37] Another salesman, Erik, remembers seeing many of his colleagues crying in the office: "It was multiple occasions where I saw my coworkers were cracking under the pressure."[38] Scott T., a former teller, was one of them: "There were numerous days where I would hide in the men's bathroom crying."[39] An anonymous salesperson found an apt way to describe the immense pressure in an email to the CEO: "I was in the 1991 Gulf War.... This is sad and hard for me to say, but I had less stress in the 1991 Gulf War than working for Wells Fargo."[40]

FRAUD AND FORGERIES

Despite the eye-watering compensation for senior management, retail banking is not a well-paid or glamorous job for most of the about 1.7 million people who work in it in the US. Most of them (84.3 percent) are women. Bank tellers earn a median hourly wage of $12.44. In 2014, a third of these bank tellers were enrolled in one or more help programs for the poor, such as Medicaid or food stamps. For bank workers alone, the public cost of such programs amounts to $900 million per year.[41]

And exactly those bank workers at Wells Fargo faced two dilemmas. In order to achieve their sales targets, they had to weigh the risk of being fired for underperformance against the risk of being caught using illegal practices. And they had to see their own interests as being opposed to those of their customers. As one employee said: "There was a constant battle of how you do right for the customer without sacrificing, you know, not paying a light bill or having shoes for the kids going back to school. You can't make that sacrifice."[42] A former employee admitted, "I had never in my life been the sort of person to see dollar signs when people walk in. I always liked building relationships. But these insane goals really affected how I saw them. I didn't think about meeting their needs, I thought about how can I meet my goals.... If someone's getting married, tell them to get a credit card.... If you heard kids in the background, the answer was a credit card."[43]

> A prevailing feeling among Wells Fargo employees was **perceived unfairness**: the carrot for a few, the stick for many. While the bosses felt that the huge board bonuses were fair compensation for their efforts to satisfy the shareholders, the employees, who only received a minimum salary but maximum pressure, felt unfairly treated, especially when they had achieved good results but it could never be enough. Going to the toilet became a privilege. Given that employees were powerless against their superiors, letting customers pay for it was a way of rebalancing things in their favor. According to *Bloomberg*, the fraud did not look like some clever-but-evil profit-making gambit, but rather like a large-scale revolt by underpaid and mistreated Wells Fargo employees against their superiors.[44]

Wells Fargo salespeople did not just sell products that customers did not need. They went one decisive and illegal step further and opened millions of saving accounts, credit cards, and debit cards without the customers' knowledge. They simply filled out the applications themselves and used the electronic signature of the customers if necessary. Checking accounts would be considered for the quota only when there was money transferred to them. In such cases, a salesperson would simply move money from one account of the customer to the new account (and back).[45] Such accounts were opened to meet the sales targets and often closed immediately afterward.[46]

Customers who were interested in products were told that these were only available in combination with other products, which was not true.[47] Moreover, salespeople would misrepresent the costs of a product or promise benefits that did not exist.[48] Phone numbers, home addresses, and email addresses of customers were often invented for fake accounts. Salespeople even opened bank accounts for themselves or their own family members to achieve their targets. A former employee at Wells Fargo explained how she learned these and other practices from her manager: "I did not agree with any of it, I really didn't, but she was my boss.... She taught me, I learned it from her, and she learned it from her bosses, and it all trickles down."[49] Numerous Wells Fargo workers confirmed that their superiors either pushed them to use such practices or looked the other way when their teams applied them.[50]

While in the end 5,300 employees were fired for illegal sales practices, it was probably hundreds of thousands of employees who applied the very same methods in order to achieve their targets. The firing barely touched the tip of the iceberg. An investigation led by PricewaterhouseCoopers estimated that approximately 3.5 million unauthorized bank accounts were opened between January 2009 and September 2016.[51] Half a million credit cards were issued without the customers knowing about it.[52] Between 2012 and 2016, some 800,000 customers were talked into buying unnecessary car insurance. Thousands of them would later lose their cars because they could not pay the premiums and had incurred debts.[53]

Employees focused many of their illegal practices on specific groups: immigrants who did not speak English well, elderly people who struggled to understand banking procedures or had memory problems, and poor and financially illiterate customers. For the latter, it was not even necessary to commit fraud. They would simply talk them into opening another bank account.[54] Kevin Pham, a former employee, compared these practices to lions hunting zebras: "They would look for the weakest, the ones that would put up the least resistance."[55]

It is not that the bank never discussed the problem. In 2004, a team of internal investigators found an increase in fraudulent sales practices. According to a memorandum they wrote, problematic cases were rising from 63 in 2000 to a projected 680 in 2004.[56] Fraudulent practices were repeatedly discussed and analyzed by the risk-management committee, the team-member misconduct committee, the ethics committee, the community-bank risk-management committee, human resources, and the board of the bank. But discussions always revolved around the magical number of 1 percent fraud, which was thought to be unavoidable, acceptable, and certainly not indicative of a pervasive problem.[57]

Even after the *Los Angeles Times* article in 2013, Stumpf and his team were convinced that Wells Fargo was demonstrating above-average integrity within the industry.[58] In a memo to the risk committee in May 2015, Tolstedt described the problem as "outlier behavior" of "only a small percentage of Retail Banking team members."[59] Tolstedt was not concerned about the firing of 3,500 employees—bad apples. For her, this simply proved that their control mechanisms were effective.[60]

Which mechanism was she referring to? Wells Fargo had a system in place to detect misconduct by its salespeople. But they applied an extremely low threshold for their monitoring. Every month, about 30,000 employees showed activities that were flagged as potentially illegal by the system. Only the top 0.01 percent of those employees, who showed the highest intensity of such activities, were investigated. US authorities would later find those monitoring practices to have been "severely deficient" and even "intentionally designed to neither prevent nor detect the vast majority of sales practices misconduct."[61] "They focused on the specific employee complaint or individual lawsuit that was before them, missing opportunities to put them together in a way that might have revealed sales-practice problems to be more significant and systemic than was appreciated."[62]

In addition to the bank's control mechanisms, managers sent their team members to mandatory ethics training, where they learned about the code of conduct and the confidential hotline they could call. However, those same managers were the ones pressuring them to meet their quotas as soon as they returned from training.

Some employees spoke up against the illegal practices that they observed around them or were supposed to apply themselves. Bill Bado was one of them. He called the ethics hotline and even sent a message to HR in September 2013: "I have been asked on several occasions to do things that I know are not ethical and would be grounds for discharge." Eight days after his message, he was fired for "excessive tardiness."[63] So was Heather Brock, another employee who had been courageous enough to speak up.[64] Ricky Hansen, a branch manager at Wells Fargo, reported multiple fraud cases in his branch to his manager, John Vasquez. Hansen was fired; Vasquez was promoted.[65] When Yesenia Guitron observed a colleague opening bank accounts for customers without their permission, she called the ethics hotline and spoke up to her manager. When nothing happened, she contacted HR. She was fired for insubordination. A former Wells Fargo HR manager later declared that the bank retaliated against employees who spoke up. They would wait for them to make a mistake. "If this person was supposed to be at the branch at 8:30 a.m. and they showed up at 8:32 a.m., they would fire them."[66]

> The Wells Fargo case shows the effect of dangerous groups operating with ambiguous rules.
>
> **Dangerous groups:** Many employees simply complied and contributed to the fraudulent practices without daring to speak out, becoming bystanders and perpetrators at the same time. Those who spoke up were fired, and those who just did what they observed their peers doing survived.
>
> **Ambiguous rules:** Those who informed HR or the top management about the fraudulent practices were fired. Torn between following the rules and achieving their sales targets, salespeople learned what the real but tacit expectations were: underachievers were fired; performing fraudsters promoted. Ethics training and rules versus sales targets—a typical double bind, with a clear hidden message: for following ethical practices there was the stick; for unethical practices there was the carrot. Moreover, it was common knowledge that "no one was ever penalized for doing the wrong thing until there was critical mass. Instead, they were promoted."[67]

It is not without a certain irony that a systemic feature of Wells Fargo helped to disguise the fact that the reason for the fraud was not a few bad apples, but deeply systemic. The bank was highly decentralized. Different parts of the business had to achieve their goals in autonomously operating units. Managers were supposed to "run it like you own it."[68] HR and risk management were decentralized, too. The assumption was that local risks or local HR problems would be best understood and managed locally. The leaders at Wells Fargo were convinced that the bank had successfully navigated through the storm of the financial crisis *because* of its decentralized risk management. But the price the company paid for this structural decision was that there was no cross-function tracking, analyzing, or reporting of problems.[69]

Another reason these topics were not discussed on the board level might have been that Stumpf was known to not appreciate bad news or being told of problems. He was not interested in how his teams achieved their goals, as long as they achieved them. As he admitted himself, "I care about outcomes, not process."[70] Stumpf had established a weekly operating-committee meeting, but it was not supposed to be a forum for discussion.[71] Tolstedt's leadership style was like Stumpf's. She was described as "intense" and "unrelentingly focused on numbers showing growth."[72] It was well known that, like Stumpf, she did not want to hear negative information and did not like to be challenged. Her managers were afraid to speak up to her.[73]

We see here a subtler version of **toxic leadership**. If you have a problem, you are a problem. Very often, it does not even require yelling to spread fear.

Wells Fargo moved forward on a **slippery slope**: (1) the behavior of employees, (2) their attitude toward customers, and (3) the corporate culture all gradually changed over time. First, salespeople started by normally selling several products to one

> customer, then they lied about their needs, misrepresented the cost of a product, or promised benefits that did not exist. If the goal was still not achieved, the salespeople opened bank accounts for family members, eventually reaching the final point of fraud by setting up fake accounts for the customers without their consent. Secondly, at the beginning of the process, a genuine long-term relationship with the customers was sought, but in the end, they were merely seen as a resource to be exploited. Finally, the culture eroded, partly because employees gradually became numb to the pressure they were under and the practices they used to save their own skin, partly because of a selection effect that left only the most unscrupulous at the end, and finally, because the best fraudsters were promoted and taught the others how to achieve sales targets.

THE SCANDAL AND ITS AFTERMATH

In May 2015, the Los Angeles city attorney filed a lawsuit against Wells Fargo branches in Los Angeles, accusing the bank of systematic illegal sales practices.[74] The house of cards started to collapse. Since 2016, in total Wells Fargo has paid $8.98 billion in penalties and $11.8 billion in consulting fees, most of it for legal services linked to their scandals.[75] Stumpf settled charges against him by paying a fine of $17.5 million. Furthermore, he lost $41 million in equity and another $28 million in compensation, which he had to return to the bank. In 2023, Carrie Tolstedt settled Securities and Exchange Commission fraud charges and agreed to pay a $3 million penalty. Separately, in a settlement with the Office of the Comptroller of the

Currency, she agreed to pay a fine of $17 million and accepted a ban from the banking industry.[76]

Under the new CEO, Timothy Sloan, Wells Fargo made a profit of $5.94 billion in the first three quarters of 2016—the year the bank was caught in the scandal around its fraudulent practices. Sloan was proud that the scandal could not thwart one of his major objectives: increasing payouts to shareholders.[77] Like his predecessor, Sloan was highly successful. In 2019, the bank made a profit of almost $20 billion.[78]

In March of the same year, the *New York Times* reported that the sales pressure on Wells Fargo workers had not changed. What had changed is that managers are more careful in how they make the pressure on their teams.[79] There is a fine line between a tough but effective corporate culture and a system that encourages abuse. When even enormous fines are dwarfed by the profits at stake, instances of bad behavior are likely to continue.

• • •

Wells Fargo is a great example of what can happen if a company tries to maximize shareholder value: it will end up destroying its own culture, its reputation, and paradoxically, create big damages for shareholders as well. The bank's leaders tried to increase the stock value by reporting ever-growing cross-sales success. However, as we have seen, this growth was based on fraud. Employees were pushed in an aggressive internal competition to achieve totally unrealistic goals. The incentive structure promoted the wrong behavior in people who were desperate and very often simply trying to survive in a disturbingly toxic work environment. We do not see thousands of bad apples in this story, but people who suffered, who developed mental and physical problems because they were humiliated by their superiors and eventually kicked out of the company when they didn't perform as expected. Knowing that goals could be achieved only through illegal practices, salespeople were caught in an inescapable double bind and felt treated unfairly, because in many cases, even achieving the goals was not enough to please their leaders. Fraud was normalized through a euphemistic language that people at Wells Fargo developed to describe their illegal business practices and to deal with their own cognitive dissonances. And since employees observed their peers doing the same and their superiors looking away or even doing it themselves, group conformity reinforced illegal business practices that unfolded gradually over time, until they became deeply engrained in the culture of the bank. The dark pattern led to the moral collapse of Wells Fargo.

7
FRANCE TÉLÉCOM—A FATAL CHANGE MANAGEMENT

Jean-Michel Laurent had worked as a technician for the French telecommunications provider France Télécom (FT) for more than three decades when he was transferred to a call center against his will. He was a shy, introverted person. He felt ashamed by what he perceived to be a demotion. He loved to work with his hands. Now he sat in front of a screen with a headset, allotted five minutes per call. When he spoke with a client for longer than that, he was yelled at. In a message to a colleague, he wrote: "For them I am nothing but an incompetent and cumbersome piece of shit." On July 2, 2008, he killed himself. His last words? "Voilà le train"—"Here comes the train." He was speaking on the phone with a union representative when he jumped. He was fifty-three years old.[1]

Christel Ciroux had been a technician at FT as well. Against her will, she became a saleswoman and was transferred to an FT shop far from where she lived. She explained to her boss that her family situation would not allow for these long and irregular working hours, because her husband was frequently traveling for business. She was thirty-seven years old, with two children aged ten and twelve. The new job required her to work until 7:00 p.m., including on some Saturdays. The HR director told her that FT was not supposed to take all her family constraints into consideration. On June 29, 2009, Christel cut her wrists in the office of the regional sales manager, in the presence of her direct manager and the HR director. She survived.

The youngest victim was Nicolas Grenoville. In August 2009, he put a cable around his neck and hanged himself. Nicolas was twenty-eight years old, and he was wearing an FT T-shirt when he died. He was a scrupulous and rather introverted technician who had also been forced into a sales job. He received no training for the new role and worked long hours. The day before he killed himself, he had done a twelve-hour shift. In a letter he wrote: "My job is hurting me.... I can't stand this job and France Télécom doesn't care.... Today, I was despised, insulted, yelled at. I called for help. People don't care."

France Télécom was hit by a wave of suicides. Employees hanged or stabbed themselves, cut their throats, shot themselves, jumped out of windows or from bridges onto motorways and into rivers, took overdoses of drugs, or set themselves on fire. Between 2008 and 2011, seventy-three FT employees died by suicide (worker representatives claimed that the real number was twice as high), and forty-one attempted suicide but survived.[2]

How could it get to this point? What went wrong at France Télécom?

THE WIND OF CHANGE

In 1992, the European Commission decided to privatize telecommunications services: "Technological development was such that monopoly was no longer appropriate. The service was often poor, the rates were much too high." The reforms were supposed to trigger competition, which would improve quality, accelerate innovation, and eventually lead to better prices for consumers.[3] In 1997, the former state-owned Direction Générale des Télécommunications, which was a department in a French ministry, mainly responsible for fixed-line telephony services, became France Télécom. The French government would become a minority shareholder.[4] What used to be a government office providing a public service now suddenly had to satisfy customers and shareholders.

Three challenges stood out in the early 2000s. First, *FT was drowning in debt*. Around 2000, the company had started to expand internationally through acquisition. Unfortunately, these investments took place during the dot-com hype. When the bubble burst in 2002, FT had accumulated a debt of EUR 70 billion. At the same time, the stock price of FT went down from a peak of EUR 219 in March 2000 to only EUR 6.94 in September 2002.[5] Second, *FT was losing money in their operations* while falling behind in an increasingly aggressive competition. Entertainment and media-content providers, with their videos-on-demand, music, or TV services, took an increasing share from FT's profits. Revenue from fixed and mobile telecommunications was shrinking fast.[6] While its customers were leaving in droves, FT had to invest billions in new licenses for European mobile-communication networks. Third, *FT had too many and wrongly skilled employees*. Most of them were technicians, trained to handle all aspects of the traditional landline telecommunications networks. They did not have the expertise to move into mobile-phone technology or internet services. FT needed engineers and programmers for the new information technologies and salespeople for their call centers and shops.

Didier Lombard, who became CEO in February 2005, was under tremendous pressure. He had to fulfill the expectations of disappointed shareholders whose investment had crashed in 2002. FT had to grow sales, profits, and market share, while fighting against increasingly international and aggressive competition in a market with rapid rates of change and innovation. Lombard wanted to make the company more agile, innovative, and efficient. "Our environment is changing, and we must change even faster," he explained in a press conference on February 14, 2006.[7] Lombard drew up an ambitious plan, which he called NExT (New Experiences in Telecom).

Lombard's plan included a goal of 22,000 departures for the coming three years, and he knew this could only be achieved if thousands of employees could be convinced to *voluntarily* leave the company. Employees at France Télécom from the old times were civil servants. They could not be fired despite the privatization of the company.[8] In early 2006, he presented his new leadership team to the top 200 FT managers: Olivier Barberot, the new HR director, and Louis-Pierre Wenès, the new deputy CEO. Wenès was internally called "the killer" and was notorious for humiliating managers in large meetings. His mission was to cut costs by EUR 3.5 billion in three years.[9] Lombard introduced his sidekicks with a warning: "Things are going to change," he said. "I'm here to introduce you to my new team, which will play in a style you don't know: it's going to be the good, the bad [he pointed to Wenès], and the ugly [he pointed to Barberot]. And the good guy is no longer here."[10]

And Lombard was right; very soon things got bad and ugly. In a management meeting on October 20, 2006, Wenès explained to his team that if the existing measures (retirement, convincing civil servants to move to other governmental organizations) were not enough to reduce the workforce, FT would have to "take more radical measures."[11] He added that productivity had to be increased by 15 percent within those three years and that he would launch a "crash program" to accelerate the transformation.

> As in all our cases, at France Télécom leaders took decisions based on **rigid ideology**. We can see right from the start: the challenges faced by France Télécom were closely linked to the restructuring of global telecommunications markets. Strictly adhering to neoliberal ideology, FT prioritized the growth of revenue, profit, and market share over the health and well-being of its employees.
>
> We can see **corrupting goals** at play here: the goal of "convincing" 22,000 employees to leave the company voluntarily was totally unrealistic from the outset. At that time, France had no real labor market. People worked at their companies for their whole life—in particular, in state-owned companies. For them, working at FT was more than just a job; many had been there for decades, and it was part of their identity. Finding an alternative job was not easy, and it was particularly difficult for the people targeted by the head-count reduction initiative at FT—older technicians whose skills were no longer in demand and women with children.

ORGANIZING HELLSCAPES

In 2006, Lombard and his team got to work. They created an internal management training center, the École de management France

(France Management School). Moreover, they gave more HR responsibility to managers further down the hierarchy—which was called the *verticalization* of HR—so that they could better implement the ACT plan: employees were expected to *adapt* their skills to the new strategy of the company, to *change* their occupation, and to be mobile geographically; that is, to understand when it is *time to move*. Otherwise, they were expected to leave the company. The latter, of course, was the main objective of ACT, as the court would later conclude. And indeed, Lombard had announced that he would "implement the departures, one way or another, either through the door or through the window."[12]

At the new training center, 4,000 managers received a ten-day course where they learned efficient methods for how to succeed at ACT (*réussir* ACT), which ultimately meant: how to convince redundant employees to leave the company. Thierry Lasselin, the director of the training center, had a clear idea of how to do this: "The challenge is to keep the pressure on mobility. More generally, we need to introduce a 'turnover culture' to help employees move: we need to shake them up a bit."[13]

In case studies, the 4,000 participants were taught how to deal with a targeted employee: Imagine you want to get rid of someone who refuses to leave the company. Further imagine that this employee is taking care of a sick mother at home. This is a pretty easy case. Move them to a new job a few hundred kilometers away from home. FT could not fire civil servants, but it could assign them to a new region so that staying at FT and taking care of their mother would become incompatible.

In one of the training elements, managers learned that FT was at war—in a fierce fight with competitors such as Free, Bouygues, and Nokia. A participant remembered that they were to make the employees "understand that the company is at war, and in any war there are casualties. And that moving, accepting change, is life."[14] In such discussions on how to convince employees to leave, civil servants were stigmatized as "dinosaurs" who were unable to adapt and thus had to disappear while smaller, more agile animals, a metaphor for young and newly hired people, would survive.[15]

> We see how **manipulative language** was systematically used in the company: the company was at war and employees were seen as potential casualties who needed to be liquidated. The use of words and metaphors around war helped to radicalize managers and make it easier for them to exert pressure. Civil servants were referred to as dinosaurs, not humans. Their time is over; they died out a long time ago (you may have noticed that Theranos used the same metaphor).

A former manager at FT, who was not among the chosen 4,000, and who was forced out of the company during this time, remembered a conversation with a colleague who returned from the training and explained that he was "advised to set unachievable objectives, so that [he could] say to the collaborator: I am sorry, but we cannot continue with you." It was not unusual that someone who returned from the training immediately became the new boss of the person who used to be their boss. A manager who was meant to leave the company remembered being told by a member of his team: "I have been mandated at the highest level to tell you that you have nothing more to expect from the company. We will do everything to make sure you leave, otherwise we will destroy you."[16]

In 2010, when the suicides appeared in the media for the first time, a journalist interviewed a senior manager at FT: "You had foreseen depression: it's written in the documents. You could have foreseen that some people would break down, couldn't you?" The response: "No. We didn't imagine it at all."[17] Well, some people did imagine it. FT had hired external organizations to oversee those trainings. The CEO of one such organization explained in the courtroom: "As part of our service to the management school, we had to report on several occasions on the discomfort felt by participants in the implementation of the NExT and ACT plans. We noticed that the discomfort was increasingly palpable, as early as 2008. We were not able to determine the causes of this malaise, as we were not present on the field."[18] Put differently: the top management claimed that they did not know what kind of training was offered at the academy, while the trainers claimed that they did not know what happened in the company during or after their trainings.

The training worked in tandem with the verticalization of HR. Top management had shifted major HR responsibilities to line managers. Why? They needed their help to find the 22,000 redundant jobs and people. Even though the process was centralized via the ACT plan, the departures themselves had to be executed further down the hierarchy.[19] In this way, local business managers were turned into HR managers. They had to set objectives, measure the performance of their team, make decisions on bonus cuts, and decide whom to target for departure, moving, or promotion. They had to constantly increase the efficiency of their teams while reducing head count. Most importantly, they had to make such decisions without necessarily having the right HR experience or knowledge. They had to make downsizing a priority and "liquidate" people.[20]

> Two additional building blocks appear at this point in our story.
>
> **Toxic leadership:** Leaders' emphasis on downsizing targets, combined with the threat of negative consequences for managers who did not meet these targets, contributed to a toxic work atmosphere. Toxic leadership traits evident in this case included a focus on results at the expense of well-being, authoritarianism, lack of empathy, manipulative tactics, and the creation of a culture of fear.
>
> **Ambiguous rules:** The managers who were selected and trained to implement the ACT plan were undoubtedly aware that they were supposed to "destroy" people. At the same time, they were told that this was the only way to ensure the survival of the company. FT was in a crisis and under heavy pressure. This was a dilemma where implementing and undermining the ACT plan were both right and wrong at the same time from an ethical perspective.

FT introduced new software to assess employee performance. What had been an annual evaluation was turned into a monthly exercise. Managers were invited to display graphs with the performance of their team members, and to put pressure on those with the worst results to improve or move on. This practice was called PIC (Performance Individuelle Comparée), which stood for "compared individual performance." The practice created a tense atmosphere in many teams, since people knew their manager was under pressure to downsize. "It triggered competition between employees, and some employees boasted about being the first, or even made fun of those who were after them on the list, which created a bad work atmosphere."[21] Andrée Courrier, who tried to kill herself on June 18, 2009, testified in court: "Every morning, we had an objective to meet. A board with our names written on it was placed in the middle of the room for everyone to see.... The sales made by each employee the day before were highlighted.... The pressure was constant, we had to reach a quota of calls without repetition, it was necessary that the average of the calls did not exceed the time allotted. The collective also had to reach its quota, otherwise everyone was penalized. I saw some salespeople selling internet-type products to elderly people who did not have a computer."[22] PIC gave managers a perfect tool to identify the best candidates for the 22,000 planned departures.

To motivate line managers to execute ACT, their bonus was connected to these departures (the same applied to HR managers). More precisely, 50 percent of the variable salary of managers, as well as their promotions, depended on reducing head count. Those who did not achieve their targets, the so-called low managers, risked finding themselves on the list of redundant employees or being demoted to a job in a call center.[23] Managers were under pressure because they knew that their own superiors would compile a comparative table of departures across business units.[24]

> Here we see **destructive incentives** at work: by linking their salary to the fulfillment of staff reduction targets, line managers and HR managers were put in a terrible dilemma. They would only get the carrot—a salary increase—if they put extreme pressure on others. Worse still, if they failed to meet their targets, they would most likely get the stick and become a target themselves.

One tactic to demoralize employees was to send them on a "mission," which often boiled down to moving them to a remote place without giving them any work. Daniel Doublet remembered such a mission. At the age of fifty-five he was sent far away from his family. His salary was cut. He was given no work to do and remembered being "known as the person doing nothing." He was told that he was a parasite. He felt ashamed.[25] Such missions often arrived abruptly. Sometimes employees were informed that they had to go on a geographically remote mission the following Monday.[26] On those "missions," employees were often isolated at their new workplace. One of the victims reported: "When I took up my duties, I was surprised to find that I was isolated from all my work and without all my files, and that I was placed alone at a desk designed for four people, located in a corridor. I was isolated from my department, with no work or tasks to perform."[27] This functional and geographical mobility was a key element in the strategy of destabilizing employees and creating anxiety.[28]

A new variation of **manipulative language** emerges in the case: the brutal HR politics were normalized by the euphemistic language used for labeling everything—a "mission," a "performance comparison," generic project titles like "NExT" or "ACT," "progress interview" for weekly scripted conversations to put pressure on people to leave, etc. It all sounded as banal and as normal as in any other company.

Some employees were drowned in work, while others sat around day in, day out with nothing to do. Some had to work with software for which they received no training. Some were given impossible objectives; then when they failed to reach them, their bonus disappeared. Or even worse, entire teams saw their bonus cut for the low performance of some individual team members.[29] Those who achieved their objectives often saw their targets increased for the following month. Those who missed their targets were constantly reminded of the fact that they needed to find something else because they were an obstacle to the success of the company.[30] Managers were supposed to reduce the "comfort" of those in so-called non-priority positions who were considered redundant.[31] As the French prosecutor summarized, FT management aimed for "the destabilization of the workers" until they volunteered to leave the company.[32]

These practices often had a side effect that reinforced the pressure on the employees. Being targeted by the management led to disunity among the employees themselves. Those selected for departure were often ostracized by their peers. Their colleagues stopped greeting them or speaking to them, as often happens to victims of harassment. For example, if one of the victims burst into tears in their office, their neighbors would just stand up, take their laptop, and move to another room.[33] Everyone else was just happy not to be targeted by these measures themselves. An employee who became a victim of such an isolation said: "It's like trench warfare, you run and hope that the shell falls not on you but on the friend next door."[34]

Many of those who killed themselves at FT were described by their colleagues as scrupulous and passionate about their work. Such people are particularly vulnerable to being mentally destabilized if they are moved onto something new; they feel a lack of expertise and take such a demotion as a lack of recognition by their company. They are quick to make a link between professional failure and the perception of *being* a failure.[35] A lack of recognition leads them to question themselves. The notes they left and the testimony of their former colleagues show that this lack of recognition was a major source of their suffering. The social isolation they experienced made it impossible for them to share their pain and to find solidarity. In the end, they were alone.

With the benefit of hindsight, how did FT managers see their own role in the tragic incidents? Some were asked to testify in court. They had interesting things to say. The manager of a technician who tried to kill herself: "In order to support the elimination of people imposed by management, I myself had instructions to regularly remind agents of the functional mobility.... I was only following the instructions that the regional management imposed on me."[36] A manager of a technician who actually set himself on fire later defended himself: "We had semester exit targets. The closer you got to the end of the semester, the more pressure you had to put on people to leave. These exit targets were treated like business objectives, except that they were the number one objective."[37] Those managers who "liquidated" members of their teams to achieve their departure goals were themselves under pressure from their superiors. The ambitious NExT plan called for them to grow the business with fewer resources. A former FT strategy director described the dilemma: "We were asking managers to achieve business objectives while depriving them of the resources to achieve them."[38] Another manager remembered: "They were told that they were being placed on 'Time to Move.'... It was a punishment, but people didn't understand why they were being punished, it was nothing personal, it was just to meet the departure objectives."[39]

Four mutually reinforcing building blocks of the dark pattern are at play here.

Corrupting goals: To make goals unachievable was an explicit part of the plan. Employees targeted to leave had to do jobs without the appropriate skills and achieve goals that kept becoming more demanding. Destabilizing people with aggressive performance targets was one of the supposed "motivators" to make them leave the company. Managers had to achieve the ever-more-ambitious goals of their unit with constantly reduced resources and fewer people. The fear of not meeting these expectations led individuals to conform to harmful practices.

Dangerous groups: Maybe the most shocking element of the case is how people targeted to leave the company were isolated by their peers. Nobody supported them; colleagues turned into silent bystanders of the suffering, just hoping not to be the next considered superfluous for the future of FT. Individuals may have been aware of the negative consequences of the practices but were reluctant to intervene due to fear of repercussions. Through the verticalization of HR functions, managers on all levels were pulled into the change plan as colluders. Nobody wanted to be considered the troublemaker, the one representing the old FT spirit. They wanted to be part of the group of people leading the company into the future.

Perceived unfairness: "It was nothing personal," as one manager aptly defended himself. For the victims, this must have been the most painful aspect of their suffering: the (perceived) randomness of the selection, the unfairness of the treatment after so many years of having done their job as a technician well and being proud of working for FT. We have seen in other cases how perceived unfairness leads people to break all kinds of rules. Sometimes, however, the unfairness breaks the people themselves. Interestingly, the top managers of FT also felt treated unfairly in this affair. Wenès referred to himself as a "scapegoat" and complained: "You think and you're sure you've been doing the right things, and suddenly you were stabbed in the back.... It's like you're running a race, and somebody gives you a sudden hit in the back and you fall over."[40]

Slippery slope: The transformation took place in small steps—a new, more aggressive culture was announced, a new mindset was trained, managers started to target individual employees. Expectations to convince people to leave grew. Many of them refused. Frustration grew. More aggressive methods were used. And all this happened in perfect harmony with what anybody around them was doing. We found no documented incident of a manager speaking up or refusing to make life uncomfortable for their team.

REACTIONS FROM THE MEDIA, POLITICS, THE COURTS, AND THE MARKETS

In July 2009, Michel Deparis's suicide made headlines in France. In a letter, he referred to France Télécom as "the only reason" for his decision to kill himself. In a press conference shortly afterward, CEO Didier Lombard commented that FT would have to stop this "fashion for suicide" (mode de suicide). He later had to apologize for his choice of words. In August, the relocation of employees was suspended, but suicides kept happening. Unions mobilized against the management and organized protests all over France.[41] On October 20, 2009, FT suspended the entire reorganization and announced the immediate cessation of the display of the individual performance comparison (PIC). FT also stopped tying manager salaries to head-count reduction.

The French Ministry of Labor decided to send labor inspectors to all of FT's 450 sites in France. When they returned from their audits, these inspectors wrote a report, in which they concluded that the management of FT was "endangering others by implementing forms of work organization capable of producing severe damage to workers." The inspectors found that there had been numerous warning signs over the years, given by unions, health-insurance companies, and FT labor physicians. They criticized the company for not having paid attention to those warnings.[42]

Louis-Pierre Wenès, the deputy CEO of FT, resigned on October 5, 2009. Didier Lombard resigned on March 1, 2010. Based on the report of the governmental labor inspectors, the labor union SUD filed a complaint against three FT managers. SUD was later joined by other unions in this lawsuit. In April 2010, the prosecutor's office in Paris started an investigation of Lombard, Wenès, and the chief human resources officer, Barberot, for moral harassment of employees and for compromising their physical and mental health. The three top managers argued that the suicide rate was not higher than the French average, that most of the employees who killed themselves had mental problems, and that managers further down the hierarchy were responsible. These people had totally misunderstood the plans elaborated by the top management. If they had known, they argued, they would have never tolerated those brutal HR practices.[43]

None of those arguments convinced the court. In December 2019, Lombard, Wenès, and Barberot were found guilty of manslaughter. Each was sentenced to one year in prison (four months firm and eight months suspended) and a fine of EUR 15,000. In September 2022, an appeal court upheld the convictions but changed the sentence to a year on probation.[44]

When Didier Lombard resigned in 2010, he was replaced by Stéphane Richard. The new CEO gave a series of interviews in the French media, announcing that his priority would be to "re-create a more humane work environment" and "put people back at the heart of our development."[45] Richard introduced a new bonus system with social-performance indicators such as employee attendance and satisfaction. The financial markets did not like Richard's new focus. As a Goldman Sachs analyst wrote, "Since the company is focusing on its employees, it seems unlikely to us that labor costs will drop in 2010." Goldman Sachs downgraded the FT stock from "buy" to "neutral."[46]

• • •

Preparing this case for the book was not easy. It gave us some sleepless nights to go through the many tragic individual stories of suicides and suicide attempts. While at Wells Fargo, people succumbed to the pressure by committing fraud; at France Télécom, some employees saw no other way out than killing themselves. And again, as in the Wells Fargo case, we find leaders who saw their only responsibility as making shareholders happy at any price. People inside the organization became an obstacle to that objective and had to be removed through ruthless psychological tactics, which were disguised in a highly effective mix of euphemistic HR terms and brutal war language for those who had to execute it. Slowly over time, the culture of the company changed. Through trainings, new incentives, and increasing pressure, France Télécom transformed into hell for many people. Ruthless leaders imposed head-count goals on their managers that could only be achieved by inflicting enough suffering on people that they would "volunteer" to leave the company. Company leaders made sure that financial incentives were well aligned with those goals. In their teams, employees were exposed to humiliating performance comparisons. What happened next is familiar from school playgrounds: people tend to take the side of the bully, not the victim. They stand silently and watch the suffering of their peers, because they do not want to become the next victim. Since those who were targeted had to perform without being given the skills or resources, a profound feeling of unfairness drove some of them to leave through the window—an option on which the CEO had loudly meditated as possible early in the process. The dark pattern, as this case demonstrates, can even kill.

8
BOEING—THE PRICE OF CUTTING COSTS

On October 29, 2018, Captain Bhavye Suneja and his copilot, Harvino, took off on Lion Air flight 610 from Jakarta, Indonesia, on a domestic flight to Pangkal Pinang. Both were experienced pilots. On that day, they were flying a brand-new 737 MAX, the latest aircraft developed by Boeing. Only thirteen minutes after takeoff, the plane crashed into the Java Sea, killing all 189 passengers and crew. The *New York Times* quickly found the culprit. "Obsessed with growth," Lion Air had failed to "build a proper safety culture." "Over the years," they wrote, "Lion planes have collided with a cow, a pig and, most embarrassingly, each other." Most importantly, the company was notorious for "passing malfunctioning equipment from plane to plane rather than fixing problems."[1] And indeed, Lion Air flight 610 was operating with a malfunctioning sensor, which was feeding erroneous information into the board computer. A mechanic had replaced and improperly calibrated the sensor, and the two pilots had badly handled the situation.[2] In their official statements, Boeing highlighted that the crash was the result of human failure.[3] Boeing CEO Dennis Muilenburg went on TV, reassuring the audience that "the bottom line here is the 737 MAX is safe. Safety is a core value for us at Boeing."[4]

Then, about five months later, on March 10, 2019, Ethiopian Airlines flight 302 was on its way from Addis Ababa Bole International Airport in Ethiopia to Jomo Kenyatta International Airport in Nairobi, Kenya. It crashed in a farm field only six minutes after takeoff. One hundred forty-nine passengers and eight crew were killed. And again, this was a brand-new 737 MAX. Something was wrong.

A FATAL MERGER

About nine years earlier, in December 2010, Airbus had surprised Boeing with the launch of a new version of the A320, which they called Neo. It came with an engine that promised to be 15 percent more fuel efficient than the previous model, which offered airlines the advantage of selling their tickets at lower prices. Boeing needed a fast answer to the Airbus challenge. They had two options: either build a new airplane from scratch or update an existing one with a more fuel-efficient engine. In 2011, the development of a brand-new airplane would come with a price tag of about $10 billion, while an update of the existing 737 was estimated to cost around $3 billion. They eventually opted for an updated version of the 737 and called it MAX.[5]

The project was under tremendous financial pressure right from the start. Boeing engineers did not only have to innovate the existing 737 but also had, in parallel, to cut costs in the process. Their previously developed airplane, the 787 Dreamliner, was not profitable, because production costs were out of control. Boeing was losing tens of millions of dollars for each plane sold, and experts predicted that even with strict cost-cutting measures put in place, the Dreamliner would never achieve profitability.[6] With total losses of over $26 billion, Boeing had to earn money with the new 737 MAX, and it had to happen fast.[7]

In 1997, Boeing had merged with its competitor McDonnell Douglas, which at that time was led by Harry Stonecipher, a former General Electric (GE) manager and protégé of Jack Welch. When Stonecipher became the CEO of McDonnell Douglas in 1996, one of his first moves was meant to impress shareholders. After only a month in office, he increased the dividend by 71 percent and made it clear in a press release that McDonnell Douglas had plans to increase shareholder value. As he had learned at GE, the best way to achieve that goal was to buy back shares and cut costs. In parallel to increasing the dividend, McDonnell Douglas bought back 15 percent of the company's shares, and within his first two years at the helm, Stonecipher cut the R&D budget of the company by 60 percent.[8]

> This is probably our clearest case of **rigid ideology** at play: there is a simple recipe if you want to maximize shareholder value. You reduce costs, and you reduce the number of shares so that the price per share goes up. Maximizing shareholder value was at the core of Jack Welch's strategy when he took over GE, and three of the Boeing CEOs who led the company into the 737 MAX disaster came from his team. They implemented what they had learned: if you focus all your attention on the shareholder, everybody will be better off in the end. Well, not really, as this and all our other scandals show.

While officially McDonnell Douglas was integrated into Boeing, McDonnell Douglas's managers elbowed themselves into key positions and soon started to dominate the new company. As a manager at Boeing remembered, "When the McDonnell Douglas guys came in, they just went through them [their Boeing colleagues] like a knife through butter." A Boeing insider described the situation of the merger as killer assassins meet Boy Scouts.[9] The newly merged Boeing company was led by Philip M. Condit, who had been Boeing's CEO since before the merger, and Stonecipher became chief operating officer. He soon demonstrated the new leadership style of the company. On one of the first occasions that Stonecipher addressed the Boeing managers, at a retreat in January 1998, he performed a typical Jack Welch stunt. He asked the managers who were responsible for commercial aircraft production to stand up in front of 200 colleagues and invited them to apologize to their peers for their bad performance. They were why the company had missed its financial goals, he said. He warned the assembled managers that from now on they were supposed to "quit behaving like a family and become more like a team," threatening that if they didn't perform, they wouldn't stay on the team. Even the *use* of the word "family" was forbidden.[10]

Destructive incentives played a key role in this scandal: McDonnell Douglas managers quickly established a climate of aggressive internal competition at Boeing. Their worldview was quite simple: The world is divided into winners and losers, and one has to aggressively fight to belong to the winners. Losers are pushed out, but before they leave, they need to be humiliated in front of their peers to teach a lesson to everybody.

Manipulative language supported the cultural change at Boeing: the aggressive climate was not only reflected in language

> but also reinforced through the words people had to use or stop using. If Boeing was not a family anymore, the only way to stay on the team was performance. There were no moral obligations that bound people together.

Stonecipher became Boeing CEO in 2003. As at McDonnell Douglas, one of his first moves was to spend $4.5 billion to buy back 15 percent of the company's shares.[11] Then he continued to transform Boeing according to the principles he had learned at GE. He introduced value scorecards to measure which of the company's businesses were creating or destroying value. Like at GE, value was mainly created by cutting costs.[12] Slowly, Boeing changed from an engineer's paradise to a company where schedules and costs began to dominate the discourse.[13]

Copying the "successful" GE strategy, Boeing started to fire people, sell plants, and outsource production. In the first two years of the new millennium, 35,000 employees were laid off. Suppliers were squeezed for the lowest possible price—another GE tactic that had become a key principle of global supply chain management.[14] Boeing continued to focus on cost cutting even beyond Stonecipher's era. In 2012, they implemented a supply chain strategy that they called "Partnering for Success." What it meant for suppliers was that they had to reduce their costs by 15 percent, while increasing production output, or risk losing Boeing's business.[15]

> **Manipulative language**, in this case euphemistic language, helps avoid cognitive dissonance. If you develop a plan to squeeze your suppliers, you cannot just call it the "Squeeze the

> Suppliers" program. You need a nice name. A name that conceals its hidden cruelty.

Stonecipher was proud of what he had achieved. As he declared in an interview with the *Chicago Tribune*, "When people say I changed the culture of Boeing, that was the intent, so that it's run like a business rather than a great engineering firm. It is a great engineering firm, but people invest in a company because they want to make money."[16]

> This is another hint at the strong **rigid ideology** at play: Stonecipher was even proud that he had transformed Boeing into a moneymaking machine. Finance people started to dominate the decisions; engineers and their views were pushed to the background. The only measure of success, the only topic that got the attention of the top management, was the ever-growing stock value of the company.

In March 2005, a new CEO took over—James McNerney, another protégé of Jack Welch. Before joining Boeing, he had been CEO at 3M. To convince him to change companies, Boeing gave him a starter package of $52 million. The financial package of the CEO was probably the only domain that was protected from concerns about costs. Like Stonecipher at Boeing, McNerney had successfully applied what he learned under Jack Welch at 3M, and when he joined Boeing, he not only continued Stonecipher's cost-cutting strategy but also installed the rank-and-yank performance-evaluation system that he had experienced at GE. As a former Boeing manager remembered: "The thing I was most offended by was the forced distribution. We had to ensure our employees were shoehorned into a prescribed distribution curve." This was a Gaussian normal distribution where the proportions of average, low, and high performers were fixed from the outset. Layoffs targeted mainly older employees. The risk of being fired doubled for Boeing engineers in their forties and tripled for those in their fifties. As a result, the company would lose its most experienced experts but save money by hiring younger and cheaper engineers.[17]

> Here we have another hint of **destructive incentives**: the struggle for survival intensified. People were rewarded or fired in a constant ranking and yanking along criteria that did not focus on engineering performance but on costs.

One of the consequences of the rank-and-yank exercise was that speaking up was increasingly perceived as a risk. One of the engineers working in the flight-test group recalled: "It was pretty intense low morale because of all the layoffs—constant grinding layoffs, year after year. So you really watch your step and were careful about what you said."[18] At Boeing, these concerns about speaking up were well known, and the company launched a program to "eliminate fear in the workplace," which was not particularly successful.[19] A former leadership coach at Boeing remembered how managers would tell her that McNerney did not want to hear bad news; he only wanted to be informed about solutions. It was creating huge safety issues—especially with the 787—people were lying because the truth wasn't on schedule and within budget.[20] A former engineer at Boeing confirms that engineers were discouraged from speaking up: "What we heard five thousand times was 'Follow the plan. Your job is to follow the plan, and if you can't follow the plan we'll fire you and get someone to follow the plan.'"[21]

> Two further building blocks of the dark pattern emerge at this point of the story.
>
> **Toxic leadership:** Especially under McNerney, Boeing developed a climate where a decision to speak up about problems risked turning into a career-terminating move. Those who had a problem were a problem and would be ranked and yanked out of the company. People at Boeing learned to follow orders and to shut up.
>
> **Ambiguous rules:** A classic double bind. You invite people to speak up and then fire them for doing so. In such an environment, the choice between "speak up about problems" and "don't mention problems" is rather easy and intuitive.

McNerney had a simple strategy. He wanted to produce "more with less."[22] In 2015 alone, Boeing reduced its workforce by another 7 percent while increasing the number of produced planes in parallel. Instead of the targeted $5.7 billion of profit, they made $8.3 billion in that year.[23] The constant cost cutting and outsourcing came at a price. Quality problems emerged first for the Dreamliner, later for the new 737 MAX. When Al Jazeera interviewed factory workers who were producing the Dreamliner, they heard frightening stories. As one of the workers anonymously told them, "I've seen a lot of things that should not go on at an airplane plant. It's been eating me alive to know what I know, and have no avenue, no venue to say anything." When they were asked whether they would themselves fly on a Dreamliner, the workers had some clear opinions: "I wouldn't fly on one of these planes, because I see the quality of the fu**ing sh*t going down around here," said one.[24] In 2015, *Forbes* warned that "Boeing will pay a high price for McNerney's mistake of treating aviation like it was any other industry."[25]

The Boeing disaster was not the result of one particular event. The company was moving forward on a **slippery slope**. There were many little decisions taken by many people on many levels of the hierarchy over all those years under several CEOs, each reinforcing and accelerating the ideas of their predecessors. All those little compromises on safety and all the small mistakes in production might be harmless. Only in combination do they slowly become systemic and dangerous over time.

Engineers were exposed to **ambiguous rules**: "Doing more with less" is a one-sentence double bind. The more you succeed at it, the more unrealistic it becomes to continue, but the more difficult to say so to your superiors—a classic double bind. In the end, people produce an airplane on which they would rather not fly.

McNerney made $231 million between 2001 and 2016 (he was CEO until 2015 and chairman of the board for one more year) and eventually retired with an additional package of $58.5 million.[26] As a former Boeing manager remembered, "A mordant joke was going around the Boeing grapevine, renaming McNerney's *more with less* initiative as *leave with more*."[27] *More with less* did not only shape the development and production of the Dreamliner; it also remained his legacy and became the slogan for the 737 MAX project as well. In July 2015, McNerney passed the CEO baton to Dennis Muilenburg. The new CEO had no intention to change the "successful" strategy of his predecessors. While McNerney had pressured suppliers to reduce costs by 15 percent, Muilenburg squeezed out another 10 percent.[28] Starting in 2016, cost reduction became a key element of the performance evaluation of managers at Boeing, and managers soon started to warn their engineers that their bonus was at risk if cost targets were not achieved.[29]

Our case displays two additional building blocks of the dark pattern.

Destructive incentives: Here it is, the tunnel vision created by the incentive scheme—people were pushed to focus on costs and speed and did not see the slowly eroding safety of the airplanes they built.

Perceived unfairness: What employees clearly saw instead was the huge gap between all the cost cutting and firing and squeezing of suppliers and the monstrous paychecks of their CEOs. The laissez-faire approach that entered into the production halls over the years, where people on different levels developed a much more relaxed approach to safety, was a typical attempt to rebalance an unfair situation.

Between 2013 and 2019, the time when the 737 MAX was designed, developed, and eventually certified, Boeing invested $43.1 billion in buying back stock and in addition paid $17.4 billion in stock dividends. This money could have been invested in the development of the plane, in its testing and safety analyses.[30] Investors did not care much. Even in December 2018, two months after the first 737 MAX crash, they praised the company as a "true dividend rockstar."[31] The Boeing leaders profited from their buyback decisions. McNerney earned $242.5 million between 2005 and 2015.[32] Dennis Muilenburg made more than $100 million in the span of only four years. When he was eventually fired over the two 737 MAX crashes, he left the company with an additional $60 million golden parachute.[33]

PHYSICAL PROBLEMS AND SOFTWARE SOLUTIONS

For the 737 MAX, Boeing engineers (together with their suppliers) developed new fuel-efficient engines. However, these new engines could not be installed below the wings as had previously been done. The wings were too low to the ground and the new engines too big. The engineers had to change the design of the new MAX by mounting the engines farther up on the wings. This new position had an effect on the center of gravity of the airplane. It influenced its aerodynamics, increasing the risk that under certain conditions, it would pitch up and risk a dangerous stall.[34] In a stall, an airplane is angled too steeply in the air and risks dropping down like a stone. When reflecting on potential remedies, the engineers realized that the best solution—a modification of the tail of the airplane—would be very expensive. They found a cheaper alternative by programming the software of the board computer to automatically push the nose of the airplane down. So essentially, they fixed a hardware problem with a software solution. The additional function was called the Maneuvering Characteristics Augmentation System (MCAS). When there was a risk of a stall, the MCAS software would take control of the plane and override the decision of the pilot.[35]

How would the MCAS make the decision to pull the nose down? A tiny instrument outside the airplane, a so-called angle of attack (AOA) sensor, would feed the information to it. This sensor measures the angle by which the airplane goes up or down. Based on the information incoming from it, the MCAS would be activated and push the nose of the plane down.[36] Flight-control experts among the Boeing engineers raised concerns about the sensor, which sits outside the aircraft close to the nose. What would happen if it were damaged by bird strike or simply sent inexact data to the software? Reports on badly functioning AOA sensors did exist, and hence the risk was real. According to an analysis by *Bloomberg* in 2019, there were "at least 140 instances since the early 1990s of [AOA] sensors on US planes being damaged by jetways and other equipment on the ground, or striking birds in flight."[37] In an email on December 17, 2015, a Boeing engineer wondered whether the MAX was "vulnerable to single AOA sensor failures with the MCAS implementation or is there some checking that occurs?" Another engineer asked a colleague in an email: "What happens when we have faulty AOA?"[38]

One of the engineers working on the MAX flight deck design was Curtis Ewbank. He repeatedly raised concerns about the MCAS software. When he argued against the poor design of the 737 MAX, his manager told him that "people have to die before Boeing will change things."[39] Some of Ewbank's colleagues shared his concerns but were too afraid to speak up for fear of retaliation.[40]

Why were the engineers so concerned about a malfunctioning AOA sensor? Because the MCAS operated with *only one* such sensor. While there were two sensors at the nose of the new airplane, the system used only one and alternated between the two from flight to flight. To measure disagreement between the two, the aircraft needed a so-called AOA Disagree Alert. This feature, however, was not installed in most 737 MAX planes. For cost reasons, it had been made optional for customers, who would have to pay an additional $80,000. Lion Air did not buy the feature. As a consequence, the pilots who crashed were not even able to find out that the data from the sensor was faulty.[41]

Boeing knew about the risks of AOA sensors feeding wrong information into the MCAS, but they simply assumed that pilots would be able to deal with critical situations. In 2012, it took a Boeing test pilot more than ten seconds to respond to the MCAS activation in a simulator, and the pilot described this as a "catastrophic" condition. In a real flight situation, the airplane would have been in huge danger. The problem appeared in various internal documents over the following years. In July 2015, Boeing did another series of flight simulations and found that when the MCAS nosed the airplane down, the average reaction time of their test pilots was four seconds, which was sufficient to solve the problem. This was documented, and again ten seconds were described as potentially "catastrophic." Then in 2016, a Boeing test pilot struggled to get back control over the MAX when, during a real test flight, the MCAS got activated repeatedly and nosed the plane down. Boeing reviewed the situation and still concluded that there was "no real requirement violation."[42]

With all these MCAS problems occurring during the tests, some engineers had serious doubts about the quality of the new airplane. As a Boeing engineer wrote to a colleague: "This airplane is designed by clowns, who in turn are supervised by monkeys."[43]

> Here we see two mutually reinforcing building blocks of our dark pattern.
>
> **Toxic leadership:** Safety was a taboo topic. Engineers and pilots shared safety concerns in a smaller circle or wrote it in a report that nobody read, but otherwise, they accepted that at Boeing, speaking up led to nothing. Cracking jokes about it was their only (cynical) way of venting their frustration.
>
> **Dangerous groups:** The implicit rule that speaking up was either not possible or led to nothing was reinforced by those exchanges between engineers. Sharing the frustration strengthened the bystander effect. After all, if the others could not do it, why would I? Then, engineers saw each other focusing on costs and speed. Why would someone challenge what seemed to be the standard operating procedure at the company?

ENSURING SAFETY: CERTIFICATION PROCESS AND PILOT TRAINING

The Federal Aviation Administration (FAA) is the government agency responsible for the regulation of private and commercial aviation in the US. Any new aircraft has to go through a certification process before it can be sold and used. Both the design and the manufacture of new aircraft must be approved. None of the trouble with the software of the 737 MAX was ever shared with the regulator.[44] Boeing even asked the regulator for permission to exclude any information on the MCAS from the flight manual, arguing that it "only operates WAY outside of the normal operating envelope." As a result, when the MCAS nosed down the 737 MAX, the pilots would not even be able to find information on the problem in the handbook.[45] The regulator agreed.[46]

Over the decades before the two MAX crashes, the FAA had gone through multiple waves of deregulation and change management. The goal was to make the organization less bureaucratic and more efficient. As in a company, salaries were made performance-dependent, and managers were rewarded for helping "customers" get smoothly through the certification process while helping reduce the costs of the entire procedure. Note that the term "customer" is new in this context; it replaced the traditional term "applicant." Results-oriented plans with quarterly performance measurement were introduced to run the FAA more like a business.[47] Managers at the FAA were even told that their bonus depended on Boeing meeting its scheduled objectives. The certification of new aircraft was included in their annual goals.[48]

> This is a clear case of **manipulative language**: frame the activities of a regulatory body like a business or a service to a business. Not only will its representatives make their decisions accordingly; companies like Boeing who are called "customers" will feel entitled to be treated as customers.

The FAA had to oversee highly complex certification processes with limited staff resources. To manage this situation, they outsourced large parts of the certification to the manufacturers themselves! Over time, the certification process increasingly shifted from FAA engineers to Boeing engineers. By 2018, Boeing already certified a stunning 96 percent of their own work.[49] This excessive delegation included the certification of the MCAS.[50] Boeing CEO Muilenburg praised the agency for its "focus on deregulation."[51]

> Again we see the effect of **dangerous groups**: regulators are there to regulate, but self-regulation led to loyalty conflicts that were of course solved by engineers choosing their primary group identity. They decided as Boeing engineers, not government representatives.
>
> **Rigid ideology** was a powerful building block of Boeing's dark pattern: praising deregulation did not sound strange to observers in the industry and beyond, simply because it represented the Zeitgeist. The taken-for-granted assumption for any industry was (and still is) that regulation is bad. It reduces the efficiency of actors in a free market.

In 2018, a total of 5,000 MAX planes were ordered by 100 different customers. The new version of the old 737 was about to become the fastest-selling airplane ever built. To deliver on all those contracts, Boeing had to accelerate production speed. In its internal magazine, *Frontiers*, Boeing proudly announced that "to meet demand, Boeing is producing its best-selling 737 jetliner at rates that once might have seemed unthinkable." Boeing had set ambitious goals, moving up from forty-two airplanes per month to forty-seven in 2017, fifty-two in 2018 (which they shortly achieved), and for 2019, a scheduled production rate of fifty-seven aircraft per month.[52] At Boeing, such goals were called "goals without a plan."[53] Quality defects rose by 30 percent and behind-schedule tasks by 10 percent. The overtime rate doubled.[54] A former mechanic remembers: "They were trying to get the plane rate up and then just kept crunching, crunching and crunching to go faster, faster, faster."[55] As a House report would later conclude, "There is no evidence that the... production issues... contributed to either of the MAX crashes. However, it is very clear that Boeing did not put safety first."[56]

> Here our case shows the impact of **unrealistic goals**: How many years can a company keep reducing costs while accelerating production speed and output without compromising quality or safety? Sooner or later, production objectives become unachievable. If speaking up is not an option and rank and yank threatens careers, people will find "solutions."

Lion Air flight 610 crashed because mechanics had made a calibration mistake when replacing the AOA sensor. During the flight, the sensor fed false information into the MCAS, and the software reacted by nosing the airplane down in the takeoff phase of the flight.[57] Adjusting the manual trim wheel, as the Boeing test pilots had done to get back control, was not only difficult, it was only lightly covered in standard trainings.[58] The two Lion Air pilots had not even been on a simulator for the new 737 MAX. Why not? When Lion Air and other customers had asked for simulator trainings, Boeing had systematically pushed back—and again, to cut costs.[59]

From the very beginning, it was clear that the updated 737 had to go through the certification process without imposing too-demanding training requirements on Boeing customers. One of the major clients of Boeing was the low-cost carrier Southwest Airlines. They had ordered 246 new 737 MAX airplanes and signaled to Boeing that they had no interest in sending thousands of pilots to expensive simulator trainings for a new airplane. Boeing guaranteed them that pilots would not have to take a training on a full flight simulator or on an aircraft. They even included in the contract with Southwest that they would pay back $1 million per airplane in the case of an obligatory simulator training. Since Southwest kept ordering airplanes and ended up buying four hundred 737 MAX airplanes, Boeing risked losing $400 million for this client alone if they could not convince the regulator to only prescribe some lighter form of training for the new 737 MAX. And indeed, Boeing was able to convince the regulator that its customers did not have to send their pilots to training. This allowed Boeing to avoid the massive paybacks that would have been due otherwise. A win-win situation, as it seemed.[60]

> Here we see **destructive incentives** at play: Boeing managers needed to avoid simulator trainings for customers at any price. And they were successful. Well, the price had to be paid later.

When the airplane nosed down, the two Lion Air pilots received "a cacophony of confusing warnings and alerts on the flight deck."[61]

In such a situation, they probably checked the manual to find out what to do. However, any reference to the MCAS had been removed from the manual, and there was no emergency checklist that they could use. They could not even know who or what was nosing down the MAX, because the redesign of the MCAS had been communicated neither to the FAA nor to the airlines.[62] The time they had to make the right decision before entering a danger zone was ten seconds. Captain Bhavye Suneja and his copilot, Harvino, desperately tried to move the aircraft back up, but the board computer pushed it down again and again. They eventually lost the fight and crashed into the sea. Five months later, the next 737 MAX crashed. This time it was an Ethiopian Airlines flight. Again, erroneous information from the AOA sensor activated the MCAS. Within 5 months, the new Boeing product had killed 346 people.

More than five years later, in January 2024, a plug door of a 737 MAX operated by Alaska Airlines detached and fell from the sky. Luckily, the pilots could land the airplane safely without any fatalities. The concern arose whether Boeing had simply continued to focus on costs after the two crashes, and its employees still had too much fear of speaking up about quality problems.[63]

• • •

Boeing is probably the perfect example of how leaders can destroy shareholder value by being overly focused on it. A series of CEOs, previous students of Jack Welch, implemented what they learned from their master. Through buybacks they artificially inflated the value of the shares, and by brutally cutting costs they improved the efficiency of their production without any consideration for the impact on employees and on the quality of the product. While the company started to shine brightly on financial markets, internally it became a world of winners and losers. Leaders established a ruthless internal competition, kicked out experienced engineers, made it risky to speak up, squeezed suppliers, and imposed ever-higher production goals on the factories, while those developing and selling the new airplane had to make sure that it did not come with too-demanding trainings for their customers. Those who saw problems often left because there was no way to communicate them to superiors. The double bind of constantly achieving more with constantly shrinking resources affected decisions across the organization. A language of cost cutting dominated all decisions, and slowly over time, quality deteriorated. And most people just executed what they were told to do. While under this pressure to keep cutting costs, employees saw the paychecks of their top leaders rise to absurd heights. Boeing also demonstrates how difficult it is to get back on track once the dark pattern holds the company in a firm grip.

9
VOLKSWAGEN—CHEATING IN THE NAME OF FAIRNESS

THE SURFACE OF THE SCANDAL

When Volkswagen CEO Martin Winterkorn arrived at work on September 18, 2015, the company was riding high. In the eight years since he'd taken over, Volkswagen had become the largest car manufacturer on the planet, at last surpassing Toyota, with annual revenues of more than EUR 200 billion.[1] And yet, the day did not end well for Winterkorn. While he was sitting in the office, the California Air Resources Board (CARB), the state regulatory body for protecting the public from air pollution, announced that Volkswagen had systematically cheated on emissions tests. Nearly half a million diesel cars in the US, and eleven million worldwide, sold between 2009 and 2015, were emitting up to *forty times* more air pollution than the company had reported.[2]

It was the start of a series of revelations that would become known as Dieselgate. It shook the entire automotive industry. Five days later, Winterkorn resigned. In his resignation statement, he declared that he was "shocked by the events of the past few days" and stunned "that misconduct on such a scale was possible in the Volkswagen Group." At the same time, however, he was of course "not aware of any wrongdoing" on his part.[3] To date, Dieselgate is estimated to have cost Volkswagen between EUR 30 billion and EUR 40 billion, making it one of the most expensive scandals in corporate history.[4]

Diesel cars emit small particles called nitrogen oxide (NO_x), which can cause asthma, cancer, and cardiovascular illness. CARB and similar agencies around the world regulate car emissions, to reduce the damage pollution does to the environment and our health. The problems for Volkswagen started when US authorities announced they were reducing the NO_x cap for 2009 from 140 milligrams per kilometer (225 mg/mile) to just 31 milligrams per kilometer (50 mg/mile). The regulation of emissions was much stricter in the US than in Europe, where the permitted threshold value was moved from 250 to 180 milligrams per kilometer in the same period.

This US ruling was a challenge to automotive engineers, who had to work out a way to filter emissions without compromising on power or efficiency. When the 31 mg/km emissions ruling was announced in 2006, Volkswagen engineers quickly realized they wouldn't be able to find a technical solution within the time and budget available.[5] There were only two options left: tell the CEO about the problem or find an alternative solution.[6] They decided on the latter. In 1999, Audi, one of the Volkswagen brands, had developed a software feature that was called "acoustic function." It made it possible to reduce the noise of the car by controlling the flow of diesel into the engine: by injecting more fuel, the noise would be reduced. Obviously, more fuel would come with higher emissions. Volkswagen engineers realized that this software could be used and further developed to solve their problem with the NO_x emission limits in the US market.[7]

Volkswagen engineers had found a solution for their problem. The software of the new EA189 engine would be programmed to sense the difference between the car being on rollers for an emissions test in the lab and the car being driven on the street.[8] Compliance with the new US regulation could be switched on in the lab and switched off on the street. While this was clearly illegal, the device was almost impossible to detect. Thousands of cars happily passed their lab tests for years.

One might wonder why this filter was switched off on the street if it was doing its job properly in the lab. The technology that Volkswagen used for filtering emissions came with two heavy tradeoffs for customers: it reduced the performance of the car, and the car had to go to a Volkswagen service center regularly for a control (a chemical solution has to be replenished, and the filter has to be cleaned). Volkswagen knew that these tradeoffs would make it more difficult to convince US customers to switch to a diesel car. So while they decided that keeping the filter on to comply with the emissions laws would hurt Volkswagen's business too much, their car would fool regulators by carefully turning on the NO_x filter whenever it was being tested for emissions.[9]

In March 2014, the International Council on Clean Transportation (ICCT), an American NGO, came up with the idea of testing diesel emissions of Volkswagen and BMW cars on the road, rather than in the lab. Such a test, which was conducted at the University of West Virginia and cosponsored by CARB, had never been done before.[10] It is important to highlight that the NGO did not do the test because there was a suspicion that Volkswagen was cheating. On the contrary. The testers wanted to show that Volkswagen was able to comply with demanding emission rules in the US and that there would be no reason not to apply the same standards in the rest of the world. The activists did not aim to challenge the official test results; they wanted to confirm them in their road tests and use them as an argument for stricter emission rules in Europe.[11] However, it turned out that the tested Volkswagen cars emitted up to forty times as much NO_x as they were allowed to emit.[12] Volkswagen was invited by CARB to explain the unusual results.[13] In numerous meetings, representatives of the Volkswagen Group lied to the authorities and even explicitly stated that they did not use software to manipulate emissions; however, they could not come up with a credible explanation for those emissions, and regulators remained unconvinced.[14]

Then, in a meeting in October 2014, Volkswagen finally acknowledged that the emissions on the street deviated from those in the lab. However, they continued to lie about the reasons for increased emissions. Volkswagen explained the variance by weather conditions, speed, and driving styles, and even told CARB representatives they didn't know how to measure emissions correctly. For a while, even experts from CARB itself believed *they* might be at fault.[15] Then the testers tried a new tactic. When measuring the cars in the lab in June 2015, they tricked the defeat device into "thinking" the car was on the road, which switched off the filter. Suddenly, emissions spiked, and from one test to the next, emissions grew.[16] In July 2015, CARB threatened not to approve the next year's Volkswagen and Audi diesel models for the US market. Under this pressure, Volkswagen finally admitted in September 2015 that they had used illegal software and violated the Clean Air Act.

NORTH KOREA WITHOUT LABOR CAMPS

On the surface, the VW scandal seems to be an open-and-shut case. Engineers illegally manipulated software to pass an emissions test. These actions were at best ill-judged, at worst criminal and immoral. But what if the staff involved thought their behavior was appropriate? And if that was the case, what might have created this impression? Why did they not go to their CEO to discuss the problem? Martin Winterkorn became the new CEO of Volkswagen at the end of 2006. Roughly two years before Dieselgate, in August 2013, the German news magazine *Der Spiegel* had published an article about Volkswagen. Two journalists who had followed Winterkorn in his daily work summarized his management style in one frightening sentence: "This is North Korea minus the labor camps."[17]

It turned out that management by fear had a long tradition at Volkswagen. The legendary Volkswagen CEO Ferdinand Piëch was a brilliant engineer. In the early 1990s, he developed the Turbocharged Direct Injection (TDI) diesel engine, which was a significant breakthrough that made diesel engines cleaner, more fuel efficient, and powerful enough for everyday vehicles. However, he was also a ruthless, terrifying, and authoritarian micromanager. The culture he created at Volkswagen during his decade-long reign would ultimately contribute to the company's downfall. When Piëch once was asked what would happen if engineers did not meet his expectations, he answered: "Then I will tell them they are all fired, and I will bring in a new team. And if they [the new team] tell me they can't do it, I will fire them, too."[18] Piëch did not tolerate the use of the word "problem." Those who had a problem were a problem. He had no patience with difficulties, especially from his top managers. As he once said,

"I would consciously allow those in whom I had lost trust to starve by the wayside."[19] To increase performance, Piëch had established an internal competition for developing new solutions. He would, for instance, have two teams working on a new engine in parallel, and while eventually the best ideas of both teams would be combined, Piëch could make it a highly unpleasant and humiliating experience to be on the losing team of such a competition.[20] When engineers argued that something was impossible, he would simply reply, "If you don't want to do it, you don't have to."[21] It was obvious to everybody what that meant.

Winterkorn had been hired by Piëch twenty-five years earlier at Audi and had soon become his protégé. He had learned from Piëch how to lead, and he showed the same intolerance for mistakes as his mentor. He strengthened the existing culture of fear and obedience. Like Piëch, Winterkorn was a gifted engineer and a micromanager with fastidious attention to detail. The only difference between his regime and the one Piëch had established was the personal flavor he gave to it. While Piëch had terrorized his managers with cold, silent aggression, Winterkorn was a shouter. He insulted and humiliated his managers when he was angry, threw stuff at them, smashed car components when he saw a quality issue. Whoever provoked his anger risked being spontaneously demoted or moved to another position. In a meeting Winterkorn would turn to the boss of the targeted employee and simply say: "I never want to see him here again." Only a small circle of managers he trusted could openly speak up without such a risk.[22] As one former employee says, "There was always a distance, a fear, and a respect.... If he came to visit or you had to go to him, your pulse would go up," and "If you presented bad news, those were the moments that it could become quite unpleasant and loud and quite demeaning."[23] "Those who spoke up were shouted down."[24]

We see already several building blocks of our dark pattern at play here.

Toxic leadership: When this group of engineers realized in late 2006 that they could not construct a NO_x trap that would reduce the emissions of their diesel engines to 31 milligrams per kilometer, they knew that the new EA189 engines would fail the lab tests. Now imagine you were one of those engineers. Would you go to Winterkorn and tell him, "Mr. Winterkorn, we have a problem"? A major driver of Dieselgate was the climate of fear created top-down in the company. Given the temper of their CEO, managers did not dare to confront him with problems.

Slippery slope: The toxic culture and the blind obedience to authority did not appear overnight. It was slowly built up over two decades.

Manipulative language: Imagine you have a problem, but you are forbidden to even use the word. Well, the problem doesn't go away simply by avoiding the word. However, you will tackle it differently. Instead of solving it, you will hide it. A problem is a sign of incompetence, as in our fairy tale of the emperor's new clothes... and as in the Boeing story.

Destructive incentives: Pitching teams against each other and humiliating the losing team neither promote collaboration nor encourage people to speak up to their colleagues about the problems they face. If you do not find the solution, someone else will. Colleagues are thus always a potential threat to your position and career.

THE DARK PATTERN

Winterkorn was also known for imposing extremely ambitious goals. As a manager working with Winterkorn has said, "Even if it was impossible to finish a project within the set deadline, nobody dared to ask for more time."[25] In a meeting of his top managers in December 2007, he announced a plan to become number one in the world, overtaking Toyota by 2018.[26] To do that, he would need to sell ten million cars worldwide, which meant tripling sales in the US in less than a decade. However, Winterkorn did not only want to beat Toyota in sales. He wanted to be number one in profitability, innovation, customer satisfaction, and sustainability, too. He wanted everything.[27] The incentive systems of the whole company were designed around beating Toyota. And Winterkorn delivered. Volkswagen sold six times as many cars in 2013 as in 2007, between 2007 and 2014 Winterkorn doubled operating profits, and in 2014, the company achieved annual revenues of EUR 200 billion for the first time.[28] Shortly before the scandal broke, Volkswagen beat Toyota in sales. They had finally become number one in the world.[29]

> Two more building blocks of the dark pattern need to be highlighted at this point of the story.
>
> **Corrupting goals:** Engineers at Volkswagen knew that the ambitious goal of becoming number one depended on the even more ambitious goal of drastically reducing emissions in a very short period and at a very low budget for the US market. Put differently, the highly ambitious goal of becoming number one in everything depended on the unrealistic goal given to the engineers. If they did not solve the "problem," Volkswagen would

not increase market shares in the US and would never beat Toyota.

Destructive incentives: The new engine was vital for growth in the US market. Failure was not an option. Without the US market, Volkswagen would not be able to achieve its ambitious goals. The bonuses of the entire company depended on becoming number one. If the engineers working on the new filter technology failed to make it happen, the bonuses of all managers worldwide were in danger. What a heavy burden on the team.

EMISSION PROBLEMS AND SOFTWARE SOLUTIONS

Volkswagen had to start producing the new cars by the end of 2008, in line with the new regulations, to get them into the US market in the 2009 calendar year. The engineers had just two years to find a solution, an unrealistic time frame for designing the new filter technology.[30] While the engineers might have been desperate, they also had a potential solution for their problem: software that was almost impossible to detect. In a meeting that also included the head of motor development, Rudolf Krebs, the engineers discussed the software manipulation as a solution to their problem. They weighed the pros and cons of this option, arguing that other car producers would manipulate emissions as well (we'll come back to this point later in our story). They finally decided to move forward with the defeat device.[31]

Some have argued that the defeat device was probably meant to be a short-term solution to guarantee the timely market entry of the new cars. Maybe they wanted to use it until a real solution was found.

"They thought they could maybe fix this later, then discovered they couldn't and went down a dark path," according to Matt DeLorenzo, a diesel expert who was interviewed by the *New York Times*.[32] Alex Gibney, who directed an episode of the documentary series *Dirty Money* about the Volkswagen scandal, tends to agree with this interpretation: "The thinking was we will solve this problem but for now—because our bosses say we have to launch—we'll come up with this cheat," he says. "We won't even call it a cheat. It is something we'll have to do for now, but we'll fix it later."[33] There is an interesting parallel to the Theranos scandal. It seems as if Volkswagen engineers played Silicon Valley's "fake it till you make it" game.

> Volkswagen moved forward on a **slippery slope**: in Europe, car producers could temporarily deactivate emission control systems if there was a risk of damage to the engine (that was the original purpose of the "acoustic function" in the software of the car). They didn't have to ask permission to do this. This loophole was used by many car producers, including Volkswagen, long before Dieselgate. The engineers thus did not invent the software—they used an existing one and added new functionalities (in a back and forth with their supplier, Bosch). The software modification did not happen overnight but over a longer period and in smaller steps. Considering it a preliminary solution for an urgent problem made it easier to continue on that path and go to the next step.

In 2011, PricewaterhouseCoopers described the company as a "light tower of compliance," and at the time of Dieselgate, Volkswagen had 550 managers officially working in the compliance department. In March 2012, Winterkorn spoke on the subject in front of 3,900 managers and told them that he had zero tolerance for rule breaking.[34] Much later, after Dieselgate, on December 10, 2015, then president of the supervisory board Hans Dieter Poetsch, and then CEO Matthias Müller, would admit in a press conference that over the years, Volkswagen had developed a "culture of tolerance for rule breaking."[35]

> Here the company even admits that it had operated with **ambiguous rules**: Volkswagen engineers were exposed to a classic double-bind situation. "Do not break the rules" was the official message; "Break the rules if necessary for achieving your objective" was the informal rule. Rule violations by successful managers were tolerated.

Before Dieselgate, Volkswagen was recognized as the global sustainability leader in the automotive industry. Their cars won awards that highlighted the power of their "groundbreaking clean diesel engine."[36] In 2014, the company was ranked number one in their industry on the Dow Jones Sustainability Index.[37] When you consider yourself the world leader in producing clean engines and you see the US authorities reducing the emissions limit from 140 to 31 milligrams per kilometer, in an unrealistic time frame, you might ask yourself: "Why are they doing this?" Well, most cars produced in Europe had diesel engines, but in the US, it was only a 2 percent niche for passenger cars. From the perspective of Volkswagen engineers, the new regulations created a special burden almost exclusively for

European manufacturers. The head of engine development at Volkswagen Group, Wolfgang Hatz, had voiced his frustration during a technology demonstration in San Francisco in 2007. He argued that the regulation was not realistic, "too aggressive," and "nearly impossible for us."[38] One of the leading German economists, Hans-Werner Sinn, would later accuse the US authorities of engaging in protectionism rather than environmental policy. While the authorities disregarded the NO_x emissions of American-made trucks, he wrote, they would try to keep the "small and efficient diesel motors for cars off the market with stricter and stricter NO_x limits, because they themselves [the Americans] did not control the technology."[39] While NO_x emissions limits were reduced for diesel cars, trucks were shielded from similar reductions by powerful lobbies.

Although diesel engines produce more carcinogens than gasoline engines, they emit less CO_2. Having signed the Kyoto Protocol in 1997, European nations needed diesel cars on the roads to help meet their climate targets. NO_x pollution was an acceptable price for lower levels of carbon dioxide. Governments incentivized producers and consumers to make the shift via low taxes on diesel engines. This of course was the result of an aggressive lobbying strategy from the automotive industry.[40] By 2014, more than half the cars on European roads were diesel, up from just 10 percent in the early 1990s.[41] The US government, on the other hand, did not ratify the Kyoto Protocol. The climate crisis was not high on the political agenda at that time, but the carcinogenic impact of NO_x pollution was. With low gas prices and no incentives for diesel, customers had no interest in buying the latter.

> An important aspect of this scandal is the **perceived unfairness** that influenced decision-makers at Volkswagen. When people

feel they have been treated unfairly, they often feel the need to rebalance things. The belief in the sustainability of their cars and the feeling they were being treated unfairly—which was fueled, among other things, by the impression that NO_x pollution from US trucks was obviously not a problem for the US government— were thus other contributing factors in Dieselgate. They helped shape how the managers and engineers at Volkswagen constructed their reality.

We see how the company was caught in a **dangerous groups** mindset: us (Volkswagen) versus them (US regulators and US competitors). As a technology leader, Volkswagen felt superior to those American actors. Volkswagen had the best technology, and now they were closing in on becoming number one in the world. At home, they had the full support of (European) regulators who did what they could to support an industry that supplied so many jobs. From their perspective, they needed to defend themselves against the attack of the US regulator.

We can safely assume that the engineers and managers at Volkswagen were convinced they had not really gone beyond some well-established practices in their industry. Three observations about the car industry make this assumption plausible: there's a history of cheating on emissions tests involving many different companies, there's a gray area of acceptable manipulations, and European regulators knew about the testing problems but saw no urgent need for stricter enforcement.

In 1998, the European Federation for Transport and Environment published a study warning that lab tests did not provide realistic results. In 2011, scientists at the European Commission's Joint Research Centre (JRC) in Ispra, Italy, found that diesel vehicles showed up to fourteen times higher emissions on the street than in the lab. Despite this, many governments blocked stricter EU regulation. Jürgen Resch, a manager of the environmental NGO Deutsche Umwelthilfe, criticized the German government for blocking stricter regulation: "The German federal government fights for the right of car manufacturers to pollute the air."[42]

The tests were either run by the car companies themselves or farmed out to third-party firms that competed for the contracts. As a result, their goal was not to accurately measure emissions but to make sure they got the next contract as well. If they were too strict, which is to say if their test results were too realistic, they risked losing the client. This competition was international. If you were certified in one EU country, for instance, other EU members had to accept the certificate. Car producers could shop for the lowest test standards.[43] In the words of the *Economist*, emissions testing as such was a "farce."[44]

In a disastrous interview in January 2016, the then new CEO Matthias Müller used a similar argument to defend Volkswagen. He claimed that Volkswagen did not have an ethical problem and that it did not lie, but it had only falsely interpreted the US law. The problem, Müller argued, was only a technical one.[45]

> Again, we see **ambiguous rules** at play: everybody, including regulators, knows that emissions tests are dysfunctional, and yet, no stricter methods or rules are introduced. In Europe, emissions regulations were lax and easy to exploit. Manipulations were not punished severely. Fraud could be settled at comparably low costs. For Volkswagen, the problem was therefore neither legal nor moral but purely technical.

Companies began to cheat as soon as the newly created Environmental Protection Agency (EPA) started regulating tailpipe pollutants in the early 1970s. The first to be caught for installing a defeat device that switched off pollution control at low temperatures was… Volkswagen! In 1973, the company paid a fine of $120,000 and settled the case without admitting any wrongdoing.[46] Fast-forward to the 1990s: in 1995, General Motors paid $45 million for circumventing pollution controls on 470,000 Cadillac luxury sedans.[47] Like Volkswagen in the 1970s, they denied any wrongdoing, arguing that this was not cheating but rather a "matter of interpretation regarding the complex issue of off-cycle emissions." In 1997, Ford paid a $7.8 million fine for having a defeat device in its Econoline diesel vans. The same year, Honda settled a case on a defeat emissions-control system, paying $267 million and Ford another case for $7.8 million.[48]

A study done by the ICCT in Europe showed, for instance, that more or less all cars by all producers significantly exceeded the official lab emissions. Other car makers were performing even worse than Volkswagen in such tests.[49] Over the years, many car producers had to settle accusations of fraud over their emissions tests. Volkswagen may have used more sophisticated technology than its competitors—one would expect nothing less from German engineering—but test manipulation was the rule, rather than the exception.

> This is another dimension of **perceived unfairness** in this case: everybody is doing it! The whole industry was involved in gaming emissions regulations to one degree or another. Volkswagen was doing the same as many of its competitors, with the tacit or explicit support of European governments. From within the

> company, the manipulation seemed legitimate, normal, and necessary. The staff did not doubt their actions as much as they should have, because in their world, what they were doing was not wrong.

It is tempting to think that the discrepancies between emissions in the lab and on the street exist only because of those illegal manipulations with defeat devices. But it's not true. Authorities tolerate a difference of up to 10 percent between emissions in the lab and those on the street. Higher deviations are taken as an indicator for an illegal manipulation. As a result, test conditions in the lab are designed to artificially reduce emissions. First and foremost, car producers do not test a randomly chosen car; they test what in the industry is called the "golden car." Cars are tested on rollers, and companies choose a car with reduced weight and optimized rolling capacities, which would lead to the best test results both with regard to emissions and fuel efficiency. Special lubricants are used for the engine, and the car uses old and low-resistance tires overinflated with special gas mixtures. The car is tested in too high a gear. Air-conditioning and navigation are switched off to reduce energy consumption; batteries are fully charged. Companies can heat the lab to about 25 degrees Celsius, as starting the engine in low temperatures produces more pollutants. The maximum speed in the lab is 120 kph, but during most of the twenty-minute test, the car accelerates slowly and runs at such a low speed that on the street it would be an obstacle. The use of a golden car and the creation of the most advantageous lab conditions possible are entirely legal. Every producer of cars uses variants of these tricks, which reduce emissions significantly so the car can comply with regulations.[50]

> Testing cars worked according to **ambiguous rules**: the rule is not "Do not manipulate emissions in the lab"; the rule is "Do not go too far in your manipulation." There is no clear right or wrong—rather, there is a gray zone where car producers are free to explore how far they can go into the darker shades of gray.

On January 7, 2017, FBI agents arrested Oliver Schmidt at Miami International Airport.[51] He had spent his Christmas holidays in Florida and was waiting to board a return flight to Germany. Schmidt had not been involved in the manipulation; he was not working on the team that tried to build the filter and failed. He was responsible for the certification of vehicles for the US market, and Volkswagen had sent him to negotiate with the authorities when the strange test results were found. In these meetings, he was supposed to defend Volkswagen's position that nothing was wrong with their diesel engines. Before traveling to Florida, Schmidt had asked the US authorities whether his legal status had changed, intending to ascertain whether he would run any risk when entering the US. He was told that his status had not changed since the year before. Schmidt arrived in Florida on December 17, and the arrest warrant was issued during his holidays on December 31, accusing him of having lied to the authorities in the negotiations with CARB. It seems that the US authorities had lured him into a trap. He was later sentenced to seven years in prison and dropped by Volkswagen.

What was Volkswagen thinking? the *New York Times* asked when the scandal erupted, speculating about the greed and ruthlessness that might have driven the engineers and their corporate leaders into the manipulation of emissions tests.[52] Stories like Dieselgate need a villain, a bad apple, and a happy and simple ending where the bad guys get caught and punished.

• • •

With toxic leaders at the helm for more than a decade, Volkswagen's culture slowly descended into fear and obedience. In such an environment, engineers could not simply go to their CEO and talk about a problem—in particular, when their challenge to build a compliant diesel filter would threaten the overall strategy of the company for becoming the number-one car producer in the world. Engineers knew that talking about their problem could be a career-terminating move. What they knew as well, however, was that rule breaking was tolerated at Volkswagen as long as it led to success—and in the case of emissions tests, it was not even clear what the rules were. Companies could manipulate results, but not too much. And many, if not most of them, did so in the lab when testing new cars. At the same time, Volkswagen felt treated unfairly. They were already considered a sustainability leader, and the reduction of NO_x particles imposed on them by the US government felt unrealistic. Could it be a move to shift market shares to US companies for whom diesel engines were not really relevant? In small steps, going back and forth between Volkswagen and their suppliers, the engineers manipulated software that had the potential for switching off a filter already built in. As in the Boeing case, we see at Volkswagen that the dark pattern sometimes builds up slowly over time. While in some cases (think about Uber) it can fall rather quickly onto an organization, others dismantle their integrity over decades.

10
FOXCONN—WELCOME TO THE MACHINE

The paper in front of me dims to yellow
with a pen I chisel down different shades of black
filled with the language of manual labor
workshop, assembly line, machine station, work certificate,
⠀⠀⠀⠀overtime, wages.......
they teach me servility
I can't shout, can't resist
can't complain, can't lay blame
but just silently endure the exhaustion
when I first stayed here
I wanted only that gray pay slip on the tenth of the month
granting me overdue comfort
to get it I have to wear down my corners, wear down my
⠀⠀⠀⠀language,
decline to skip work, decline sick days, decline personal leave
decline to arrive late, decline to leave early

*I stand like iron on the assembly line, hands flying
and how many days, how many nights
do I just fall asleep on my feet*
—Xu Lizhi, "I Just Fall Asleep on My Feet"
(translated by Eleanor Goodman)

This poem was written by Xu Lizhi on August 20, 2011, about half a year after he started working as an assembly line worker at Foxconn in Shenzhen, China.[1] On September 30, 2014, he jumped to his death from the seventeenth floor of one of the company's dormitories, apparently in despair over the situation in the factories.[2] He had just turned twenty-four.

Xu Lizhi was not the only one. Four years earlier, in 2010, there had already been a series of seventeen suicide attempts in Foxconn factories, in which thirteen people died and four were injured.[3] These incidents, which occurred mainly at the Longhua and Guanlan plants in Shenzhen, attracted a lot of attention.[4]

What was going on in this company?[5]

THE COMPANY

Founded in 1974 by Terry (Taiming) Gou in Taiwan, Foxconn Technology Group is the world's largest contract manufacturer of electronics and was ranked twenty-seventh in the *Fortune* Global 500 in 2023. Foxconn's well-known customers include Apple, Nokia, Sony, Samsung, Xiaomi, HP, and many others.[6] The name "Foxconn," the international brand name of Hon Hai Precision Industry, stands for the company's goal of connecting, assembling, and shipping electronic products with the speed of a fox.[7] The company describes its "five core competencies" as "speed, quality, engineering, flexibility, and cost."[8] As an original equipment manufacturer for multinational brands, Foxconn produces on a large scale. A highly centralized and hierarchical management system controls hundreds of thousands of low-wage workers on the assembly lines with an iron fist.[9] With low profit margins, the company must constantly compete with its rivals in terms of price, quality, and delivery times. To remain competitive and win orders from customers, Foxconn is forced to minimize costs, resulting in cost pressures being passed on to the workers on the assembly line.[10]

In 1988, Foxconn expanded from Taiwan into mainland China. The first production facility was opened in Longhua in the north of Shenzhen. As we write these lines, in August 2024, there are more than forty Foxconn factories in mainland China with more than one million employees.[11] This rapid expansion in mainland China has been driven by the need to increase production and reduce manufacturing costs. For local governments, the arrival of a giant company like Foxconn, bringing with it massive investment, GDP growth, and job creation, was undoubtedly extremely attractive. Foxconn was met with pro-capital policies everywhere, not only in preferential treatment in terms of land, factories, taxes, and tariffs but also in local governments' efforts to recruit workers for manufacturing companies suffering from labor shortages.[12]

Many Foxconn factories are not just factories within a city but cities themselves. The Longhua campus, for example, with its 300,000 employees, has an area of between 2 to 3 square kilometers. Consider that a city with such a population would normally occupy an area ten times as large. There are restaurants, supermarkets, banks, and even a company hospital, a soccer stadium, and a kind of academy.[13] Above all, however, there are assembly plants and dormitories. Interestingly, there are no warehouses. Truck after truck brings components and transports finished products directly to the customers. This machinery cannot stop, cannot take a break, and cannot slow down.[14]

Former chairman and CEO Terry Gou, who has been described as a "modern-day Genghis Khan," ran the company with an iron hand.[15] His management practices included demanding impromptu reports at meetings or factory inspections, and those who could not respond appropriately had to expect public reprimands or had to stand for hours as punishment. Gou emphasized the importance of strict discipline: "If you allow deception and careless behavior to become part of the company's culture, then we cannot continue as a manufacturer."[16] He freely admitted that he often required his employees—but only senior managers—to stand for punishment, just as he had to stand for punishment at school and in the military. He claimed to hold himself to the same standards that he applied to others and argued that he would lead by example, never asking his employees to do anything that he wouldn't do himself. His working hours were long, he traveled around the world at short notice to be able to act immediately, and he thought quickly and at a high level, making it exhausting for those around him to keep up. Foxconn's senior executives are employees who have stood by Terry Gou's side for several decades, since the company's beginnings.[17]

THE SUICIDES

After the first suicides, Gou was shocked and described them as "the biggest crisis Foxconn had faced in its 37 years of operation."[18] "It might as well have been me thrown from the building," and "I've only been sleeping 4 hours a night," he later admitted. Moreover, these frequent, unusual incidents put him and Foxconn in the media spotlight—and in the moral hot seat.[19] After the seventh suicide on May 10, 2010, Gou summoned key executives to a meeting in Longhua to discuss responses to the suicide crisis, and he launched the Loving Heart Safety Project. He took charge of this crisis management himself; made his vice president, Terry (Tianzong) Cheng, the deputy director; and invited numerous medical, religious, and psychological experts to assist.[20]

In two articles, written nine years after the crisis and seven years after leaving Foxconn, Cheng divided the Foxconn employees who died by suicide into three categories.[21] First, there were those who had a history of mental illness, who had already regularly visited hospitals and were on medication. However, after leaving their hometowns to work at Foxconn, some of them stopped seeking treatment and taking medication, leading to many unusual behaviors before jumping.[22] Second, some were struggling with romantic or family problems.[23] In one case, eyewitnesses said, a person argued with her partner on the phone, became impulsive, threw the phone off the building, and then jumped.[24] The third category Cheng mentioned was people who sacrificed their life for the good of their families, based on the assumption that Foxconn would pay compensation.[25] External psychologists referred to such cases as "martyr" suicide.[26] Cheng's three categories can be condensed into one simple conclusion: for him, all those suicides had nothing to do with the company itself.

And yet, after the internal crisis-management team had completed its mission, Foxconn admitted that it had not taken sufficient care of the company's employees and introduced several measures to improve and strengthen workers' welfare.[27] They rolled out a plan for an average wage increase of 20 percent for more than 800,000 workers on the mainland and promised to introduce a system of one day off per week.[28] In addition, Foxconn implemented various preventive measures, including the establishment of care centers, the establishment of psychological counseling hotlines in each plant with staff on duty 24/7, the formation of *care and love groups* of twenty people each, with the group leader taking care of the members and immediately referring abnormal emotions to medical professionals, and the organization of two to three evening recreational events per week in each plant, inviting professional singing and dancing groups to help workers relax.[29] In addition, access to roofs and open windows was blocked, and the company installed 1.5 million square meters (!) of safety nets.[30] While all these measures were primarily aimed at the mentally ill and mentally unstable, the way to stop martyr suicide was quite simple: On May 25, 2010, Foxconn announced the so-called Suicide Disclaimer Agreement, which essentially stated that suicides were no longer considered as work accidents and would no longer result in compensation for families of the deceased. However, after heavy criticism from employees and society in general, Foxconn stopped demanding that its employees sign this agreement.[31]

Next to discussing the three types of suicides and prevention measures, Cheng also presented some statistics to provide benchmarks, all of which were much higher than the suicide rate at Foxconn.[32] So in his two articles, Cheng essentially said the following: The motives and reasons for the suicides are not work related, Foxconn has made great efforts to prevent further incidents, and the rates are comparatively very low anyway. Reading his articles, one almost gets the impression that Foxconn is the victim. Not a word is offered about the work culture at the company. Chen even went so far as to accuse the media of exaggerating the situation and turning the suicides into an "epidemic."[33] This reaction is almost identical to the France Télécom case, where top managers also blamed the victims themselves and complained about the "suicide fashion."

Based on such an assessment, the so-called Foxconn suicide scandal may not even deserve the name, and the question arises as to why it is covered in this book. Well, our examination has two more sections. Each of them suggests that the real scandal lies elsewhere—and that the suicides, tragic as they are, seem rather to be the tip of a much larger iceberg.

THE MACHINE

An important question that the Loving Heart Safety Project also had to ask itself was whether the workload and pressure on Foxconn workers exceeded their capacity. In fact, there have been allegations of sweatshop conditions against the company since 2006. Some Foxconn employees describe their lives as follows: "We work harder than a donkey, eat worse than a pig, get up earlier than a chicken, finish work later than a prostitute, behave more obediently than a grandchild, [our lives] look better than everyone else's, but we age faster than anyone else in five years."[34] Triggered by the media coverage of the suicides, the Chinese central government sent a delegation to the Longhua factory to investigate whether Foxconn was a "sweatshop." It reached the conclusion that Foxconn's management and workers' welfare were better than those of state-owned and foreign companies and that the "sweatshop" label did not apply to Foxconn.[35]

Even though the allegation of exploitation was officially disproved, the suicide "epidemic" was stopped, and the public discussion about the jumping incidents gradually subsided in the following years, the concern about the reasons for these incidents, the plight of the one million Foxconn workers, and the questioning of Foxconn's management and operation models has never ceased.[36] One of those who fueled these concerns was Liu Zhiyi, an intern reporter for the *Southern Weekly* publication, who applied to Foxconn to conduct a twenty-eight-day undercover investigation. His testimony speaks for itself: "The 28 days I worked undercover were deeply shocking, not because I understood why they died, but because I learned how they lived."[37]

So, how did they live? In a nutshell, like wheels in a machine. Foxconn has been honed into a highly controlled, efficiently operating precision machine that also "mechanizes" its employees, turning them into mere "components" of the process.[38] The functioning of the people is entirely determined by the functioning of the vast machinery and the various machines that the workers must operate. People are essentially turned into cogs in a machine. Xiao Qin, who worked on one of Foxconn's assembly lines: "People were like machines, just walking corpses."[39]

> The **rigid ideology** displayed at Foxconn, as in some of our other cases, is a large-scale and constant cost-cutting effort. For a company that engages in mass production and makes massive use of assembly line manufacturing, making a profit hinges on efficient production, which of course also means cutting costs wherever possible. To achieve this, Foxconn uses scientific methods to analyze and optimize tasks and work processes (also known as scientific management, which in turn is rooted in the basic idea of Taylorism).[40] The company's management philosophy is to "deconstruct the entire enterprise's processes, identify key points, simplify, establish norms and standards, implement them and achieve greater benefits with minimal

> resources."[41] This enables Foxconn to integrate employees into the production system as standardized "parts." Workers no longer have to think, they just have to follow management's instructions and mechanically repeat a few simple operations. As Karl Marx predicted at the beginning of industrialization, workers feel disconnected from the results of their work and see themselves as interchangeable parts rather than as valuable individuals. A phrase like "we are just machines" and the description of work as "tiring, monotonous, and boring" vividly illustrate the extent to which workers are alienated and dehumanized.[42]

To ensure the proper functioning of workers in this machinery, a strict hierarchy and a culture of obedience are introduced through a series of strict regulations and measures. Thousands of security guards ensure that order is maintained and almost all public and work areas are monitored by surveillance cameras[43]—which is of course reminiscent of George Orwell's novel *Nineteen Eighty-Four*, with its famous slogan, "Big Brother is watching you."[44] The workers feel deprived of their freedom by the control system, as if they were in a prison.[45] Opposition is nipped in the bud by the "silence mode": Employees are forbidden to say anything unrelated to work after entering the workshop, and even if they do talk about work, it is only in pairs. Conversations with more than three people must be discussed in the team leader's office, and violators may be punished or dismissed.[46] On the streets in Foxconn's areas, workers are allowed to walk side by side only in pairs. If there are three of them, they must form a line.[47]

Supervisors who are under immense pressure to fulfill production tasks often resort to harsh treatment of workers. A line manager from one of the two plants in Kunshan commented: "To avoid

THE DARK PATTERN

being scolded yourself, you have to scold others as often as possible." It is indeed a humiliating experience for employees at the bottom of the pyramid to be constantly berated. Typical comments from superiors: "Do it well if you want to do it, or fuck off!," "If you don't want to work, fuck off!," "You're useless, a failure, an idiot, trash!" A Foxconn employee revealed: "Do you know the most commonly used expression in Foxconn management? It's 'motherfucker'!" An employee of the Foxconn factory in Langfang wrote: "Before, I didn't understand why people at Foxconn would commit suicide; I thought they had personal issues. After joining Foxconn, I understand. Now, I also want to commit suicide! Here, the supervisors don't see you as a human being; they only care about their performance bonuses and don't see employees as people."[48]

Foxconn's management system illustrates four building blocks of the dark pattern.

Toxic leadership: In Foxconn's pyramid management model, managers at all levels pass the pressure from top to bottom. "Strict management" and "inhumane" are the words workers use most often to describe their impression of Foxconn.[49]

Manipulative language: Foxconn's brutal "scolding culture," with its dehumanizing vocabulary, exacerbates the destructive potential of the system. It contributes to workers not only selling their labor but also losing their dignity.[50]

Corrupting goals: The company's production speed audit departments and management calculate the time it takes workers

> to complete each operation in seconds and set their production quotas based on this.
>
> **Slippery slope:** Despite the heavy pressure exerted by these quotas, a given quota is constantly increased, and in small steps. If it is met today, it will be increased tomorrow. If it is met tomorrow, it will be increased the day after tomorrow—until it can no longer be met. The time of physical or mental collapse cannot be predicted a priori but can only be observed post hoc. Survey data shows that 12.7 percent of Foxconn employees already have experienced fainting on the job.[51]

Foxconn's meticulous planning of the assembly line leads not only to strong alienation for the workers but also to their fragmentation. Workers are randomly assigned to positions on the assembly line, where they are strictly bound to their assigned places and are not allowed to move or communicate with each other during working hours. Interaction between workers from different workshops is also strictly forbidden. In one workshop at the Foxconn plant in Tianjin, there is even a rule that prohibits more than two workers from the same hometown from working together on the same assembly line. It seems as if Foxconn is deliberately destroying the existing social networks of workers, presumably to minimize cohesion and prevent joint action. As a result, workers feel isolated as individuals and are prone to feelings of helplessness and loneliness.[52]

In this isolation, they go to work, leave work, sleep, and do so over and over again—this clockwork-like existence leaves little time for anything else, including socializing.[53] They hardly know each other, not even their names. Liu Zhiyi: "Among hundreds of thousands of people on the factory site, they are like shadows for each other and become the most familiar strangers."[54] In the factories and dormitories, they refer to each other as "dickhead" (diǎo máo, 屌毛), which carries a vulgar and derogatory connotation related to male genitalia. It is often used to describe someone as unpleasant, unimportant, inferior, and/or of relatively low social standing. There is rarely friendship between the "dickheads." The high turnover rate among employees—which is already remarkable in itself—also contributes significantly to the difficulty of building and maintaining social relationships.[55]

More than half (52.9 percent) of Foxconn employees live in employee dormitories.[56] Typically, a dormitory houses eight to twelve people. While the place is physically very dense and crowded, people are socially miles apart. Roommates are typically from different departments and speak different dialects, making it difficult to socialize. Tian Yu, a seventeen-year-old suicide survivor: "We were strangers to each other."[57] When a new "dickhead" arrives at the dorm, there is no welcoming ceremony, and it is only when the roommates find a bed empty in the ten-person room that they realize a "dickhead" has left."[58] After Ma Xiangqian had jumped to his death on January 23, 2010,[59] it turned out that his roommates did not even know his name.[60] The workers living in the same dormitory often have different schedules due to their work assignments and shifts, making the dormitory a place where rest and relaxation are nearly impossible. Personal space is nonexistent. Access is strictly controlled, which also prevents interaction between workers from different dormitories. A worker from Taiyuan: "Someone from dormitory area B cannot go freely to area C. Door-to-door visits are not permitted.... Even if you live near the dormitory, the tight schedules make it difficult to meet up, which makes communicating with friends very difficult."[61]

> Foxconn shows a very interesting kind of **dangerous group** that we have not yet discussed: workers have lost their individuality, their uniqueness, and their dignity. They have become deindividualized individuals. This shared experience—of being atomized, fragmented, and lonely—creates a very strange group identity. These familiar strangers are members of a group, but they are not socially integrated. Rather, they are members of a set in the mathematical sense—the set of people who are disintegrated and who have lost their ability to help themselves and to help others. Hannah Arendt described this as the worst form of group pressure in totalitarian structures: the eradication of the group idea itself and the transformation of people into an amorphous and de-solidarized mass.[62] A few decades before her, the French sociologist Émile Durkheim, the founder of suicide research, identified lack of social integration as one of the risk factors for suicide.[63]

Why would anyone want to be part of such a machinery? One plausible answer is the lack of better alternatives, especially for workers from rural areas.[64] The fact is that Foxconn, with its standardized salaries and benefits, such as health insurance, has long been a popular choice in the labor market.[65] Every day, thousands of workers line up outside the recruitment offices, often waiting for hours,[66] even though Foxconn's base salary is barely above Shenzhen's minimum wage.[67] And yet they come, and those who have managed to get in want to stay, at least for a while.

> The lack of better alternatives creates a rather dangerous kind of **destructive incentive**, one that we haven't seen in any other chapter: if employment at Foxconn, as humiliating and dehumanizing as it may be, is still better than losing one's job, then workers have a strong incentive to endure hardship there. The strongest source of power in a negotiation is typically the ability to walk away.[68] Most Foxconn workers cannot just go somewhere else, and that means they have no power; they can't negotiate better terms. Not only are there very few other options for them, they also know that people queue up in front of the factory to get their job in case they don't perform.

Since 2010, Foxconn has announced significant wage increases in response to social and public pressure, but a comprehensive report by a workers' rights group found that actual implementation has been minimal and subject to various restrictions and hurdles. Tactics such as increasing labor intensity, setting longer probation and evaluation periods, cutting benefits previously provided to workers, relocating experienced workers to inland locations where labor costs are lower, and withholding overtime pay have been used to circumvent keeping promises in order to cut costs. Recall that maintaining low costs was the key to Foxconn's success—and also the driving factor behind its expansion from coastal regions into the interior.[69]

To ensure twenty-four-hour continuous operation of the machines, Foxconn has introduced a system of "day and night shifts," each lasting twelve hours. Some 75 percent of employees have on average only four days off per month; 8 percent of employees even less. In addition, 73.3 percent of employees report an average daily working time of ten hours or more. The average monthly overtime worked by employees is 83.2 hours, which is a serious violation of the Labor Law (Article 41), which stipulates that monthly overtime must not exceed thirty-six hours.[70] Why do those workers do overtime at all? At the 2010 shareholder meeting, Gou stated that "80 to 90% of employees are happy to work overtime to earn more money to buy houses in their hometowns."[71] While this wording suggests that employees do this voluntarily in order to move up the socioeconomic ladder from middle to upper class, it obscures the fact that many are effectively forced to work overtime in order to move up from below minimum to the minimum. One worker from Shenzhen explained: "The work here barely covers personal expenses, so there is nothing left for anything else."[72]

> Unsurprisingly, workers have accumulated a lot of **perceived unfairness**: the reported averages do not include time for meetings, which is usually between fifteen and sixty minutes per day, as that time is not counted as working time. Similarly, if quotas are not met, employees have to stay longer to make up for what they have missed, and this additional working time is not counted either. Finally, "supervisors don't report our overtime that exceeds 80 hours because the regulations don't allow it"—and unsurprisingly, these hours are not compensated with overtime pay. After the suicides in 2010, Foxconn promised that frontline workers would get at least one day off a week. However, during the peak production of iPhones and iPads in 2011, workers had to revert to a schedule of one day off in thirteen days—another

> broken promise. After the successive suicide incidents, Foxconn promised that the monthly overtime would not exceed eighty hours—for many another broken promise.[73] The workers feel all this is unfair—but just like Xu Lizhi, they "can't shout, can't resist / can't complain, can't lay blame."[74]

THE GLOBAL MARKETS

While Foxconn can be seen as a huge machine, with its workers as cogs, there is an even larger machine of which Foxconn is just a little cog itself: the global markets. When the Berlin Wall came down, the Western economic model and its ideological credo were globalized. Companies started to outsource to suppliers who would be under constant pressure to produce "more with less," similar to what we saw in the Boeing case. Just as water flows downhill, capital flows into the countries where wages are lowest. At the same time, there are not many countries as capable as China of supplying assembly workers and highly skilled engineers in high numbers, and with the flexibility to meet the demands of multinational brands.

Here is a telling example. When Apple decided on short notice to make an important design change for an already announced new iPhone, mainly involving the display, this change request reached the Foxconn factory in China shortly before midnight. The manager in charge there immediately woke up 8,000 workers and ordered them into the production hall, where they changed the planned production within 30 minutes and, in just 96 hours, achieved a daily output of 100,000 iPhones—all with 12-hour shifts and hourly wages of a bit more than a dollar.[75]

Foxconn and Apple need each other, but their relationship is not symmetric. Foxconn produces for Apple, not the other way around. Apple and numerous other Western companies are therefore still at the top of the food chain. With their market share, they can easily exert pressure on manufacturers and pit them against each other. And as long as they auction production orders and as long as manufacturers know that they are competing with each other, there will be pressure to produce cheaply.

But wait a minute: Are Western brands really at the top of the food chain? On closer inspection, this only applies to the B2B relationship between Apple and Foxconn. According to the motto "the customer is king," there are millions of kings over Apple. First, there are the shareholders, who at least formally own the company and want high dividends. And second, there are the customers, who want not only good products but also cheap ones; otherwise, they will run to the competition. These millions of shareholders and customers exert pressure on the brands, which in turn pass this pressure on to the manufacturers, who in turn pass it on to their employees.

> Global production networks expose suppliers such as Foxconn to **ambiguous rules**. Just like its competitors, Foxconn finds itself in a dilemma. Western politicians and NGOs publicly admonish them to respect human rights and treat their workers well. At the same time, the manufacturers assume that the contract will be awarded to the one who submits the lowest bid. Low cost and worker welfare are too often contradictory expectations, but suppliers cannot communicate to their customers that they must choose between fast and cheap delivery and human

> dignity. Customers want both, and they do not want to know how their suppliers make it happen.
>
> With the global expansion of production, the **rigid ideology** of neoliberalism, with its pressure on costs and the ever-growing expectations of shareholders, now vibrates across transnational supply chains, with powerful actors squeezing their weaker business partners to the breaking point.

To what extent are Western brands responsible for the working conditions in their production and supply chain? While Steve Jobs, like Gou, had no objection to harsh working conditions, Tim Cook, who replaced Jobs as CEO in 2011, has a different attitude.[76] He commissioned the Fair Labor Association to work with Apple and develop measures to improve the situation of the workers. The association's first report, published in 2012, contained 360 "remedial action items," including pay and hours worked, overtime pay, health and safety training, unemployment insurance, child labor, and ending the exploitation of interns. As always with such improvement plans, there was praise and criticism: while Ted Smith, founder and former CEO of the Silicon Valley Toxics Coalition and chairman of the Electronics TakeBack Coalition, praised Apple for remarkable improvements, most of which he attributed to Cook's leadership, Heather White, in her film *Complicit*, criticizes Apple for not doing more.[77] We don't want to take sides and evaluate Apple's achievements and failures in its efforts to improve working conditions in the manufacture of its products. But we do want to point out that Foxconn operates in a context, and that each of us is involved in the huge global-markets machinery and may contribute to exerting pressure through our purchasing behavior. Every product purchased initiates an order to the manufacturer to make that exact product again, and that has repercussions, usually in places many thousands of miles away. Note that this causal chain works even without bad apples. Its potentially destructive power comes, at least in theory, from the invisible hand of anonymized markets designed to increase efficiency and create general prosperity. But efficiency in a globalized world does not necessarily lead to prosperity for all, and perhaps the invisible hand is invisible because, in a world where knowledge and power are not equally distributed, it may not even exist as the textbooks claim.[78] And ultimately, a central question in this distribution problem that concerns each and every one of us is this: How much are we willing to pay for a smartphone?

• • •

In 2010, Foxconn hit the headlines with its suicide scandal. As tragic as these suicides were, we see through them, as a kind of window, and glimpse the world of the machine and what it does to people. The dark pattern emerges again. First, we see the many machines at Foxconn that unskilled workers have to operate in a mindless manner. Worse still is Foxconn as a precision machine that has perfected scientific management à la Taylor, which presses the people working there into process sequences, deindividualizes them, and takes away their dignity. There is no place for humanity in this world. Leaders on all levels ruthlessly push and yell and insult and replace those who do not perform. On an even higher level, we see the functioning of global markets as something machinelike, where pressure is built up and passed on. Unrealistic goals get formulated and constantly increased in interorganizational production networks designed for maximum efficiency. At the same time those Western brands, pressured by NGOs, demand decent treatment of workers, which for the factory owners is incompatible with the parallel pressure on costs. Not even 200 years ago, machines entered the development of civilization on a grand scale. They have the potential to serve humans, but in the case of Foxconn and the global markets, much seems to indicate that it is human beings who must serve the machine and its laws.

11
THE BRIGHT PATTERN

Ethical blindness is not a tragic destiny, descending upon you and your organization, leaving you helplessly entangled in the *dark pattern*. You can fight these dynamics of moral failure. The power of context is not an excuse for unethical behavior—on the contrary, you can and should leverage it to promote a healthy organizational culture. "But where the danger lies, also grows the saving power," writes the poet Friedrich Hölderlin. In this chapter, we introduce the *bright pattern* that will help you build an ethically robust organization. Mirroring the dark pattern, the bright pattern offers nine antidotes to the nine toxic building blocks:

1. *Rigid ideology* can be fought with *holistic responsibility*. While in the past, companies could simply focus on shareholder value maximization, today they face a multitude of responsibilities they need to balance.

2. *Toxic leadership* loses its dangerous impact when organizations are able to establish a *speak-up culture*.
3. *Manipulative language*, which reinforces and drives immoral decisions, can be fought with a normalization of *moral conversations* in the company.
4. *Corrupting goals* can be avoided through the formulation of *integrity goals* that set a moral limit on what a company wants its managers to achieve.
5. *Destructive incentives* can have a devastating effect on the integrity of decision-makers, while *constructive incentives* help employees perform and flourish without being pitted against each other.
6. *Ambiguous rules* disappear when companies create *moral clarity*, helping employees navigate moral dilemma situations.
7. *Perceived unfairness* is reduced when leaders are sensitive to the conditions that drive *organizational fairness*.
8. The effects of *dangerous groups* can be thwarted by helping people become *courageous upstanders*.
9. Finally, instead of moving forward on a *slippery slope*, companies can promote a *virtuous circle*.

Let us look now in detail at these building blocks of the bright pattern.

HOLISTIC RESPONSIBILITY

When the Berlin Wall came down in 1989, we, the people west of the wall, assumed that the whole world would now become like "us": with the global spread of Western-style liberal market democracies, "the end of history" had arrived, as Francis Fukuyama wrote in

1989. Western liberal democracy had won this competition of ideologies and thus proven to be the best of all possible systems. It was, as Fukuyama wrote, "an unabashed victory of economic and political liberalism" and "the ultimate triumph of Western liberal democracy."[1] In 1996, following the enthusiasm of Fukuyama, Thomas Friedman came up with the "Golden Arches Theory of Conflict Prevention," proposing the McDonald's formula of world peace: Never had two countries with McDonald's restaurants been at war with each other.[2] Fast-food restaurants—as a symbol of the American way of life—were markers on the road to global peace, stability, and prosperity. We just needed to let the magic of the free market enchant the entire planet and work its magic.

Fast-forward to January 2020, to Davos, a little village in the Swiss mountains. "Capitalism as we have known it is dead," disenchanted Salesforce CEO Marc Benioff noted at the World Economic Forum in Davos, criticizing the "obsession that we have with maximizing profits for shareholders alone."[3] In her speech at the same event, then German chancellor Angela Merkel concurred: "The whole way that we do business, that we live and that we have grown accustomed to in the industrial age will have to be changed. We will have to leave that behind us in the next 30 years."[4] The disillusionment expressed at the World Economic Forum is in part due to the accelerating ecological crisis. The alarming decline in biodiversity, rampant deforestation, and rising global temperatures are stark reminders of this crisis.[5]

Doubts about the magic of the (now global) market already were voiced in the early 1990s, when companies started to organize their production in global supply chains, designing them for speed, efficiency, and profit maximization. Milton Friedman had imagined his theory in a time when capitalism was limited to three *well-regulated* democratic places: the US, Europe, and Japan. However, since the 1990s, multinational companies often operate in conflict zones and in countries with repressive regimes and corrupt regulatory systems. What Friedman had postulated as the rule for companies, namely "to maximize profits within the limits of the law," suddenly led to trouble. Who is responsible if governments are not willing or able to regulate well? And what about dictators whose regulatory effectiveness is hardly compatible with the idea of democracy? So companies started to write codes of conduct for their suppliers, engaged in human-rights audits, and followed private social standards developed by NGOs. In short, they engaged in what we have called "political corporate social responsibility," filling the global regulatory vacuum with self-regulation.[6]

Since then, companies have been confronted with ever-growing expectations. Just one decade after this emerging debate on *human rights in global production*, a string of big corruption scandals pushed *compliance and risk management* onto their agenda. In fact, this book would not exist without some of the iconic scandals of the early 2000s. Another decade later, with the above-mentioned acceleration of the ecological crisis, managing *sustainability* moved center stage. A few years ago, investors discovered those topics and Environmental, Social, and Governance (ESG) accounting, and ESG investment started to become fashionable. Currently, mere presence in countries with repressive regimes is questioned, and many international brands avoid such countries for ethical reasons. Add to this the need to manage diversity, the emerging discussion on purpose, and the pressure to use (or not) the corporate voice in political discussions, and you will see that the (corporate) world has changed since Milton Friedman drafted his idea of shareholder value maximization.

All the above challenges are shot through with ethical questions, and yet, decades of managers got their business-school degrees without any training in ethics management. On the contrary, as we have argued, they were trained to consider ethics as something private or optional, disconnected from their job. In a time of global turmoil this is slowly changing.[7] A narrow focus on shareholder value becomes problematic. Maximizing means that the organization tries to achieve the highest possible outcome for one single goal. Mathematically speaking, only one goal can be maximized at any given moment. Strategically speaking, all resources, efforts, and attention must then be focused on that goal. In reality, however, companies face a multiobjective optimization problem with conflicting interests, expectations, and values. Leaders must learn to balance expectations in their stakeholder network to be successful. This requires them to be as sensitive to their moral responsibility as they are to their profit responsibility. Our analysis of recent scandals has demonstrated that a too-narrow focus on profit can paradoxically threaten the economic success or even the existence of a company. Instead of rigidly concentrating on just one aspect of their multiple responsibilities, decision-makers in organizations must carefully observe their network of stakeholders with what Sigmund Freud once called "evenly hovering attention."[8]

Rigid ideological thinking leads corporations into trouble. Instead, leaders need to learn to think holistically and see the company as a highly interconnected and socially and environmentally embedded system in which a too-rigid focus on one aspect will threaten the success of the whole. Holistic responsibility requires taking multiple perspectives, the ability to identify and manage ethical-dilemma situations, and a deep understanding of historical, political, ecological, and cultural context.

This is not an easy task! It might require not just a strategic reorientation but a deep transformation of the entire value chain. Furthermore, companies need experts with totally new skill sets who are able to manage human rights, CO_2 reduction, biodiversity, and other topics that have not been on the agenda of companies so far. Leaders need to develop the competence to manage ethics in all its dimensions, decisions need to be embedded in dialogues with multiple stakeholders, and shareholders must be informed along a triple bottom line of people, planet, and profit.[9]

SPEAK-UP CULTURE

In each of the scandals we have investigated in this book, there have been people who at one point courageously spoke up against the immoral and illegal practices they observed. These people were ignored (France Télécom, Boeing), fired (Wells Fargo, Uber, Theranos), silenced (Uber, Volkswagen), and even sued (Theranos). In fact, critical voices were crushed in pretty much *any* organization that ended up in the headlines for the wrong reasons. In toxic organizations where legal rules are broken, bullying and harassment are the standard operating procedure, and speaking up is a career-terminating move.

Economist Albert O. Hirschman famously argued that people or groups have exactly three options when they are dissatisfied with their organization: exit, voice, and loyalty.[10] They can remain *loyal* despite their disagreement, keep doing their job, and remain silent. They can use their *voice* and speak up, or they can *exit* the organization and vote with their feet, as some did at Theranos, Boeing, Uber, and Wells Fargo.

If we could only give a single recommendation to tremendously reduce the risk of ethical blindness, it would be to encourage people to speak truth to power, to create an environment where anybody on any level of the organization can raise moral concerns. But how do you do this? Pretty much any company is currently communicating to their employees that they are invited to use their voice, and yet, most organizations (not just the really bad ones) miserably fail to create the right conditions for speaking up. People will not speak up just because you ask them to do so.

We need to understand why people choose to remain silent. Late MIT professor and corporate culture guru Edgar H. Schein has observed that "what really drives the culture—its essence—is the learned, shared, tacit assumptions on which people base their daily behavior."[11] Most of the time, the tacit assumptions about the voice option are not very encouraging: our scandal analysis shows the most obvious reason—the fear of drastic forms of retaliation. Then, there is also the fear that superiors might retaliate in a subtler form: your boss might "forget" to invite you to an important meeting or to share information with you that you need to do a decent job. Sometimes retaliation even happens unconsciously. Ethan Burris found that "managers view employees who engage in more challenging forms of voice as worse performers and endorse their ideas less than those who engage in supportive forms of voice."[12]

Furthermore, some people experience that while speaking up might not expose them to a retaliation risk, it doesn't change much either. Superiors do not follow up; raising concerns is thus pointless. Or worse, they trivialize the concerns: "That person is a bully? Yes, sure, we know his leadership style is a bit rough, but he doesn't really mean it and he is a high performer. After all, there must be something he does right, don't you think?" And finally, there is role modeling: people do not observe their own superiors speaking up. How can you expect your team to speak up if you do not dare to speak up to your own superior?

Schein's tacit assumptions that dominate an organization are not simply updated because the compliance department runs a nice internal speaking-up communication campaign. Even after toxic leaders have been removed and new leaders have taken over—for example, when a company starts to clean up after a big scandal—employees might sit and wait for years before they really dare to speak up. Who knows how long those new leaders will stay before the old order is reestablished?

People will only speak up if they consider it psychologically safe to do so.[13] However, such a safe environment does not fall from heaven and cannot be willed into existence by a benevolent CEO. Companies need to invest in the necessary skills and create the conditions that promote speaking up.

First, if people are expected to speak up, leaders on all levels of the hierarchy must be trained in how to listen. And managers very often have a distorted perspective of their own approachability.[14] While they might tell everybody that their door is always open, that open door might feel like a threat to their team (as in the case of Volkswagen CEO Martin Winterkorn). They need to learn how to reduce power distance and how to react properly (for instance, don't get angry, don't propose solutions before you have finished listening). In their teams, leaders must normalize speaking up: they could integrate it systematically in team-meeting routines and let their team members voice their opinion on an issue before they speak themselves. They could formally encourage employees to take on the role of devil's advocate so that employees do not have to speak for themselves but can easily hide behind this role, thereby lowering the threshold for saying something critical.[15] Leaders need to learn how to ask the right questions, how to signal their openness to critical questions, and how to follow up. All that doesn't just happen naturally.

Similarly, employees need speak-up training because they can make plenty of mistakes as well. A speak-up conversation needs to be carefully prepared. It shouldn't be done spontaneously. What is the best timing and place? How can you focus on facts and refrain from being judgmental? What do you want to achieve? What are your arguments and observations? What do you propose as a solution? What do you say if your superior doesn't react well to your concerns?

Second, speaking up requires a supportive institutional environment. The Finnish-Swedish multinational company Stora Enso is one of the world's largest producers of pulp, paper, and packaging materials. Its roots trace back to the thirteenth century. Speaking up is one of the focus areas of its ethics-and-compliance strategy. Hundreds of managers have been trained in psychological safety, and so-called ethics ambassadors are trained to serve as contact points for those who want to voice concerns. In their employee survey, Your Voice, they measure how comfortable employees feel speaking up, and they also measure how often managers encourage employees to use the speak-up tools provided by the company. Most importantly, Stora Enso has set up a process to assist employees who speak up and protect them against all forms of (even subtle) retaliation.

Implementing a sustainable speak-up culture brings challenges for leaders and employees alike. Ideally, followers trust their leaders, but to achieve this, leaders need to know that trust is hard to earn and easy to lose.

MORAL CONVERSATIONS

Some years ago, I (Guido) coached the CEO of a multinational company on how to communicate the importance of ethics to his global team. I persuaded him that the strongest signal he could send about the company values was to talk about a personal experience regarding one of those values. He picked safety, which was an important value in that company due to the hazardous working conditions in their factories. We produced a video in which he shared a story of his grandfather, who became deaf after an accident at work, and the CEO explained how he regretted that he could not have a real conversation with him when he was a child. He made it clear that he had strong and authentic reasons for putting safety first in his company. The video and the message were a success, but it took some discussions to convince him that talking about ethics in such a personal way would not make him look weak in front of his employees. In fact, the opposite was the case, but this concern is widespread. Managers have not learned to integrate ethics into their decisions or their communication. They have not learned to use a moral vocabulary in a work environment and talk about dilemmas, values, principles, and moral success or failure. What they have learned when studying at business school is that they are not supposed to voice moral sentiments on their job. As a result, many managers are morally mute. Already in 1989, Frederick Bird and James Waters observed that managers often fear that moral talk is dysfunctional: "Managers are concerned that moral talk will threaten organizational harmony, organizational efficiency, and their own reputation for power and effectiveness."[16] Not much has changed since then.

What people in an organization consider normal and appropriate behavior results from the narrative web that they weave together in their daily communication. The web is built around stories that answer relevant organizational questions: How do managers make their decisions? What do they talk about? How do they talk about it? If a *moral vocabulary* does not appear systematically in organizational conversations, it isn't considered important. How can employees know that values are important if they are not discussed in team meetings, are not made explicit in decisions, and as a result, are not observed in the daily operations across all ranks? Group conformity pressure is powerful in both directions. Whatever gets normalized as behavior will be copied and thus reinforced. AtkinsRéalis, a world-leading engineering and project management company (formerly known as SNC-Lavalin Group), was charged with fraud and corruption in 2015 and spent eight years under the supervision of a World Bank monitor. To change the culture and leadership style of the company was one of the main objectives when a new CEO and a new chief compliance officer came in. They both understood well that psychological safety and the willingness to speak up among their employees depended on the right signals sent by their managers. Their pragmatic and simple solution was to make a part of the bonus of the top 1,000 managers dependent on ethics. At least four times per year, each of them had to engage their teams in an ethical conversation or send an ethical message to them—and they had to make it personal. Compliance developed a tool kit to inspire them and help them in those conversations. The impact was impressive. In an annual ethics survey, year after year the proportion of employees who perceived their situation as safe enough to speak up increased.

    Employees easily sense whether ethics counts. It doesn't take much for them to understand the general atmosphere of their organization. Psychologist Jonathan Haidt has argued that people intuitively assess moral situations through their gut feelings.[17] Within fractions of seconds, using verbal cues or observations, they sense that something is morally wrong.[18] As our analysis of scandals shows, when struggling with such cognitive dissonances, many people will simply blend in and follow the herd.

After the Swiss pharmaceutical company Novartis was involved in a global corruption scandal, it set up a new compliance and ethics program (we come back to that in Chapter 12). The newly built Ethics, Risk, and Compliance (ERC) department does a global ethics survey of the more than 150,000 employees of the company. One of the goals is to use the results for the promotion of a speak-up culture. They found that people are more likely to speak up if they observe their colleagues behaving ethically. The more their work environment was characterized by unethical practices, the less they were willing to speak up.[19] Ethical behavior promotes ethical behavior. It's contagious. As we have demonstrated in our chapter on the dark pattern, the way we speak, think, and act are strongly connected. Organizations that facilitate moral conversation will normalize moral behavior and thereby make it easier to express discomfort with morally problematic situations. The power of language—not only *that* something is said but also *how* it is said—can be used not only manipulatively, for worse, but also for better.

Do people share stories about peers who spoke up successfully or stories of retaliation? Do they expect their leaders to follow core values, even in rough times, or discount them if necessary? Do they see their peers speaking up? Do they experience moral conversations and the accepted and promoted practices as aligned? Or are they cynical about corporate values? How they *speak* about all this will determine how they will tend to *act* themselves.

INTEGRITY GOALS

I (Guido) once was invited to do a workshop with the top 200 managers of a globally operating pharmaceutical company. They were having their annual strategy meeting, and my workshop on ethical blindness was scheduled for the afternoon of the first day. In the morning, they gave awards to their best salespeople. When the winner went onstage, the compliance people next to me got nervous, and I asked them what was wrong. "This guy," they told me, "is known for cutting corners wherever he can. He is breaking the rules to achieve his success. We always have trouble with him." His behavior was well known to his peers. During the break, we went to the CEO and explained the situation. I told him that if this were true, then he was giving his team two different messages on that day. In the morning, the message was that they can break the rules as long as they are successful, while in the afternoon, with me as a guest speaker, we were going to talk about the importance of doing business with integrity. Everybody would know this was just cheap talk. The company was promoting exactly the dark pattern that I was there to speak about. The CEO was new to the company and did not know about the salesman and his notorious disregard for compliance rules. I urged him to interrogate the situation, and if necessary, send a strong signal and fire his best salesman, which he did one week later. It may sound drastic, but it was necessary and sent the right signal to the rest of the company.

There is a difference between *learning goals* and *outcome goals*. While outcome goals are simply about achieving very specific results ("Sell ten insurance policies per day"), learning goals focus on the process of goal achievement and on improvement along the way

("Put yourself in your customer's shoes"). Outcome goals are extrinsically motivating (you want to get this bonus), while learning goals motivate intrinsically. Learning goals come with the explicit right to fail, to learn new skills, to ask for different tools or additional resources, and to adapt one's sales strategy. As David Welsh and colleagues summarize existing research: "Learning goals are associated with deeper processing of the task and a greater focus on planning, monitoring, and personal progression," and most importantly for skeptics, they also enhance performance. There is no business case for shortcuts.[20]

It may not seem like it at first, but learning goals can be very ambitious. They might on the surface even look like outcome goals (you still are expected to sell those ten insurance policies). However, in contrast to narrow outcome goals, they are constantly accompanied by a clear, top-down ethical message: we do not want you to achieve your goals at any price. This is of particular importance in times of high pressure on sales teams, as when operating in markets with aggressive competition, during a market crisis, or toward the end of the year when people are closing in on their goals. Leaders need to constantly ask themselves whether their short-term goals are sufficiently aligned with the long-term interests of the company, whether the risk of not meeting goals might push their people into taking too-high risks, and whether they have sent the right message about zero tolerance for rule breaking.[21]

So, would *you* also fire your best salesman to protect your principles and values? If you believe in outcome goals, you probably wouldn't, but with a learning-goal approach that considers corporate values as important, and if you want to avoid the dark pattern dynamic, you would have no other choice. Whatever organizational leaders decide in such a situation, it sends a message in one or the other direction.

Learning goals need to be understood as an ongoing conversation with constant feedback. Who is struggling with their goals, why are they struggling, what can be done to help them? Do we need to adapt the goals because of unforeseen events that created new obstacles? Employees must have the opportunity to ask questions about their goals to understand the thought process behind the goals and the underlying assumptions, as well as the internal and external pressures that drive the goals.[22]

How can their leaders keep employees who fail to achieve their goals motivated without nurturing too big a risk appetite? What happens if goals are not met must be clear to any employee. How will they be evaluated? What will be the consequences? Reserve capacity might help buffer the pressure that comes with tough goals. It supports the learning and improvement and mitigates risks of unethical behavior.[23]

Integrity is not promoted by formulating specific ethics-related goals, but rather by embedding business goals into a broader values-based context. Siemens, the German global technology company, is sending such a message to their managers. After being caught in a huge corruption scandal in 2008, paying $1.6 billion in fines, and spending another billion on investigations and reform efforts, the company has learned a painful lesson about too-rigid outcome goals.[24] Under the supervision of a monitor, they implemented a strict compliance system and installed a hotline for internal whistleblowers. With their "integrity initiative," they engage in collective action to fight corruption in those industries where they operate. Managers who arrive at their beautiful leadership training center on Lake Starnberg in Bavaria, Germany, are greeted in the entrance hall by a sentence of the company's founder, Werner von Siemens: "I don't sell the future for instant profit."[25]

CONSTRUCTIVE INCENTIVES

Handelsbanken is a highly successful Swedish bank. While their competitors in global financial markets stumbled or fell during the financial crisis, they remained unharmed. The bank has a rather unusual approach to rewarding their employees. They pay no bonuses. As CEO Mikael Sorensen explains: "If you have to do 10 mortgages per month, or 100 credit cards, then you're not focused on your customer. We don't have those kinds of targets.... Many people believe that the only way to motivate your staff is to give bonuses. We think it's the worst thing to do."[26]

Handelsbanken's approach is fully aligned with what researchers on organizational behavior have found out about performance evaluation, bonus schemes, and employee rankings. Performance evaluations are unavoidably biased and subjective. They can lead to frustration and reduce motivation because employees rarely feel correctly evaluated by their superiors. They often consider the feedback unfair. Furthermore, the measures used by companies are too often not even valid indicators of performance. As a result, performance-based pay is not very effective.[27]

For employee rankings, research results are not better. In a recent series of experiments, Jan Woike and Sebastian Hafenbrädl found, for instance, that if the performance of people is ranked, feedback on individual performance leads to competitive behavior while feedback on the overall group performance promotes collaboration.[28] Already the taken-for-granted assumption that the performance of individual team members would normally distribute over a Gaussian curve, with most people falling near the average and fewer people being classified as high and low performers, is highly questionable: rather, most organizations have a few star performers, with small and rather irrelevant differences between the rest of their people. Promoting the stars and treating the others well might be much better for the corporate bottom line than forcing everybody onto an imagined distribution curve, pitting them against each other.[29]

What does work, instead, is to implement a process of employee coaching that provides skills and information and promotes behavioral changes to achieve goals.[30] Such a coaching process needs to focus on care (a concern for the well-being of each employee) and enabling structures that help people to be motivated, perform, and feel at home in the organization.[31] With such an approach, organizations might create performance-management systems that support employees, promote collaboration within and across departments, and unite people under the overarching strategic goals of the company. They can flourish without this constant pressure to demonstrate that they perform better than "the enemy" next door. Incentive structures need to be aligned with the values and ethical principles of the company and focus on long-term results instead of short-term maximization.

Some years ago, Zappos, a leading online retailer that was well known for its innovative corporate culture, engaged in a fascinating experiment. They replaced annual performance evaluations with regular evaluation meetings that happened daily to monthly, depending on the goals. A goal department led by a "head coach" helped employees to define their individual professional and personal goals, framed as a thirty-day challenge. The performance evaluation itself was 50 percent focused on how employees contributed to the corporate culture (spelled out in ten different corporate values such as "Be humble," "Build a positive team," or "Pursue growth and learning").[32] As *Forbes* raved in 2012, "Zappos.com is consistently rated as one of the best places to work in the country and has built a reputation as the gold standard in customer service."[33] We write this in the past tense, because the successful company was bought by Amazon, and this new owner slowly dismantled the management approach that founder Tony Hsieh had established, instead enforcing a culture that we have already seen in our case analyses: losers leave or are fired in annual culling of the staff—"purposeful Darwinism," as a former Amazon manager summarized the approach in a conversation with the *New York Times*.[34] According to the *Wall Street Journal*, "By 2019, Amazon was pressuring Mr. Hsieh and his team to meet certain growth targets."[35] Zappos had to operate with outcome goals, individual performance evaluation, rank and yank, and individual bonus schemes. It was the sad end of a promising initiative.

MORAL CLARITY

Ethical decisions in organizations are not easy. Very often, managers are confronted with options that seem to be equally right or wrong. This is what philosophers call "dilemma situations": values and principles clash in those options (shall I be honest to my client or loyal to my team?), and the interest of stakeholders might be incompatible (a higher salary for workers comes at the expense of the shareholder; investment in sustainability makes the product more expensive for customers). What makes decisions even more complex is that consequences are often uncertain and unpredictable and solutions rarely straightforward. If several options make sense from one or the other value or principle held by the manager and the company, the choice is not between right and wrong, but between right and right or between wrong and wrong.[36] Such decision-making situations involve trade-offs between values and are unavoidably ambiguous.

Wait, now you might be confused: Didn't we describe ambiguity as one of the building blocks of our dark pattern? Yes, we did, but it is a different kind of ambiguity. You might compare it to the good and bad cholesterol in your bloodstream. Good cholesterol reduces the risk of heart disease by removing the plaque in your arteries, while bad cholesterol does the opposite: it forms the plaque in your arteries and increases the risk of heart diseases. Good cholesterol represents our right-against-right situation, where several options make sense from an ethical perspective. Bad cholesterol is the ambiguity we have seen in our case studies. These are right-versus-wrong situations. What is morally right clashes with what superiors pressure their teams to do or what teams have developed as tolerated routines: faking compliance with diesel regulation, manipulating blood tests to prove that the analyzer works, taking performance-enhancing drugs, harassing female employees, cheating customers.

From the perspective of the decision-maker, both types of situations are ambiguous: however, the good and unavoidable ambiguity comes from the clash of values. The bad and avoidable ambiguity results from the clash of corporate decisions and routines with moral and legal rules. Therefore, aiming for moral clarity does not mean removing ambiguity from the decision-making situations in an organization. This is not possible. To remove it means to impose one interpretation of a situation on everybody else—we have seen in our cases where such an authoritarian leadership style can lead.

When making a decision in a right-versus-right dilemma, people might come to different legitimate conclusions when examining a trade-off between principles and values. When defending one value, applying one principle, or promoting one outcome, we do so at the expense of other values, principles, and outcomes. The moral clarity an organization needs therefore does not come from the *result* of a decision, but rather from the *process* of decision-making a company establishes for difficult decisions.

Some companies have developed a standardized decision-making process for ethical dilemma situations. Siemens has, for instance, set up a framework that is based on six ethical principles, covering the ethical domains relevant for the company:

- Integrity in transactions
- Legal compliance
- Human rights
- Sustainable production
- Occupational safety
- The duty to "explore ethical concerns"

Those domains need to be navigated with five behavioral principles:

- We behave correctly.
- We respect each other.
- We create trust.
- We protect our company.
- As managers, we have a special responsibility to set the right tone from the top.

Managers are supposed to follow a decision-making process in four steps:

- Analyze the situation
- Evaluate the decision options

- Apply the ethical principles
- Decide and document[37]

The Japanese pharmaceutical company Takeda has defined four core values: to do what is right for the patient, to build trust in society, to protect the reputation of the company, and to achieve sustainable business results. When making their decisions, managers must process their options through these four lenses and in that order: the patient first, the profit last.[38] This might all sound like a long and winding process, but when applied regularly, people routinize the use of company values and principles in their decisions. Ethics is like a muscle. If you do not use it, it gets weak. If you use it, it becomes a habit.

To turn the use of such decision-making tools into a powerful habit, it is important to train employees at all levels of the organization to see and understand their potential ethical dilemma situations (thereby reducing the risk of ethical blindness). Standard compliance trainings that let employees go through annual online tests by clicking on the appropriate answer are not the right tool for this objective. Effective trainings need to be designed around realistic dilemma stories that people do experience or could experience in their respective jobs and at their respective level of responsibility. A top manager in the sales department and a salesperson will have different day-to-day dilemma situations. A manager in procurement will not share the same potential dilemma situations with a manager in accounting or production. While the situations differ, the principles and the decision-making process remain the same. Help people find this common ground and focus on it: this is how you create a robust ethical culture.

ORGANIZATIONAL FAIRNESS

In 2022, Citibank fired a senior analyst who had asked for the reimbursement of expenses after a business trip. While his expense claim was well within the EUR 100 limits of the bank, Citibank found out that he had traveled with his partner, and the meals for which he wanted to be reimbursed had actually been for two people. This was against the rules, and when the case was investigated, the analyst lied about it.[39] Was the decision to fire him right? On the surface, this sounds like a great demonstration of what we argue with regard to rule breaking: since small rule violations spiral very often into big transgressions, there should be no tolerance even for small rule breaking (see "Virtuous Circle" below, the ninth building block of our bright pattern).

However, there are a few questions we would need to ask Citibank to seriously evaluate the decision: Would they have fired someone higher up in the hierarchy for the same behavior? Would they fire someone for this violation of the rules regardless of whether they are a high or low performer? Or someone who is well protected by their superiors? Or someone who breaks other types of rules in the organization to achieve targets? We don't know the answers. And to be honest, it doesn't really matter what the official answers of Citibank would be. What counts is what the employees of the bank *believe* their organization would do in such cases. Would leaders of the bank be coherent? Make exceptions? If yes, for whom and why?

In such cases, people inside the organization will ask one main question: *Was the decision fair?* As we have demonstrated, the perception of unfairness is a key building block of our dark pattern, and consequently, a climate of fairness is important for the integrity of an organization. But how do people evaluate fairness in the first place? Three types of fairness considerations can be differentiated: *distributive*, *procedural*, and *interactional* fairness.

First, *distributive fairness* is about how resources, rewards, or punishments are distributed. In assessing it, what matters is not the actual distribution, but the extent to which it matches a person's ideas about what a fair distribution across recipients should look like.[40] Moreover, these fairness perceptions depend on who is distributing the resources (or rewards, or punishments), who is receiving them, who is observing (and judging) this, what the resource is, and what the context is.[41] Various principles can be used to establish and evaluate distributive justice. One principle for distributing resources, rewards, or punishments is *equality*: everyone simply gets the same. Another principle is *equity*: allocation is proportional to a person's input or contribution. Finally, allocations can be made based on *need*, ignoring whether everyone gets the same amount (as the principle of equality would require) and what the recipients have done or contributed (as the principle of equity would require).[42] Overall, from a distributive-fairness perspective, regardless of which principle is applied, people will ask themselves whether there is a balance between what they give and what they receive—and how their balance compares to that of others. This will also include the question of resources made available to them for their assignments.

Second, *procedural fairness* relates to how employees perceive organizational processes like resource allocation, conflict resolution, and performance evaluation.[43] A fair process typically uses clear formal procedures. Leaders need to be transparent about how they arrive at their decisions, and they must be open to feedback on it. Their decisions must be consistent, based on accurate information, and free of biases. Ideally, they explicitly link decisions with an ethical dimension to their values and those of the organization. People must be convinced that decisions can be corrected if information or evaluations turn out to be problematic.[44]

Finally, *interactional fairness* is about the human interactions during the enactment of procedures—specifically, whether the people involved are treated with respect, empathy, and dignity. Answering emails quickly, a respectful tone, or empathically listening during a phone conversation may all influence interactional-justice perceptions. An analysis of everyday life events that respondents regarded as unjust revealed that "a considerable proportion of the injustices which were reported did not concern distributional or procedural issues in the narrow sense but referred to the manner where people were treated in interpersonal interactions and encounters."[45] Most companies underestimate the damage they do, for instance, when they mass-layoff people—or when they rank and yank them. The damage they do to their culture very often doesn't come from *whether* they do it, but *how* they do it: very often by violating the dignity both of those who are forced out and those who survive the process. Leaders must develop the ability to sense and restore perceptions of unfairness, making fairness a fundamental leadership value.

COURAGEOUS UPSTANDERS

Generations of students in many countries have read William Golding's novel *Lord of the Flies* at school. Stranded on a deserted island, a group of boys slowly descends into savagery. Any attempt to establish order and promote cooperative behavior fails. The story conveys a simple and frightening message that philosopher Thomas Hobbes had already proclaimed centuries earlier: remove the thin layer of civilization, leave people in a "state of nature," and man becomes the wolf of man. Even children would turn into wild beasts and kill each other, as in Golding's story. His novel was translated into more than thirty languages and sold tens of millions of copies. It has shaped (or at least reinforced) our pessimistic outlook on human nature.

Some of our cases seem to confirm such a negative view on humanity. One of the shocking details of the France Télécom case is the total lack of solidarity among colleagues: instead of supporting a suffering colleague, people distanced themselves, left the room, stopped communicating with the victims. At Uber, victims of sexual harassment were told by HR managers that they themselves, not the perpetrators, were responsible for the trouble. It is maybe the most disturbing aspect of corporate scandals: the immense human suffering happening in silence and isolation and the lack of solidarity with the victims. The Jewish philosopher Hannah Arendt, who escaped the Holocaust in Germany, once described this experience very well. "The problem, the personal problem" she argued, "was not what our enemies did, but what our friends did.... It was as if an empty space was forming around you."[46] But is this really who we are? Silent bystanders, devoid of empathy? Wolves who fight each other ruthlessly?

In 2019, two scholars—physician and sociologist Nicholas Christakis in his book *Blueprint*, and historian Rutger Bregman in his bestseller *Humankind*—investigated what happened after real shipwrecks. Both find that castaways in real cases often cooperate and demonstrate solidarity with each other. Christakis finds two interesting differences between groups of survivors who fight against each other and those who cooperate: the latter *started* their adventure with acts of kindness. By helping someone with broken bones, for instance, a group of shipwrecked sailors set the default for cooperation. Furthermore, cooperative groups had leaders who promoted solidarity within the group.[47]

Research in behavioral economics and in social psychology confirms those findings. Game theory shows that people are willing to cooperate instead of simply following their own self-interest under the right conditions. When people experience others cooperating in repeated interactions, when they build the belief that others will reciprocate their cooperative behavior, and when defectors are punished by enforcement mechanisms, people will choose cooperation over fighting.[48] The beginning of the "game" is often decisive. Psychologist Steven Gilbert has argued that small decisions can be "precedent setting."[49] While he made this observation for transgressions, the same can be argued for situations where moral decisions set a different precedent and the first move is made in a spirit of cooperation, as Christakis showed for the shipwrecked sailors. Dennis Gioia, the engineer from our Ford Pinto case, who later became a management professor, added one more important dimension: people often display wrong moral behavior because they do not have the cognitive script available for the situation.[50] This is the case for both victims and observers of a transgression. Victims often "play dead" as an instinctual survival response, and observers play deaf and blind. Both simply do not know how to react, what to say, what to do.

If companies want to create a culture where people collaborate, stand up for each other, and support those who speak up, they can leverage those insights from research. We recommend six different measures:

1. Many organizations try to encourage their employees to speak up. However, we have not seen many examples where they invite them to stand up for each other and interfere in cases of observed harassment or other unethical behavior.

2. Upstanding needs to be included in codes of conduct, value statements, and policies to make this expectation explicit.
3. Leaders need to include the topic in their moral conversations.
4. Bystander intervention trainings can sensitize people for situations where their upstanding is expected and provide the moral scripts on how to intervene.[51]
5. Furthermore, those trainings need to train employees in the importance of searching for allies—for instance, when they plan to speak up.
6. Finally, cases of upstanding need to be communicated and celebrated to set the default. If those measures are taken, a culture of mutual support can be created.

VIRTUOUS CIRCLE

Big ethical and legal problems often start with small transgressions. They seem to be so harmless and insignificant that it is easy to rationalize the rule breaking. And even if an actor on that slippery slope might have the feeling that what they do is wrong, this emotional response will fade away over time. They become ethically blind, because "the brain adapts to dishonesty."[52]

Minor transgressions do not only precede more serious ones on a slippery slope—they may also be warning signals that something more serious is already going wrong in the background. I (Guido) once worked with a company in its postscandal process of cultural transformation, and one of the stories I learned in this company illustrates this: the manager who was the main instigator in a corruption scheme that had spread in the organization used to smoke in the office even though smoking was not allowed.

How can this dynamic of small steps be stopped or even prevented from happening in the first place? One of our favorite movies that we regularly show to our students when we teach the dark pattern is *The Devil's Advocate*. Kevin Lomax (played by Keanu Reeves) is a highly successful and ambitious defense attorney based in Florida. He represents a schoolteacher who is accused of having sexually harassed a young girl. In the court room, Lomax realizes that his client is guilty, which puts him in a moral dilemma. Shall he defend a teacher who harassed one of his students? He asks the judge for a break, goes to the bathroom, and looks into the mirror. There, he sees a fictional preview of what his life will be like if he takes this first step on the path to success at any cost. He sees himself rising through the ranks of a leading law firm in New York, making one compromise on his values after another, driven by his growing appetite for success and power. On this steep career path, he eventually destroys his modest but happy life with his wife. In the mirror, Lomax sees his entire life in *fast-forward*. He sees the slippery slope on which he would move forward at an ever-faster pace if he is willing to make this first compromise of his personal values defending the guilty (and gullible) schoolteacher. After imagining the consequences of that decision, he has the strength to resist the temptation and not even take the first step. Lomax tells the judge that he can no longer represent his client.

Research confirms what Kevin Lomax understood intuitively. In Stanley Milgram's famous obedience experiment, people were invited to give electric shocks of increasing intensity to another person, and 65 percent of participants were willing to go up to a lethal dose. A shockingly high number. However, it is often forgotten that 35 percent did *not* obey. They refused to "kill." Most of those who disobeyed did so *early on in the process*, and others stopped when they realized that from one step to the next there was a *qualitative difference*—the harm done by the next electric shock would be significantly more dangerous than the previous ones.[53] All these participants saw a line they did not want to cross because, like Kevin Lomax in the movie, they imagined the endpoint of the process.

This is also what the late Harvard professor Clayton Christensen had in mind when he warned against the easy rationalization of deviating from one's norms and principles *just this once*. "That's the lesson I learned," he wrote. "It's easier to hold to your principles 100 percent of the time than it is to hold to them 98 percent of the time. The boundary—your personal moral line—is powerful because you don't cross it.... Decide what you stand for. And then stand for it all the time."[54] If people anticipate the consequences of their decision on their future self, their values get activated and they tend to resist the temptation more than people who do not engage in such moral imagination. Sometimes, being reminded of an upcoming temptation can trigger a person's self-control, helping them resist the urge.[55]

What follows from those insights for organizations and people in organizations? Organizations should implement a zero-tolerance policy for small rule breaking, and leaders must carefully observe how and when their teams transgress seemingly harmless limits to achieve their goals. This does not mean they should punish people for small infractions (after all, you do not want to establish a climate of fear). However, the clear signal top-down must be that there are ethical and legal limits to business success.

And what about each employee and their vulnerability to the slippery slope? In ancient Greece, the priestess of the Temple of Apollo in Delphi was supposed to be a medium through which mortals could speak with the gods. People traveled to Delphi for advice. The temple had the inscription "Know Thyself." Before asking for guidance through the gods, know who you are, what your place in the world is, and what your values are. This advice is as valid today as it was 2,500 years ago. Values are the most stable element of our identity, but we rarely reflect upon them. They help us to draw the red line we are not willing to cross. Know your values. Then imagine the endpoint of your decision well before you are caught up in the heat of the moment. If the pressure is high, engage in a little thought experiment: Ask yourself: *What would I decide if I had no fear?*

In the late 1920s, anthropologist Edward E. Evans-Pritchard investigated the impact of witchcraft and magic among the Azande, an ethnic group in southern Sudan. His observation of how powerful belief systems are created holds beyond the Azande for any social setting: "If one must act as though one believed, one ends in believing…as one acts."[56] We either move down the slippery slope of unethical behavior or up the virtuous ladder of integrity by taking one step after another. With each step, we reinforce the direction we have chosen. And each step makes the next one not only easier but also more probable and unavoidable—the notorious escalation of commitment. We rationalize the first steps by either ignoring our ethical concerns down on the slippery slope or resisting our fear up on the virtuous ladder. The deeper we slide and the higher we climb, the more firmly we keep going. The first steps are decisive for the magic of integrity to unfold.

12
AFTER THE FALL

THE DANGEROUS BUSINESS AS USUAL

We make a very simple argument in this book: too often, our behavior is strongly influenced by a context that promotes unethical decisions and makes ethical behavior more difficult. It distorts the perception of reality in a way that people are numbed to all the warning signals as they slide down the slippery slope. Under these conditions, even good people struggle to do the right thing. This is, however, neither how scandals are discussed in public nor how they are processed internally by the affected organizations. The simple bad apple stories are much more attractive for the media and an easy way out for the managers who have to bring their struggling organization back on track: after the fallout, those leaders who survive will most probably highlight their total innocence, denying any responsibility for what went wrong. In the best case, new leaders are brought in from outside who also have no interest in digging too deeply into what went wrong. After all, they are paid to look forward, not backward. The company will fire a few people and hire some others further down the hierarchy. Lawyers in the compliance department will write a new code of conduct and strengthen some control measures. Then, after a certain cooling-off period, the company will go back to business as usual.

However, business as usual is almost always the problem in those cases. After a few years or even sooner, some of those companies are caught in the next scandal and are forced to repeat the exercise, never learning their lesson. In January 2024, a door plug on a Boeing 737 MAX on an Alaska Airlines flight fell from the sky; several whistleblowers report there are ongoing quality problems. There are reports that the same pressure on costs and speed that we—in our analyses above—identified as a major driving force of the two 737 MAX crashes continues to dominate the company culture. Boeing engineers complain about the fear of speaking up and have reported punishment of those who dared to raise critical issues. It seems to be indeed business as usual at Boeing. Apparently, the scandal did not trigger any deeper reflections on why things had gone wrong in the past.[1] Similarly, at Wells Fargo, systematic legal problems continued after the big scandal. When, a few years later, federal regulators again imposed additional fines and restrictions on the bank due to its mishandling of home-loan customers' portfolios, US senator Elizabeth Warren even proposed revoking their license to operate.[2] Some industries, such as defense, pharma, or medtech, are also well known for the cyclical return of systemic compliance problems.

It doesn't have to be like this. When a scandal happens, a company can choose a different path. After the fall, both leaders and followers are in an ideal situation for deep ethical introspection. What went wrong top-down and bottom-up? How did we end up in this mess? Why did we not see it coming? Why did we not listen to those who spoke up? Or was there no one in our organization who spoke up, and if so, why not? What can we learn from what happened? In many companies, these are multibillion-dollar questions because that is the price tag of their moral collapse. As in the case of Boeing and Wells Fargo, the wrong conclusions might set up the company for the next wave of expensive fines.

Of course, fighting the dark with the bright pattern that we discussed in the previous chapter applies to any organization, including companies in a postscandal phase. However, a scandal puts a company in the perfect situation for two additional initiatives. First, an organization that is shaken by a scandal needs to process what has happened in a period of collective grief instead of just moving on. Looking back is painful, but important for healing. Second, they have the unique opportunity to set up an ethics-and-compliance program that is broader and more effective than the more or less ineffective legalistic minimum approach.

LOOK BACK!

After a crisis, companies often focus on immediate causes that permit quick solutions—such as firing the ringleaders of a corruption scheme, the bad apples. In a postscandal situation, most, if not all, companies will make the big mistake of disconnecting from the past as soon as possible. The worst thing top leaders in an organization can do—and still most of them do it—is enforce silence, tell people to focus on bringing the business back on track, shift the blame to a few, and argue that otherwise nothing was wrong. They want to look forward, not backward. In many cases, the ugly past even becomes a taboo: corporate lawyers highly recommend not talking about it anymore to avoid further legal trouble, and corporate communication specialists, paid to make the company shine, do the same because they want to limit the reputational damage. After a short period of shame, the company tries to give the impression that they have moved to a better place. References to what went wrong disappear, and if references cannot be avoided, the story is whitewashed. Soon after Dieselgate, Volkswagen claimed that it had learned from what happened and that it had started a new era. And Boeing wrote in 2020, "The events and lessons learned have reshaped our company and further focused our attention on our core values of safety, quality, and integrity."[3] Four years later, it was under scrutiny again with that door plug. The disturbing indications were that "the events" did not lead to much learning, nor did they reshape anything. Analyzing how companies speak about their past scandals is often very revealing. The language they use often tends to "minimize the scale and seriousness of the ongoing scandal," as Olivier Boiral and colleagues write. Volkswagen, for instance, referred to Dieselgate in its internal and external communication as the "diesel issue."[4]

Bold announcements of learning and transformation might be credible, and the attempt to neutralize the negative impact and turn the page is even understandable. However, it entirely misses an important point of postscandal management, wastes an opportunity for a deeper moral introspection, and diverts attention from fundamental issues such as the corporate culture that led to the problems in the first place. This culture still shapes the collective identity and influences the behavior of people in the organization and will not just disappear by itself. As William Faulkner once wrote, "The past is never dead. It's not even past."[5]

While the companies we examined hit the news because of problems with software in cars or airplanes, blood analyzers, or bank accounts, our analysis demonstrates that behind the scenes, there is enormous and yet mostly invisible human suffering. People have been humiliated, kicked out, yelled at, silenced, demoted, harassed, and pushed into illegal practices or suicide. In any scandal, there are always instigators, perpetrators, colluders, and victims. For all of them, being at the epicenter of a scandal can be a deeply distressing and disturbing experience. They are experiencing *moral injury*, which is defined as "the damage done to one's conscience or moral compass when a person perpetrates, witnesses, or fails to prevent acts that transgress one's own moral beliefs, values or ethical code of conduct."[6] In a situation where many good people engage in unethical practices—the consequence of the dark pattern—employees might be emotionally and morally damaged, regardless of whether they see themselves as perpetrators, colluders, victims, or a mix of all those identities. As Brett Litz and colleagues highlight, "The critical elements to moral injury are the inability to contextualize or justify personal actions or the actions of others and the unsuccessful accommodation of these potentially morally challenging experiences into preexisting moral schemas, resulting in concomitant emotional responses (e.g., shame and guilt) and dysfunctional behaviors (e.g., withdrawal)."[7]

Put differently, a postscandal situation is emotionally complex. Many people will be in shock and disbelief, especially if they learn about the misbehavior of leaders or peers whom they trusted. Employees who participated in unethical practices, whether knowingly or unknowingly, will experience intense shame. They feel guilt and self-blame for their role in the misconduct, even if they were coerced or pressured into participating. They will experience cognitive dissonance and struggle to reconcile their actions with their values. This can lead to a profound sense of personal failure and a crisis of conscience. Those who were victims might feel a deep sense of betrayal. For many people, their job and company are important elements of their identity. Being associated with a scandal-tainted company, they might now face social stigma. Some will feel anger and betrayal for being misled, involved in unethical or illegal practices, and harmed. Some will be in a state of denial. I (Guido) once overheard a conversation between two managers of a company that had just been hit by a big scandal where one of them asked his colleague, "What's the problem? We just had the most successful year of our history!" After all, things cannot be too bad, as long as the company is successful. It is important that organizational leaders address all these complex sentiments.

Cultural change doesn't happen overnight, and it doesn't happen because a company communicates on all internal and external channels that it has learned its lesson and miraculously transformed somehow into a morally updated version of its previous broken self. Instead of ignoring or repressing past suffering, the company needs to engage in a process of *moral healing*, which involves discussing, interpreting, and remembering traumatic experiences. At this point, we would have loved to discuss an example of a company managing such a process well, but we can't. We are not aware of any. Moral healing is definitely going beyond just setting up a more effective compliance system to reduce the risk of getting into trouble again. There are good examples (albeit not many and difficult to find as well) of such forward-looking transformations, and we will show you one later. In contrast to such more process-oriented changes, moral healing seems to be a topic that companies either do not see as important or find too difficult to tackle. Therefore, we can only theoretically present the idea of this important backward-looking dimension of a postscandal transformation.

First and foremost, it is important to develop a shared understanding of what went wrong. The company must create an accurate and transparent narrative of its moral collapse. Put differently, they must do internally what we have done for this book: dig through all available information and find their own manifestation of the dark pattern. Acknowledging what went wrong is the critical first step in the healing process. For those affected by the scandal, understanding what happened and why it happened is important for closure. People cannot move past the incident if the new resounds too much like the old and they feel as silenced as before. Daring to look into their moral and psychological abyss and address the scandal head-on demonstrates that the company is willing to take responsibility for its past immoral actions. Such accountability and transparency can help rebuild trust with stakeholders, including customers, employees, and investors. Engaging in a process of moral healing makes it more probable that lessons will be learned and improvements will be made.

Then, a company needs to create a protected environment where employees can meet, share, and discuss this narrative and their own experiences with what happened, as well as express their potential postscandal anxieties. As we highlighted in the chapter on the bright pattern, creating a culture where followers speak up and leaders listen is already difficult to achieve in a normal organization. It is even more difficult in a postscandal situation. People will sit and wait because they first want to see how serious top management is about change. They might sit and wait for years. If a company doesn't create protected environments for conversation about the past, it begins its cultural transformation on the wrong foot, sending the wrong signal right from the start. In all the scandals that we have analyzed, speaking up was a career-terminating move. Just imagine such a company launching a speak-up campaign in a context where speaking about what happened is suppressed. The already existing culture of fear, distrust, and cynicism will be reinforced rather than transformed.

To make their people speak up about future problems, a company needs cathartic conversations about past problems, pain, shame, and suffering. In a postscandal situation, conversations can have a therapeutic effect. Protected environments can be town-hall meetings, smaller circles initiated by the company or the employees themselves, or even anonymous feedback mechanisms as confidential channels for voicing grief. The latter is important because there will obviously still be much fear and distrust in the organization. In scandals where people died, working with coaches who are experienced in trauma awareness and resilience-building techniques could be necessary.

Creating protected environments for an expression of individual and collective grief, shame, and suffering is important for signaling to employees that the company cares about their well-being. It will help to rebuild relationships and foster a sense of community and solidarity. When initiating protected environments, a company acknowledges the negative emotional impact the previous corporate culture and leadership had on employees, and importantly, it creates opportunities for top leaders to listen to those in grief and anger. After all, victims of abuse will seek answers and accountability for the injustices they have suffered. Healing conversation can empower and energize leaders and followers to engage for a better future. It's the training ground for a strong speak-up culture. This requires honest communication from top leadership and also, if appropriate, the courage to ask for forgiveness.

Of course, the organization needs to find the right balance between commemoration and moving forward. The past should not absorb the energy necessary to succeed in the future, nor should it promote negative thinking. Over time, such a process of moral healing must be transformed into a *politics of memory*. The moral collapse of the past moves to the background, but it is important to keep it in everybody's memory. Over the years that follow a scandal, fewer and fewer people will remember what happened; most employees might not even have been at the company when it hit the news. When leaders and employees start to argue that this could only happen in the past and would not happen to them, they take a dangerous first step toward the dark side again. The scandal needs to be memorialized to avoid toxic leadership ever taking root again in the organization. This could be done through annual reflections, dedicated communication from top management, and the integration of lessons learned into corporate values, but also through making the past an element in how people are hired, promoted, and trained. A company could even produce a film (or use the one on Netflix if its scandal were big enough) as training material for new employees or leaders who move up in the hierarchy.

MOVING ETHICS AND BEHAVIORAL SCIENCES CENTER STAGE

If you work in compliance, avoiding a scandal under your watch is paramount. If you can't, you are normally one of the first to be fired. However, being in a company *postscandal* can be a unique and rewarding challenge. When the cleanup begins, the entire organization is in moral shock, the CEO's attention is focused on your topics, and you'll receive all the resources you need. This is especially true when investigating authorities impose a monitorship on the company. In severe cases and after settling their legal issues, companies often fall under the oversight of an independent third party. This monitor assesses whether the company is making adequate progress in implementing an effective compliance program, including appropriate policies, procedures, control mechanisms, and training to prevent future misconduct. The monitor regularly reports to regulatory bodies or the court, and negative reports can lead to further penalties for the company. While this process demands significant time and energy from organizational leaders, compliance moves center stage. The moral shock of the postscandal phase is an opportune moment for a (usually newly formed) compliance team to develop a robust program, innovate, and dare to implement new ideas.

Klaus Moosmayer experienced this firsthand when he transitioned as chief ethics, risk, and compliance (ERC) officer from Siemens to the Swiss pharmaceutical company Novartis after the latter had been embroiled in a major corruption scandal in 2018. The scandal centered around accusations of illegal payments made to doctors and other health-care professionals in various countries to boost sales of Novartis drugs and influence prescription decisions (put differently, the typical compliance trouble in the pharmaceutical industry). Novartis was investigated in several countries, from the United States to Greece, Türkiye, and South Korea. The illegal practices turned out to be systemic. In total, Novartis paid almost $1.3 billion in fines in a legal settlement.[8]

Without going into details, investigations revealed numerous elements of our dark pattern, from aggressive pressure on sales targets, to a culture of fear and silence, unclear rules, and lack of accountability, to a tolerance and normalization of questionable practices within certain regions or divisions. As at Volkswagen before Dieselgate, the word "problem" had been forbidden at Novartis and could easily become a career-terminating word. In short, as in all the cases you have seen so far in our book, Novartis had established a culture where short-term sales goals were prioritized over ethical considerations.

In contrast to many other companies involved in a big scandal, Novartis acknowledged the need for cultural and organizational change, including strengthening its compliance program, enhancing transparency and accountability, and fostering a culture of integrity and ethical conduct. Most importantly, they decided to focus their attention on what we have discussed in our book so far: they broadened their understanding of risk management by including human risks and focused on the organizational context that drives the wrong or right behavior of people.

As Moosmayer argues, "In the event of a major compliance crisis, there is no remedy other than to quickly build a compliance program to tackle detected deficiencies, including a solid control system. As an analogy when you suffer a severe road accident, you need immediate intensive care. But what comes afterwards? Is the corporation committed to investigate deeper into why the 'accident' happened and whether existing compliance measures are sustainable and effective over the long term?" When he took over the compliance department at Novartis, he fused compliance and risk management into one function and extended the latter with a new focus on human risk. This "integrated assurance concept" was then embedded in a broader ethical framework to promote a leadership mindset that would protect the organization against the return of the previous toxic culture.[9]

In a first step, the incoming ERC team at Novartis developed a new code of ethics as a normative reference point for the company, involving thousands of employees bottom-up in the process. However, most companies—including those that we examined in this book—have codes and corporate values. Between the ambitious expectations coming with a code of ethics and the real behavior in day-to-day operations, a gray zone can open—we showed this in our scandal analyses. In this space, all kinds of distorted incentives and problematic implicit expectations can drive decision-makers to the dark side—whether or not the company has some nice values posted on the wall and printed in colorful brochures. A proper analysis of the risks that emerge in this gray zone cannot be done by a legalistic approach to compliance. The law is blind for the ethical and psychological perspective. Instead, such an analysis requires the insights of behavioral sciences. Just developing a code, defining organizational values, and communicating them would not have much impact on real behavior. But how do you impact behavior? By understanding how people make decisions, by understanding the pitfalls of those decisions, and by influencing the context of those decisions. As Antoine Ferrère, the global head of behavioral and data science on the Novartis ERC team, explains: "Early on it became very clear that, if our goal was to drive ethical behaviors, we would need to go beyond the Code and investigate the ways in which we could remove 'what gets in the way' of our associates being their best ethical selves."[10]

Novartis incorporated insights from behavioral science into its compliance program to better understand the factors that influence (un)ethical decision-making and behavior. By leveraging principles from psychology, neuroscience, and behavioral economics, the company sought to design interventions and incentives that would encourage employees to make ethical choices and resist the temptation to engage in misconduct.[11] The team of behavioral scientists at Novartis, specializing in ethics, risk, and compliance, examined decades of experimental evidence to identify factors that increase the likelihood of unethical behavior—such as cheating, remaining silent when one should speak up, following bad examples, and succumbing to pressure.

Crucially, they refused to operate with the bad apple theory and rather focused on the organizational context to identify risks. Instead of focusing on personality traits, the behavioral scientists in the ERC team dug into the literature on the drivers of ethical and unethical behavior and designed a questionnaire with fifty-plus questions. The questionnaire focuses on those psychological measures and constructs that influence ethical and unethical behavior according to research, adding questions on behavior around critical aspects such as speaking up, perceived fairness, or psychological safety. Readers of this book will not be surprised about the constructs they integrated as drivers of (un)ethical behavior: perception of conflicting goals and unclear expectations (we discussed this as the double bind), moral disengagement, sense of control, psychological safety, fairness, and trust.

The survey was launched across the organization and sent out to more than 150,000 people in over one hundred countries. The first questionnaire in 2021 was answered by over 38,000 people, and 32,000 employees participated in the last survey in 2023. The data that emerges from the global ethics survey is interpreted and key findings and action points are made available to ERC professionals at the company on a digital platform, called the ERC Control Tower. ERC country heads are then responsible for using those insights to take local measures and promote ethical conversations within their country leadership teams.

With their survey, Novartis, for instance, found out that people in the lab, compared to those in field forces, manufacturing sites, or office settings, were *more* likely to observe unethical behavior and *less* likely to report it—a highly dangerous combination. Two further findings explained potential reasons. Lab and manufacturing leaders were rated lower in ethical leadership skills, a common issue in many companies where the culture tends to be rougher than in office settings. Additionally, when concerns are raised, a rougher culture results in poorer reactions from leaders at all levels of the hierarchy. Those insights gave Novartis a clear indication of where and how they needed to improve the organizational context.

Using behavioral sciences to understand how people make decisions, then changing the context so that the probability of ethical decisions increases—a program very aligned with what we argue in this book. Behavioral change is then the result of an analysis of three aspects of a decision:

1. Do the people have the skills for the right behavior?
2. Has the company removed barriers that block such behavior?
3. And finally, are people motivated to engage in such a behavior?

Based on their large data set, Novartis's ERC team can develop, test, and globally scale potential actions. At the core of such a program is the idea that the best way to mitigate human risks is to empower leaders with the ethical and behavioral-science-based skills so that they can take ownership in the process of creating a culture of psychological safety and speak up. Both ethics and behavioral sciences are integrated in leadership education programs and executive onboarding. The training program for managers is called "Why good people do bad things," pretty much in the spirit of the analysis we offer here in this book. In fact, it was explicitly inspired by the MOOC (massive open online course) we offer (for free) on Coursera: Unethical Decision Making in Organizations.[12]

Even though the ERC team at Novartis scaled a steep learning curve, it certainly made mistakes on its way. For instance, in our view, their first wave of trainings focused too much on biases. Not only is the impact of bias trainings contested, it dangerously shifts the focus away from context toward the individual. Bias training too easily loads the responsibility on the decision-makers instead of challenging the context and its systemic problems like destructive incentives, ambiguous rules, or other elements of our dark pattern. However, broadening the understanding of compliance by focusing on ethics and social psychology creates a much more effective protective shield against the dark pattern. It is a game-changing transformation of compliance and the only way of reducing the human risks that drive the moral collapse of an organization.

EPILOGUE

Which scandals should we choose for our book? The choice was not easy. There are so many, and we did not want to overwhelm our readers with too many stories and too many details. The list of potential candidates was long, and new cases kept coming up in the headlines as we were writing. Just to mention a few cases that did not make it in the book: **3M** paid $12.5 billion to settle their legal trouble over forever chemicals. They were accused of knowingly poisoning the entire planet for decades.[1] In France, **Orpea**, one of the globally leading chains of retirement homes, was caught maximizing profit for shareholders to the point that elderly residents were systematically mistreated and neglected in understaffed nursing homes.[2] The investment in such nursing homes is also called "gray gold"—there's a lot of money to be made for investors off people with gray hair. **Norfolk Southern Corporation**, a major American transportation company that operates one of the largest freight railroad networks in the US, was involved in a series of train derailments, including a major incident in East Palestine, Ohio, in February 2023, which resulted in a hazardous chemical spill. Just another company trying to do "more with less" like Boeing, as critics have argued.[3] The **UK Post Office** wrongfully prosecuted hundreds of employees due to faulty data from their IT system, which falsely showed financial discrepancies. These inaccuracies led to criminal convictions, job losses, bankruptcies, social stigma, and suicides.[4]

Then there are also those subliminally occurring scandals that remain just below the surface because instead of making one big boom, these companies have myriads of smaller incidents. Just google the lawsuits, settlements, and accusations of legal violations involving companies such as Tesla, Twitter/X, Facebook, or Amazon.[5] You can spend days going through that stuff. Then google the work climate and the leadership style in those organizations or go through any of our building blocks of the dark pattern. It's probably there. In plain sight.

Below the surface are also the many scandals happening in small- and medium-size companies, that struggle as much with abusive leaders, corrupt business practices, fraud, and other morally and legally problematic issues. They never make the news, because they are simply too small to catch the interest of journalists. Most people reading this book will not be involved in Boeing-level scandals. However, they could easily find themselves in smaller, but nonetheless dangerous and damaging, situations—both as perpetrators and victims. It can happen to any of us.

Who is next? This is a question we often get from our students or managers when we do workshops in companies. Can you predict the next scandal? No, we can't. But what we can certainly do—and you should now be able to do the same with the help of our book—is to see the warning signals, the red flags that indicate a growing risk of ethical blindness in an organization. Just watch out for the dark pattern. Many companies dance on the edge of the moral cliff, and sometimes, they fall. But which one will fall and when? They fall when the dark pattern is sufficiently strong and their success story is faltering, while external expectations and internal hubris remain high. The company needs to keep the story going. But it is not possible. Admitting it and speaking up internally is not possible either, because there is this culture of fear. At that point, something will break.

Everywhere in the world, companies keep ending up on the wrong side of the law. The bad apple theory miserably fails to explain such scandals, where hundreds and sometimes thousands of people turn into perpetrators and colluders. Instead, if you dig a bit deeper in all those cases, you find the dark pattern. People succumb to the pressure, engage in some imagined Darwinist endgames, and become ethically blind. And then there are the victims. In all those cases, beyond some often-banal violation of laws, there is tremendous human suffering happening backstage.

We have highlighted already that ethical blindness is not a destiny befalling otherwise good people, helplessly exposing them to the pressure of context. Humans are not machines. There is always a choice, and with our bright pattern we offer a list of recommendations for how organizations and individuals can strengthen their self-defense and become mindful when contexts push them into mindless execution of doubtful routines. There are always people who are strong enough to resist. Many of them just leave the toxic organization, but some of them—actually very few of them—become whistleblowers and are ready to pay the price for upholding their ethical principles. In particular for those heroes, who are often not just unsung but even stigmatized and destroyed, and for all the victims who were made to suffer in toxic organizational cultures of fear, we must make a final point. Late Stanford psychologist Philip

Zimbardo, whose famous prison experiment of the 1970s taught us an important lesson on the power of context, once highlighted that when we understand how the pressure of context can distort human behavior, it doesn't release perpetrators and colluders from their moral and legal responsibility. As he argued, "Understanding the 'why' of what was done does not excuse 'what' was done. Psychological analysis is not 'excusiology.' Individuals and groups who behave immorally or illegally must still be held responsible and legally accountable for their complicity and crimes."[6]

Therefore, with our analysis we do not intend to excuse the behavior of people who break rules in organizations. We all must be held accountable for what we do. Rather than *subtracting*, the dark pattern *adds* a layer of responsibility by demonstrating how those who break the rules might be pushed to do so by an organizational context that in turn is created mainly by leaders of the organization.

There seems to be an amazingly flat learning curve in organizations. The pattern repeats itself again and again, jumping from company to company, from industry to industry. And those not (yet) affected stand there and watch with curiosity, never making a link to their own organization, because, after all, "we" are not like "them."

As the poet William Butler Yeats once wrote, "In dreams begins responsibility." We have a duty to imagine. This is what, according to Hannah Arendt, drives most of our unethical behavior: the lack of moral imagination. It is important to imagine what might follow from our decisions when we give or follow doubtful orders. Contexts are made by people, in particular by those with power. The *golden rule of ethical leadership* is thus very simple: as a leader you should never create a situation for followers where they are pushed to believe that breaking moral and legal rules is the only option they have to achieve their goals.

The dominating explanation for scandals out there is the behavior of some bad apples in an otherwise healthy barrel. We showed that this is too simple because very often, the entire barrel is rotten. When we wrote this book, we discussed the priority in which we wanted to order the nine building blocks of our dark pattern. We decided to start with rigid ideology because this seems to be the most powerful driver. The phenomenon we explain in this book is global. It doesn't depend on a particular national culture—it rather emerges from a globally shared understanding of business. What if this understanding itself is the problem? What if the prevailing economic system is the problem? Adhering to a rigid shareholder value ideology, knowing full well that it provides fertile ground for monsters to grow—perhaps this is in the end the real scandal.

ACKNOWLEDGMENTS

This book marks a milestone on a long journey that started with an idea: What if unethical decisions have less to do with a person's character traits and more with the context in which they make their decisions? Together with our colleague Franciska Krings, we developed a theory on why good people do bad things and called it "ethical blindness." Since then, we engaged with thousands of our students in Lausanne, virtual students in our Coursera MOOC, and managers around the world in this idea, hopefully helping them to better navigate the psychological pitfalls of ethical blindness in their private and professional lives. We are thankful for the many discussions we had with them, for the experiences they shared, and for their encouragement to write this book.

We want to thank all those people who were there when it happened and who were willing to anonymously speak with us for this book project. With your help we could much better narrate what happened at Enron, Uber, Volkswagen, France Télécom, Boeing, Wells Fargo, the Tour de France, and Karolinska.

ACKNOWLEDGMENTS

A conversation with Martin Lüdicke inspired the title of the book, and Pink Floyd as well as the Scorpions inspired some of our chapter titles and subtitles. The connoisseur will know which these are.

We thank numerous colleagues, both at our faculty and across the world, for fruitful discussions and pointers to relevant literature. And we thank our student assistants who helped us in our research on the scandals used in this book, and/or edited text and/or references: Barnaby Dicker, Dan Luca Fulger, Joana Goy, Larisa Mijatovic, Lorenzo Parma, and Yue Wu.

We are grateful to Alison Taylor. When this book was just an idea in our minds, she helped us find an agent. And we could not have found a better agent than Connor Eck from the Eck Agency, who helped us turn this idea into a book proposal and find the best publisher for *The Dark Pattern*. We thank Colleen Lawrie and Emily Taber, the editorial directors at Basic Venture, for their critical feedback and guidance. Their vision helped shape this book. We also thank Joseph Gunther and Susan Gollnick for their copyediting. Both have a sharp eye for detail that really made a difference.

Finally, we would like to express our deepest gratitude to our families and friends, whose unwavering support, encouragement, and expertise were the most important prerequisites for this project.

NOTES

Introduction: Good Managers Gone Bad
1. US Senate, *An Examination of Wells Fargo's Unauthorized Accounts and the Regulatory Response*, Hearing Before the Committee on Banking, Housing, and Urban Affairs, September 20, 2016, https://www.govinfo.gov/content/pkg/CHRG-114shrg23001/pdf/CHRG-114shrg23001.pdf.

2. Watching the video, which is well worth viewing, one gets the impression that she is acting as the spearhead of angry and furious customers who have gathered in large numbers with protest placards on the street to vent their displeasure at elitist bankers exploiting the poor masses: "Senator Elizabeth Warren Questions Wells Fargo CEO John Stumpf at Banking Committee Hearing," September 20, 2016, YouTube video, https://www.youtube.com/watch?v=xJhkX74D10M; see also US Senate, "An Examination of Wells Fargo's Unauthorized Accounts and the Regulatory Response," Committee on Banking, Housing, and Urban Affairs, September 20, 2016, https://www.banking.senate.gov/hearings/an-examination-of-wells-fargos-unauthorized-accounts-and-the-regulatory-response.

3. For a discussion on how context influences (un)ethical decisions, see Philip Zimbardo, *The Lucifer Effect: How Good People Turn Evil* (Random House, 2007), 230–231, and Gerd Gigerenzer, *The Intelligence of Intuition* (Cambridge University Press, 2023), 140.

4. Guido Palazzo, Franciska Krings, and Ulrich Hoffrage, "Ethical Blindness," *Journal of Business Ethics* 109, no. 3 (2012): 323–338.

5. About 25,000 enrolled during the first year and another 25,000 have enrolled since the course was redesigned in 2015, such that students no longer take it together as a cohort starting at a fixed time but can enroll whenever they want; see https://www.coursera.org/learn/unethical-decision-making.

Chapter 1: Ethical Blindness
1. Constantine Sedikides et al., "Behind Bars but Above the Bar: Prisoners Consider Themselves More Prosocial Than Non-prisoners," *British Journal of Social Psychology* 53, no. 2 (2014): 396–403.

NOTES TO CHAPTER 1

2. Shadd Maruna and Ruth E. Mann, "A Fundamental Attribution Error? Rethinking Cognitive Distortions," *Legal and Criminological Psychology* 11, no. 2 (2006): 155–177.

3. Jennifer J. Kish-Gephart, David A. Harrison, and Linda Klebe Treviño, "Bad Apples, Bad Cases, and Bad Barrels: Meta-Analytic Evidence About Sources of Unethical Decisions at Work," *Journal of Applied Psychology* 95, no. 1 (2010): 1–31.

4. Troy Segal, "Enron Scandal: The Fall of a Wall Street Darling," *Investopedia*, November 26, 2021, https://www.investopedia.com/updates/enron-scandal-summary/.

5. Matthew T. Lee and M. David Ermann, "Pinto 'Madness' as a Flawed Landmark Narrative: An Organizational and Network Analysis," *Social Problems* 46, no. 1 (1999): 30–47, https://doi.org/10.2307/3097160.

6. Psychologist Gerd Gigerenzer calls this a simplistic "one-word explanation": see Gerd Gigerenzer, "On Narrow Norms and Vague Heuristics: A Reply to Kahneman and Tversky," *Psychological Review* 103, no. 3 (1996): 594.

7. Douglas O. Lindner, "Famous Trials," UMKC School of Law, accessed November 14, 2024, https://www.famous-trials.com/enron/1791-stockchart; Segal, "Enron Scandal."

8. "Greed, for lack of a better word, is good. Greed is right. Greed works. Greed clarifies, cuts through, and captures the essence of the evolutionary spirit." This is corporate raider Gordon Gekko speaking, the protagonist of the movie *Wall Street*. Yes, it's just a movie. So, what about Ivan Boesky's statement "greed is healthy," built into a graduation speech at the University of California, Berkeley? "You can be greedy and still feel good about yourself," Boesky told the students. Unlike Gekko, he was not an invention of scriptwriters in Hollywood. Boesky was a real rogue trader involved in one of the big insider-trading scandals of the 1980s; see Bob Greene, "A $100 Million Idea: Use Greed for Good," *Chicago Tribune*, December 15, 1986, https://www.chicagotribune.com/news/ct-xpm-1986-12-15-8604030634-story.html; for a more general discussion, see Venkat R. Krishnan, "Impact of MBA Education on Students' Values: Two Longitudinal Studies," *Journal of Business Ethics* 83, no. 2 (2008): 233–246.

9. Dennis Gioia, "Pinto Fires and Personal Ethics: A Script of Missed Opportunities," *Journal of Business Ethics* 11, no. 5/6 (1992): 379.

10. Ulrich Hoffrage, "How People Can Behave Irresponsibly and Unethically Without Noticing It," in *Responsible Management Practices for the 21st Century*, ed. Guido Palazzo and Maïa Wentland (Pearson Education France, 2011), 173–182; Gioia, "Pinto Fires," 380.

11. While most philosophers distinguish between "moral" and "ethical," often these two terms are used indistinctly in debates, so we will not separate them sharply either. Moreover, often they are used in established terms such as "moral disengagement" or "ethical blindness," and then of course we use the standard vocabulary as well.

12. Hannah Arendt, "Eichmann in Jerusalem—I," *New Yorker*, February 8, 1963, https://www.newyorker.com/magazine/1963/02/16/eichmann-in-jerusalem-i.

13. Hannah Arendt, *Eichmann in Jerusalem: A Report on the Banality of Evil* (Viking Press, 1963); Hannah Arendt and Gershom Scholem, "The Correspondence: 1939–1964," ORF, April 8, 2017, https://oe1.orf.at/artikel/263219/Der-Briefwechsel-1939-1964.

14. Christopher R. Browning, *Ordinary Men: Reserve Police Battalion 101 and the Final Solution in Poland* (HarperCollins, 1992, repr. Penguin Books, 2001); Daniel Jonah Goldhagen, *Hitler's Willing Executioners: Ordinary Germans and the Holocaust* (Vintage, 2007).

15. Philip Zimbardo, *The Lucifer Effect: How Good People Turn Evil* (Random House, 2007), 231, 372.

NOTES TO CHAPTER 1

16. Adrian Raine and Yaling Yang, "Neural Foundations to Moral Reasoning and Antisocial Behavior," *Social Cognitive and Affective Neuroscience* 1, no. 3 (2006): 203–213.

17. Victoria Bryan, "Goldman Sachs Boss Says Banks Do 'God's Work,'" Reuters, November 8, 2009, https://www.reuters.com/article/us-goldmansachs-blankfein-idUSTRE5A719520091108.

18. Ann E. Tenbrunsel and David M. Messick, "Ethical Fading: The Role of Self-Deception in Unethical Behavior," *Social Justice Research* 17 (2004): 223–236.

19. Guido Palazzo, Franciska Krings, and Ulrich Hoffrage, "Ethical Blindness," *Journal of Business Ethics* 109, no. 3 (2012): 323–338.

20. Definition adapted from J. Edward Russo and Paul J. H. Schoemaker, *Winning Decisions: Getting It Right the First Time* (Random House, 2002), 21.

21. Francis Bacon, with foreword by Basil Montagu, *The Works of Francis Bacon V1* (1884) (Kessinger, 2010), 171.

22. Frederic Charles Bartlett, *Remembering: A Study in Experimental and Social Psychology* (Cambridge University Press, 1932).

23. Elizabeth Loftus, "Our Changeable Memories: Legal and Practical Implications," *Nature Review Neuroscience* 4, no. 3 (2003): 231–234.

24. Kimberley A. Wade et al., "A Picture Is Worth a Thousand Lies: Using False Photographs to Create False Childhood Memories," *Psychonomic Bulletin & Review* 9, no. 3 (2002): 597–603.

25. Marcia K. Johnson and Carol L. Raye, "False Memories and Confabulation," *Trends in Cognitive Sciences* 2, no. 4 (1998): 137–145.

26. Brady Wagoner, "What Makes Memory Constructive? A Study in the Serial Reproduction of Bartlett's Experiments," *Culture & Psychology* 23, no. 2 (2027): 186–207.

27. Leon Festinger, Henry W. Riecken, and Stanley Schachter, *When Prophecy Fails: A Social and Psychological Study of a Modern Group That Predicted the End of the World* (University of Minnesota Press, 1956).

28. Will Storr, *The Science of Storytelling* (William Collins, 2019).

29. Jeff Guinn, *The Road to Jonestown: Jim Jones and Peoples Temple* (Simon & Schuster, 2017).

30. Pat Beall, "Purdue Pharma Plants the Seeds of the Opioid Epidemic in a Tiny Virginia Town and Others," *Palm Beach Post*, 2018, https://heroin.palmbeachpost.com/purdue-pharma-plants-seeds-of-opioid-epidemic/.

31. Barry Meier, "The Delicate Balance of Pain and Addiction," *New York Times*, November 25, 2003, https://www.nytimes.com/2003/11/25/science/the-delicate-balance-of-pain-and-addiction.html.

32. Ryan Hampton, *Unsettled* (St. Martin's Press, 2021), 70.

33. Beall, "Purdue Pharma."

34. Harry Wiland, *Do No Harm: The Opioid Epidemic* (Turner Publishing Company, 2019), 32.

35. Patrick Radden Keefe, *Empire of Pain: The Secret History of the Sackler Dynasty* (Doubleday, 2021), 228, 385.

36. Hampton, *Unsettled*, 57, 60.

37. Bethany McLean, "'We Didn't Cause the Crisis': David Sackler Pleads His Case on the Opioid Epidemic," *Vanity Fair*, June 19, 2019, https://www.vanityfair.com/news/2019/06/david-sackler-pleads-his-case-on-the-opioid-epidemic.

NOTES TO CHAPTER 1

38. Supreme Court of the State of New York, *The City of New York Against McKinsey & Company, Inc. and McKinsey & Company, Inc. United States*, https://www1.nyc.gov/assets/law/downloads/pdf/McKinsey%20Complaint.pdf.

39. McLean, "'We Didn't Cause the Crisis'"; Jan Hoffman, "Purdue Pharma Is Dissolved and Sacklers Pay $4.5 Billion to Settle Opioid Claims," *New York Times*, September 12, 2021, https://www.nytimes.com/2021/09/01/health/purdue-sacklers-opioids-settlement.html; Andrew Edgecliffe-Johnson, "McKinsey Pays Out Another $230mn to Settle Opioid Cases," *Financial Times*, September 27, 2023, https://www.ft.com/content/df746e59-352b-47a0-9090-913ac2707b84.

40. McKinsey & Company, "Our Purpose, Mission, and Values," accessed September 16, 2024, https://www.mckinsey.com/about-us/overview/our-purpose-mission-and-values.

41. Albert Bandura, "Moral Disengagement in the Perpetration of Inhumanities," *Personality and Social Psychology Review* 3, no. 3 (1999): 193–209; see also Albert Bandura, "Albert Bandura Discusses Moral Disengagement," October 4, 2011, YouTube video posted by Jeffrey Zeig, 10:45, https://www.youtube.com/watch?v=JjuA4Xa7uiE.

Chapter 2: The Power of Context

1. We compiled our modified version of Hans Christian Andersen's (1805–1875) fairy tale "The Emperor's New Clothes" from various French, German, and English versions.

2. Jennifer S. Lerner and Philip E. Tetlock, "Accounting for the Effects of Accountability," *Psychological Bulletin* 125, no. 2 (1999): 255.

3. Florian M. Artinger, Sabrina Artinger, and Gerd Gigerenzer, "CYA: Frequency and Causes of Defensive Decisions in Public Administration," *Business Research* 12 (2019): 9–25.

4. Philip Zimbardo, *The Lucifer Effect: How Good People Turn Evil* (Random House, 2011).

5. Jean-Paul Sartre, *No Exit: Four Contemporary French Plays*, trans. by Stuart Gilbert (Random House, 1967).

Chapter 3: The Dark Pattern

1. Adapted from Aristotle's *Metaphysics*, this quote became the motto of Gestalt psychology in the early twentieth century. For its origin, original meaning, and later use, see SE Scholar, "Who said 'The Whole Is Greater Than the Sum of the Parts'?," June 6, 2019, https://se-scholar.com/se-blog/2017/6/23/who-said-the-whole-is-greater-than-the-sum-of-the-parts.

2. Milton Friedman, "A Friedman Doctrine—the Social Responsibility of Business Is to Increase Its Profits," *New York Times*, September 13, 1970, https://www.nytimes.com/1970/09/13/archives/a-friedman-doctrine-the-social-responsibility-of-business-is-to.html; Alan B. Thomas, *Controversies in Management* (Routledge, 1993), 56.

3. Harrison M. Trice and Janice M. Beyer, *The Cultures of Work Organizations* (Prentice Hall, 1993).

4. Daniel Kahneman, *Thinking, Fast and Slow* (Farrar, Straus and Giroux, 2011), 277: Once we "have accepted a theory and used it as a tool in [our] thinking, it is extraordinarily difficult to notice its flaws. If you come upon an observation that does not seem to fit the model, you assume that there must be a perfectly good explanation that you are somehow missing. You give the theory the benefit of the doubt."

5. Mark J. Perry, "Quotation of the Day on the 'Magic of the Marketplace,'" American Enterprise Institute, September 26, 2013, https://www.aei.org/carpe-diem/quotation-of-the-day-on-the-magic-of-the-marketplace/.

NOTES TO CHAPTER 3

6. Bill Goldstein, "Word for Word / 'Greenspan Shrugged'; When Greed Was a Virtue and Regulation the Enemy," *New York Times*, July 21, 2002, https://www.nytimes.com/2002/07/21/weekinreview/word-for-word-greenspan-shrugged-when-greed-was-virtue-regulation-enemy.html.

7. Joseph L. Bower and Clayton M. Christensen, "Disruptive Technologies. Catching the Wave," *Harvard Business Review*, January/February 1995, https://hbr.org/1995/01/disruptive-technologies-catching-the-wave.

8. Henry Blodget, "Mark Zuckerberg on Innovation," *Business Insider*, October 1, 2009, https://www.businessinsider.com/mark-zuckerberg-innovation-2009-10.

9. Ronald Reagan Presidential Foundation & Institute, "Ronald Reagan's Inaugural Address: January 20, 1981," accessed May 30, 2024, https://www.reaganfoundation.org/ronald-reagan/reagan-quotes-speeches/inaugural-address-2/.

10. Maurice Punch, *Dirty Business: Exploring Corporate Misconduct* (Sage, 1996); John T. Jost et al., "Fair Market Ideology: Its Cognitive-Motivational Underpinnings," *Research in Organizational Behavior* 25 (2003): 53–91; John R. Carter and Michael D. Irons, "Are Economists Different, and If So, Why?," *Journal of Economic Perspectives* 5, no. 2 (1991): 171–177; Venkat R. Krishnan, "Impact of MBA Education on Students' Values: Two Longitudinal Studies," *Journal of Business Ethics* 83, no. 2 (2008): 233–246; Long Wang, Deepak Malhotra, and Keith J. Murnighan, "Economics, Education, and Greed," *Academy of Management Learning & Education* 10, no. 4 (2011): 643–660; Björn Frank and Günther G. Schulze, "Does Economics Make Citizens Corrupt?," *Journal of Economic Behavior and Organization* 43, no. 1 (2000): 101–113.

11. Ronald R. Sims and Johannes Brinkmann, "Enron Ethics (Or: Culture Matters More Than Codes)," *Journal of Business Ethics* 45 (2003): 243–256.

12. Sarah Bahr, "In 'Super Pumped,' the Uber Founder Disrupts His Own Rise," *New York Times*, February 22, 2022, https://www.nytimes.com/2022/02/22/arts/television/super-pumped-uber-showtime.html.

13. Norbert Bischof, *The Oedipus Riddle* (Psychosozial-Verlag, 2020), 305–307; authors' translation from German.

14. Robert Hogan, *Personality and the Fate of Organizations* (Erlbaum, 2007).

15. Delroy L. Paulhus and Kevin M. Williams, "The Dark Triad of Personality: Narcissism, Machiavellianism, and Psychopathy," *Journal of Research in Personality* 36, no. 6 (2002): 556–563.

16. Robin M. Kowalski, ed., *Behaving Badly: Aversive Behaviors in Interpersonal Relationships* (American Psychological Association, 2001), 210.

17. Robert D. Hare, *Without Conscience: The Disturbing World of Psychopaths Among Us* (Guilford Press, 1999).

18. Paul Babiak, Craig S. Neumann, and Robert D. Hare, "Corporate Psychopathy: Talking the Walk," *Behavioral Sciences & the Law* 28, no. 2 (2010): 174–193.

19. Clive Boddy, Richard Ladyshewsky, and Peter Galvin, "The Influence of Corporate Psychopaths on Corporate Social Responsibility and Organizational Commitment to Employees," *Journal of Business Ethics* 97 (2010): 1–19; John Clark, *Working with Monsters: How to Identify and Protect Yourself from Workplace Psychopaths* (Random House, 2005); Simon Croom, "12 Percent of Corporate Leaders Are Psychopaths. It's Time to Take This Problem Seriously," *Fortune*, June 6, 2021, https://fortune-com.cdn.ampproject.org/c/s/fortune.com/2021/06/06/corporate-psychopaths-business-leadership-csr/amp/; Katarina Fritzon et al., "Problem Personalities in the Workplace: Development of the Corporate Personality Inventory," in *Psychology and Law in Europe: When West*

Meets East, ed. Par Anders Granhag et al. (CRC Press, 2016); Frederick S. Stinson et al., "Prevalence Correlates, Disability, and Comorbidity of DSM-IV Narcissistic Personality Disorder: Results of the Wave 2 National Epidemiologic Survey on Alcohol and Related Conditions," *Journal of Clinical Psychiatry* 69, no. 7 (2008): 1833–1845.

20. Elena Fernández-del-Río, Pedro J. Ramos-Villagrasa, and Jordi Escartín, "The Incremental Effect of Dark Personality over the Big Five in Workplace Bullying: Evidence from Perpetrators and Targets," *Personality and Individual Differences* 168 (2021): 1–6.

21. Benjamin R. Walker and Chris J. Jackson, "Moral Emotions and Corporate Psychopathy: A Review," *Journal of Business Ethics* 141, no. 4 (2017): 797–810; Ormonde Rhees Cragun, Kari Joseph Olsen, and Patrick Michael Wright, "Making CEO Narcissism Research Great: A Review and Meta-Analysis of CEO Narcissism," *Journal of Management Scientific Reports* 46, no. 6 (2020): 908–936, https://doi.org/10.1177/0149206319892678.

22. Maaike Cima, Franca Tonnaer, and Marc D. Hauser, "Psychopaths Know Right from Wrong but Don't Care," *Social Cognitive and Affective Neuroscience* 5 (2010): 59–67; Rebecca Michalak and Neal M. Ashkanasy, "Working with Monsters: Counting the Costs of Workplace Psychopaths and Other Toxic Employees," *Accounting & Finance* 60, no. 51 (2020): 729–770.

23. Dong Liu, Raymond Loi, and Hui Liao, "The Dark Side of Leadership: A Three-Level Investigation of the Cascading Effect of Abusive Supervision on Employee Creativity," *Academy of Management Journal* 55, no. 5 (2012): 1187–1212; Salar Mesdaghinia et al., "How Leaders Drive Followers' Unethical Behavior," *Journal of Management* 9, no. 7 (2022), https://doi.org/10.1177/01492063221104031.

24. Leonid Schneider, "How Macchiarini Was Recruited to Karolinska," *For Better Science*, August 8, 2018, https://forbetterscience.com/2018/08/06/how-macchiarini-was-recruited-to-karolinska/.

25. Maureen McKelvey, Rögnvaldur J. Saemundsson, and Olof Zaring, "A Recent Crisis in Regenerative Medicine," *Science and Public Policy* 45, no. 5 (2018): 608–620; Eve Herold, "A Star Surgeon Left a Trail of Dead Patients—and His Whistleblowers Were Punished," *Leaps*, October 8, 2018, https://leaps.org/a-star-surgeon-left-a-trail-of-dead-patients-and-his-whistleblowers-were-punished/particle-2; Alison Abbot, "Culture of Silence and Nonchalance Protected Disgraced Trachea Surgeon," *Nature*, September 2, 2016, https://www.nature.com/articles/nature.2016.20533.

26. Bess Levin, "Dick Fuld's 'I'll Fucking Kill You, Like Actually Put a Shotgun in Your Mouth and Pull the Trigger 'til It Goes Click' Style of Management Has Kept Lehman Brothers Safe from Things Like $8.4 Billion Writedowns, So Far. But Is He Going Soft?," *Dealbreaker*, October 29, 2007, https://dealbreaker.com/2007/10/dick-fulds-ill-fucking-kill-you-like-actually-put-a-shotgun-in-your-mouth-and-pull-the-trigger-til-it-goes-click-style-of-management-has-kept-lehman-broth.

27. Lawrence G. McDonald and Patrick A. Robinson, *Colossal Failure of Common Sense: The Inside Story of the Collapse of Lehman Brothers* (Crown, 2009), 89, 98, 101, 105, 129.

28. United States Bankruptcy Court Southern District of New York, *Report of Anton R. Valukas, Examiner Volume 1 of 9* (Jenner & Block, 2010), 4, https://jenner.com/lehman/VOLUME%201.pdf (accessed May 32, 2024).

29. Steve Fishman, "Burning Down His House," *New York*, November 27, 2008, https://nymag.com/news/business/52603/.

30. John L. Austin, *How to Do Things with Words* (Oxford University Press, 1975).

31. Varda Liberman, Steven M. Samuels, and Lee Ross, "The Name of the Game: Predictive Power of Reputations Versus Situational Labels in Determining Prisoner's

NOTES TO CHAPTER 3

Dilemma Game Moves," *Personality and Social Psychology Bulletin* 30, no. 9 (2004): 1175–1185; Paul H. Thibodeau and Lera Boroditsky, "Metaphors We Think With: The Role of Metaphor in Reasoning," *PLOS One* 6, no. 2 (2011): 1–11.

32. Dennis W. Campbell and Ruidi Shang, "Tone at the Bottom: Measuring Corporate Misconduct Risk from the Text of Employee Reviews," *Management Science* 68, no. 9 (2021): 7034–7053.

33. Terri L. Rittenburg, George Albert Gladney, and Teresa Stephenson, "The Effects of Euphemism Usage in Business Contexts," *Journal of Business Ethics* 137 (2016): 315–320.

34. Amanda Montell, *Cultish: The Language of Fanaticism* (HarperCollins, 2021).

35. Maurice E. Schweitzer, Lisa Ordonez, and Bambi Douma, "Goal Setting as a Motivator for Unethical Behavior," *Academy of Management Journal* 47, no. 3 (2004): 422.

36. Thomas Gryta and Ted Mann, *Lights Out: Pride, Delusion, and the Fall of General Electric* (Mariner Books, 2020), 14.

37. Jessica Höpfner and Nina Keith, "Goal Missed, Self Hit: Goal-Setting, Goal-Failure, and Their Affective, Motivational, and Behavioral Consequences," *Frontiers in Psychology* 12 (2021).

38. Daniel Kahneman and Amos Tversky, "Prospect Theory: An Analysis of Decision Under Risk," *Econometrica* 47, no. 2 (1979): 263–292.

39. Brian R. Dineen et al., "Green by Comparison: Deviant and Normative Transmutations of Job Search Envy in a Temporal Context," *Academy of Management Journal* 60, no. 1 (2017): 295–320; Mary B. Mawritz, Robert Folger, and Gary P. Latham, "Supervisors' Exceedingly Difficult Goals and Abusive Supervision: The Mediating Effects of Hindrance Stress, Anger, and Anxiety," *Journal of Organizational Behavior* 35, no. 3 (2014): 358–372.

40. Siri Schubert and T. Christian Miller, "At Siemens, Bribery Was Just a Line Item," *New York Times*, December 20, 2008, https://www.nytimes.com/2008/12/21/business/worldbusiness/21siemens.html.

41. Mo Chen and Chao C. Chen, "The Moral Dark Side of Performance Pressure: How and When It Affects Unethical Pro-Organizational Behavior," *International Journal of Human Resource Management* 34, no. 7 (2021): 1–31.

42. Kenneth E. Goodpaster, "Teleopathy," *Business Ethics* 2 (2015), https://doi.org/10.1002/9781118785317.weom020213.

43. Kenneth E. Goodpaster, "Ethics or Excellence? Conscience as a Check on the Unbalanced Pursuit of Organizational Goals," *Ivey Business Journal* (March/April 2004): 5.

44. Goodpaster, "Teleopathy."

45. Albert Bandura, "Selective Moral Disengagement in the Exercise of Moral Agency," *Journal of Moral Education* 31, no. 2 (2002): 107, https://doi.org/10.1080/0305724022014322.

46. Thomi Richards, "What Pilots Can Teach Us About Managing Our Attention," *Fast Company*, October 1, 2019, https://www.fastcompany.com/90411290/pilots-and-attention-management; Darryl B. Rice and Natasha Reed, "Supervisor Emotional Exhaustion and Goal-Focused Leader Behavior: The Roles of Supervisor Bottom-Line Mentality and Conscientiousness," *Current Psychology* 41, no. 12 (2022): 8758–8773.

47. "Creating Success: Building Leaders at Every Level," *Business Recorder*, June 30, 2011, https://www.brecorder.com/news/.

48. Francesco Guerrera, "Welch Condemns Share Price Focus," *Financial Times*, March 12, 2009, https://www.ft.com/content/294ff1f2-0f27-11de-ba10-0000779fd2ac.

NOTES TO CHAPTER 3

49. Geoffrey Colvin, "The Ultimate Manager," *Fortune*, November 22, 1999, in *CNN Money*, https://money.cnn.com/magazines/fortune/fortune_archive/1999/11/22/269126/index.htm.

50. Peter Robison, *Flying Blind: The 737 MAX Tragedy and the Fall of Boeing* (Random House, 2021), 147.

51. Gryta and Mann, *Lights Out*, 15, 18.

52. Kinsey Grant, "How to Fire People Like Former General Electric CEO Jack Welch," *The Street*, November 14, 2017, https://www.thestreet.com/opinion/how-to-fire-people-like-jack-welch-14315785; Peter Cohan, "Why Stack Ranking Worked Better at GE Than Microsoft," *Forbes*, July 13, 2012, https://www.forbes.com/sites/petercohan/2012/07/13/why-stack-ranking-worked-better-at-ge-than-microsoft/.

53. Gryta and Mann, *Lights Out*, 19.

54. Grant, "How to Fire People."

55. Gryta and Mann, *Lights Out*, 74; Robison, *Flying Blind*, 149.

56. Troy Segal, "Enron Scandal: The Fall of a Wall Street Darling," *Investopedia*, November 26, 2021, https://www.investopedia.com/updates/enron-scandal-summary/; Douglas O. Lindner, "Famous Trials," UMKC School of Law, accessed November 14, 2024, https://www.famous-trials.com/enron/1791-stockchart.

57. C. William Thomas, "The Rise and Fall of Enron," *Journal of Accountancy* (March/April 2002): 41–48.

58. Frank Ahrens, "Houston, City of Texas-Size Calamities," *Washington Post*, February 2, 2002, https://www.washingtonpost.com/archive/business/2002/02/23/houston-city-of-texas-size-calamities/080594fb-f5e1-43bc-a654-4c503342dfdb/.

59. Tea Young Park, Sanghee Park, and Bruce Barry, "Incentive Effects on Ethics," *Academy of Management Annals* 16, no. 1 (2022): 297–333.

60. Pascal Boyer and Michael Bang Petersen, "Folk-Economic Beliefs: An Evolutionary Cognitive Model," *Behavioral and Brain Sciences* 41 (2018): e158; Russell Roberts and Shai Davidai, "The Psychology of Asymmetric Zero-Sum Beliefs," *Journal of Personality and Social Psychology* 123, no. 3 (2022): 559–575, https://doi.org/10.1037/pspi0000378.

61. Jan K. Woike and Sebastian Hafenbrädl, "Rivals Without a Cause? Relative Performance Feedback Creates Destructive Competition Despite Aligned Incentives," *Journal of Behavioral Decision Making* 33, no. 4 (2020): 523–537.

62. Andrew L. Molinsky, Adam M. Grant, and Joshua D. Margolis, "The Bedside Manner of Homo Economicus: How and Why Priming an Economic Schema Reduces Compassion," *Organizational Behavior and Human Decision Processes* 119, no. 1 (2012): 27–37; Amos Schurr and Ilana Ritov, "Winning a Competition Predicts Dishonest Behavior," *Proceedings of the National Academy of Sciences* 113, no. 7 (2016): 1754–1759; Willy Bolander et al., "Managing New Salespeople's Ethical Behaviors During Repetitive Failures: When Trying to Help Actually Hurts," *Journal of Business Ethics* 144 (2017): 519–532; Steven L. Grover and Chun Hui, "How Job Pressures and Extrinsic Rewards Affect Lying Behavior," *International Journal of Conflict Management* 16, no. 3 (2005): 287–300.

63. A. J. Hess, "Ranking Workers Can Hurt Morale and Productivity. Tech Companies Are Doing It Anyway," *Fast Company*, February 16, 2023, https://www.fastcompany.com/90850190/stack-ranking-workers-hurt-morale-productivity-tech-companies.

64. Gregory Bateson, *Steps to an Ecology of the Mind: A Revolutionary Approach to Man's Understanding of Himself* (University of Chicago Press, 1972), 215–216; Gregory Bateson et al., "Toward a Theory of Schizophrenia," *Behavioral Science* 1 (1956): 251–264.

65. Bateson, *Ecology of the Mind*, 215–216.

NOTES TO CHAPTER 3

66. Bateson, *Ecology of the Mind*, 271–278; Bateson et al., "Theory of Schizophrenia."

67. Ralph Hertwig and Christoph Engel, "Homo Ignorans: Deliberately Choosing Not to Know," *Perspectives on Psychological Science* 11, no. 3 (2016): 359–372.

68. Matthias Geyer and Udo Ludwig, "The Last Liar," *Der Spiegel*, June 26, 2013, https://www.spiegel.de/sport/der-letzte-luegner-a-75a83f4a-0002-0001-0000-000099311860.

69. US Anti-Doping Agency, "Report on the Proceedings Under the World Antidoping Code and the USADA Protocol," Claimant v. Lance Armstrong, 2012, 29–30, https://www.usada.org/wp-content/uploads/ReasonedDecision.pdf.

70. Christian Ewers and Joachim Rienhardt, "Jan Ullrich on His Crashes: 'It Turns You from a Human Being into a Monster,'" *Der Stern*, November 20, 2023, https://www.stern.de/sport/jan-ullrich-im-stern-interview-ueber-drogen--alkohol-und-dopingbetrug-34215052.html.

71. Tyler Hamilton and Daniel Coyle, *The Secret Race: Inside the Hidden World of the Tour de France* (Transworld Publishers, 2012), 138.

72. Jerald Greenberg, "Employee Theft as a Reaction to Underpayment Inequity: The Hidden Cost of Pay Cuts," *Journal of Applied Psychology* 75, no. 5 (1990): 561–568, https://doi.org/10.1037/0021-9010.75.5.561; Jerald Greenberg, "Stealing in the Name of Justice: Informational and Interpersonal Moderators of Theft Reactions to Underpayment Inequity," *Organizational Behavior and Human Decision Processes* 54, no. 1 (1993): 81–103; Gerold Mikula, Birgit Petri, and Nober K. Tanzer, "What People Regard as Unjust: Types and Structures of Everyday Experiences of Injustice," *European Journal of Social Psychology* 20, no. 2 (1990): 133.

73. Blair H. Sheppard, Roy J. Lewicki, and John W. Minton, *Organizational Justice: The Search for Fairness in the Workplace* (Macmillan, 1992).

74. George C. Homans, *Social Behavior: Its Elementary Forms* (Harcourt, Brace & World, 1961); John M. Jermier, David E. Knights, and Walter R. Nord, *Resistance and Power in Organizations* (Taylor & Francis/Routledge, 1994).

75. Daniel Houser, Stefan Vetter, and Joachim Winter, "Fairness and Cheating," *European Economic Review* 56, no. 8 (2012): 1645–1655; Jerald Greenberg, "Stealing in the Name of Justice: Informational and Interpersonal Moderators of Theft Reactions to Underpayment Inequity," *Organizational Behavior and Human Decision Processes* 5 (1993): 81; Maureen L. Ambrose, Mark A. Seabright, and Marshall Schminke, "Sabotage in the Workplace: The Role of Organizational Injustice," *Organizational Behavior and Human Decision Processes* 89, no. 1 (2002): 947–965; Sylvia W. DeMore, Jeffrey D. Fisher, and Reuben M. Baron, "The Equity-Control Model as a Predictor of Vandalism Among College Students," *Journal of Applied Social Psychology* 18, no. 1 (1988): 80–91; Robert Folger and Daniel P. Skarlicki, "A Popcorn Metaphor for Employee Aggression," in *Dysfunctional Behavior in Organizations: Violent and Deviant Behavior*, ed. Ricky W. Griffin and Anne O'Leary-Kelly (JAI Press, 1998), 43–81.

76. Christopher R. Browning, *Ordinary Men: Reserve Police Battalion 101 and the Final Solution in Poland* (HarperCollins, 1992, repr. Penguin Books, 2001). Citations refer to the Penguin Books edition.

77. Browning, *Ordinary Men*, 57.

78. Gerd Gigerenzer, "Moral Intuition = Fast and Frugal Heuristics?," in *Moral Psychology*, ed. Walter Sinnott-Armstrong, vol. 2, *The Cognitive Science of Morality: Intuition and Diversity* (MIT Press, 2008), 1–26.

79. Eric J. Johnson and Daniel G. Goldstein, "Do Defaults Save Lives?," *Science* 302, no. 5649 (2003): 1338–1339.

80. Solomon E. Asch, "Effects of Group Pressure upon the Modification and Distortion of Judgments," in *Groups, Leadership, and Men*, ed. Harold Guetzkow (Carnegie Press, 1951): 222–236, https://www.gwern.net/docs/psychology/1952-asch.pdf.

81. Russell D. Clark and Larry E. Word, "Where Is the Apathetic Bystander? Situational Characteristics of the Emergency," *Journal of Personality and Social Psychology* 29, no. 3 (1974): 279–287; Linda Z. Solomon, Henry Solomon, and Ronald Stone, "Helping as a Function of Number of Bystanders and Ambiguity of Emergency," *Personality and Social Psychology Bulletin* 4, no. 2 (1978): 318–321.

82. Bibb Latané and John M. Darley, *The Unresponsive Bystander: Why Doesn't He Help?* (Appleton-Century-Crofts, 1970).

83. Jingyu Gao, Robert Greenberg, and Bernard Wong-On-Wing, "Whistleblowing Intentions of Lower-Level Employees: The Effect of Reporting Channel, Bystanders, and Wrongdoer Power Status," *Journal of Business Ethics* 126, no. 1 (2015): 85–99. It should be added that this was a vignette study, prompting the question of whether the results generalize to real behavior in a real situation.

84. Henri Tajfel et al., "Social Categorization and Intergroup Behaviour," *European Journal of Social Psychology* 1, no. 2 (1971): 149–178; Charles Efferson, Rafael Lalive, and Ernst Fehr, "The Coevolution of Cultural Groups and Ingroup Favoritism," *Science* 321, no. 5897 (2008): 1844–1849.

85. Henri Tajfel and John Turner, "An Integrative Theory of Intergroup Conflict," in *The Social Psychology of Intergroup Relations*, ed. William G. Austin and Stephen Worchel (Brooks/Cole, 1979), 33–47.

86. Irving Janis, *Victims of Groupthink: A Psychological Study of Foreign-Policy Decisions and Fiascoes* (Houghton Mifflin, 1972), 9.

87. Janis, *Victims of Groupthink: A Study*; see also Irving Janis and Leon Mann, *Victims of Groupthink: A Psychological Analysis of Conflict, Choice, and Commitment* (Free Press, 1977).

88. Agnieszka Golec de Zavala et al., "Collective Narcissism and Its Social Consequences," *Journal of Personality and Social Psychology* 97, no. 6 (2009): 1074–1096.

89. Jonathan Vaughters, *One-Way Ticket: A Memoir* (Penguin, 2019), 192.

90. Hamilton and Coyle, *Secret Race*, 66.

91. Hamilton and Coyle, *Secret Race*, 45; Vaughters, *One-Way Ticket*, 139.

92. Thomas Dekker, *Descent: My Epic Fall from Cycling Superstardom to Doping Dead End* (VeloPress, 2017), 62.

93. Hamilton and Coyle, *Secret Race*, 58.

94. Vaughters, *One-Way Ticket*, 146, 154.

95. Daniel Pauly, "Anecdotes and the Shifting Baseline Syndrome of Fisheries," *Trends in Ecology and Evolution* 10, no. 10 (1995): 430.

96. Peter H. Kahn Jr., "Children's Affiliations with Nature: Structure, Development, and the Problem of Environmental Generational Amnesia," in *Children and Nature: Psychological, Sociocultural, and Evolutionary Investigations*, ed. Peter H. Kahn Jr. and Stephen R. Kellert (MIT Press, 2002), 93–116.

97. Andrea Sáenz-Arroyo et al., "Rapidly Shifting Environmental Baselines Among Fishers of the Gulf of California," *Proceedings of the Royal Society B: Biological Sciences* 272, no. 1575 (2005): 1957–1962.

98. Masashi Soga and Kevin J. Gaston, "Shifting Baseline Syndrome: Causes, Consequences, and Implications," *Frontiers in Ecology and the Environment* 16, no. 4 (2018): 222–230.

NOTES TO CHAPTER 4

99. Carole S. Kleinman, "Ethical Drift: When Good People Do Bad Things," *JONA's Healthcare Law, Ethics, and Regulation* 8, no. 3 (2006): 72–76.

100. Daniel F. Chambliss, *Beyond Caring* (University of Chicago Press, 1996), cited in Kleinman, "Ethical Drift," 74.

101. Fethiye Erdil and Fatos Korkmaz, "Ethical Problems Observed by Student Nurses," *Nursing Ethics* 16, no. 5 (2009): 589–598.

102. Kleinman, "Ethical Drift," 73–74.

103. For academia, see Yudhijit Bhattacharjee, "The Mind of a Con Man," *New York Times Magazine*, April 26, 2013, https://www.nytimes.com/2013/04/28/magazine/diederik-stapels-audacious-academic-fraud.html; for corruption, see Blake E. Ashforth and Vikas Anand, "The Normalization of Corruption in Organizations," *Research in Organizational Behavior* 25 (2003): 1–52; for accounting, see Constance E. Bagley, "Winning Legally: The Value of Legal Astuteness," *Academy of Management Review* 33, no. 2 (2008): 378–390, http://www.jstor.org/stable/20159403; Marc Street and Vera L. Street, "The Effects of Escalating Commitment on Ethical Decision-Making," *Journal of Business Ethics* 64, no. 4 (2006): 343–356; David T. Welsh et al., "The Slippery Slope: How Small Ethical Transgressions Pave the Way for Larger Future Transgressions," *Journal of Applied Psychology* 100, no. 1 (2015): 124.

104. John M. Darley, "Social Organization for the Production of Evil," *Psychological Inquiry* 3, no. 2 (1992): 208.

105. Bethany McLean and Peter Elkind, *Smartest Guys in the Room: The Amazing Rise and Scandalous Fall of Enron* (Portfolio, 2003), 128.

Chapter 4: Theranos—the Empress's New Clothes

1. John Carreyrou, *Bad Blood* (Picador, 2018), 81–82.

2. Carreyrou, *Bad Blood*, 15.

3. Mad Money, "Theranos CEO Elizabeth Holmes: Firing Back at Doubters," CNBC, October 2015, YouTube video, 9:31, https://www.youtube.com/watch?v=rGfaJZAdfNE.

4. Roger Parloff, "A Singular Board at Theranos," *Fortune*, June 12, 2014, https://fortune.com/2014/06/12/theranos-board-directors/.

5. Kevin Loria, "This Isn't the First Time People Have Raised Troubling Questions About Theranos," *Business Insider*, October 15, 2015, https://www.businessinsider.com/science-of-elizabeth-holmes-theranos-update-2015-4.

6. Sophia Kunthara, "A Closer Look at Theranos' Big-Name Investors, Partners, and Board as Elizabeth Holmes' Criminal Trial Begins," *Crunchbase*, September 14, 2021, https://news.crunchbase.com/health-wellness-biotech/theranos-elizabeth-holmes-trial-investors-board/.

7. Carreyrou, *Bad Blood*, 16.

8. Cameron Scott, "Small, Fast, and Cheap, Theranos Is the Poster Child of Med Tech—and It's in Walgreen's," *Singularity Hub*, November 18, 2013, https://singularityhub.com/2013/11/18/small-fast-and-cheap-theranos-is-the-poster-child-of-med-tech-and-its-in-walgreens/.

9. Loria, "This Isn't the First Time," 15.

10. Joseph Rago, "Elizabeth Holmes: The Breakthrough of Instant Diagnosis," *Wall Street Journal*, September 8, 2013, https://www.wsj.com/articles/elizabeth-holmes-the-breakthrough-of-instant-diagnosis-1378526813.

11. Charlotte Hue, "A Former Apple Employee Inspired Theranos CEO Elizabeth Holmes' Change from 'Frumpy Accountant' to Her Signature Steve Jobs-style Black

NOTES TO CHAPTER 4

Turtleneck," *Business Insider*, September 5, 2018, https://www.businessinsider.nl/how-elizabeth-holmes-came-up-with-her-iconic-jobsian-look-2018-5/.

12. Carreyrou, *Bad Blood*, 31.

13. Zaw T. Tun, "Theranos: A Fallen Unicorn," *Investopedia*, February 12, 2014, https://www.investopedia.com/articles/investing/020116/theranos-fallen-unicorn.asp; Carreyrou, *Bad Blood*, 295.

14. Freya Berry, "I'm a Corporate Fraud Investigator. You Wouldn't Believe the Hubris of the Super-Rich," *Guardian*, January 24, 2023, https://www.theguardian.com/lifeandstyle/2023/jan/23/fraud-investigation-super-rich.

15. Carreyrou, *Bad Blood*, 17–20, 29.

16. Matt Wynn, "How Did Theranos' Holmes Fool So Many Smart People?," *MedPage Today*, June 25, 2018, https://www.medpagetoday.com/practicemanagement/informationtechnology/73677.

17. Kevin Loria, "What We Know About How Theranos' 'Revolutionary' Technology Works," *Business Insider*, October 19, 2015, https://www.businessinsider.com/how-theranos-revolutionary-technology-works-2015-10.

18. Loria, "What We Know."

19. Ken Auletta, "Blood, Simpler," *New Yorker*, December 8, 2014, https://www.newyorker.com/magazine/2014/12/15/blood-simpler.

20. Tim De Chant, "Theranos Swiped Logos from Pfizer and Another Pharma Giant for Fake Reports," *Ars Technica*, November 3, 2021, https://arstechnica.com/tech-policy/2021/11/theranos-swiped-logos-from-pfizer-and-another-pharma-giant-for-fake-reports/.

21. Joel Rosenblatt, "Tale of Theranos Devices Saving Soldiers Haunts Holmes at Trial," *Bloomberg*, November 19, 2021, https://www.bloomberg.com/news/articles/2021-10-19/tale-of-theranos-devices-saving-soldiers-haunts-holmes-at-trial.

22. Christopher Weaver and John Carreyrou, "Craving Growth, Walgreens Dismissed Its Doubts About Theranos," *Wall Street Journal*, May 25, 2016, https://www.wsj.com/articles/craving-growth-walgreens-dismissed-its-doubts-about-theranos-1464207285.

23. Kate Briquelet and Noah Kirsch, "Former Theranos Employees Get Ready to Relive the Sh*tshow," *Daily Beast*, September 7, 2021, https://www.thedailybeast.com/elizabeth-holmes-trial-dredges-up-toxic-memories-for-theranos-workers.

24. The roots of today's very powerful translation machines lie in computational linguistics, which in turn paved the way for LLMs (large language models) as used by ChatGPT. To secure funding, the developers of computational linguistics did not shy away from using tricks to create positive impressions about the performance of their early prototype. For instance, in a public demonstration they used a "lexicon of just 250 words" that "comprised only the vocabulary required to translate the carefully selected sentences." Had they taken random sentences from a larger corpus, this could easily have meant the end of their project; see John Hutchins, "The First Public Demonstration of Machine Translation: The Georgetown-IBM System, 7th January 1954," March 2006, archived at Internet Archive Wayback Machine, 12, https://web.archive.org/web/20071021224529/http://www.hutchinsweb.me.uk/GU-IBM-2005.pdf.

25. Berry, "Corporate Fraud."

26. Parloff, "Singular Board."

27. Parloff, "Singular Board."

28. Carreyrou, *Bad Blood*, 22.

NOTES TO CHAPTER 4

29. Seth Fiegerman and Sarah Ashley O'Brian, "Theranos Employees Struggle to Put Scandal Behind Them," *CNN Business*, March 14, 2019, https://edition.cnn.com/2019/03/14/tech/theranos-employees/index.html.

30. James Clayton, "Elizabeth Holmes: Has the Theranos Scandal Changed Silicon Valley?," *BBC News*, January 4, 2022, https://www.bbc.com/news/technology-58469882.

31. Stephanie Fairyington, "Why We Need to Talk About Elizabeth's Destructive Work Ethic," *Thrive Global*, March 25, 2019, https://thriveglobal.com/stories/how-elizabeth-holmes-work-ethic-burnout-theranos-inventor-hbo/.

32. Carreyrou, *Bad Blood*, 21.

33. Heather Somerville, "Inside Theranos: Stress, Pressure, and Shifting Priorities," *Wall Street Journal*, September 21, 2021, https://www.wsj.com/livecoverage/elizabeth-holmes-trial-theranos/card/hXH3lOeZ2iJgBWMv34Du.

34. Zack Morrison, "My experience working for Sunny Balwani, former COO of the infamous blood testing startup Theranos, has forever shaped my management philosophy," LinkedIn post, December 2022, https://www.linkedin.com/feed/update/urn:li:activity:7011042805741490176/.

35. John Carreyrou, "Theranos Inc.'s Partners in Blood," *Wall Street Journal*, May 18, 2018, https://www.wsj.com/articles/theranos-inc-s-partners-in-blood-1526662047.

36. Heather Somerville, "In Elizabeth Holmes Trial, Ex-Theranos Employees Cite Culture of Fear and Isolation," *Wall Street Journal*, November 13, 2021, https://www.wsj.com/articles/in-elizabeth-holmes-trial-ex-theranos-employees-cite-culture-of-fear-and-isolation-11636812000.

37. Robert Law, "The Role of H-1Bs in the Theranos Scam," CIS, January 6, 2022, https://cis.org/Law/Role-H1Bs-Theranos-Scam; Carreyrou, *Bad Blood*, 164.

38. Monica Torres, "4 Ways Elizabeth Holmes Manipulated Her Theranos Employees," *Huffington Post*, November 18, 2019, https://www.huffpost.com/entry/elizabeth-holmes-office-employees_l_5c92abe3e4b01b140d351b6f.

39. Emilie Wasserman, "Theranos Grabs FDA Approval for Finger-Stick Herpes Test," *Fierce Biotech*, July 6, 2015, https://www.fiercebiotech.com/medical-devices/theranos-grabs-fda-approval-for-finger-stick-herpes-test.

40. Carolyn Y. Johnson, "FDA Approves Theranos $9 Finger Stick Blood Test for Herpes," *Washington Post*, July 2, 2015, https://www.washingtonpost.com/news/wonk/wp/2015/07/02/fda-approves-theranos-9-finger-stick-bloodtest-for-herpes/.

41. Carreyrou, *Bad Blood*, 163.

42. Ken Alltucker, "As Theranos Drama Unwinds, Former Patients Claim Inaccurate Tests Changed Their Lives," *USA Today*, July 5, 2018, https://eu.usatoday.com/story/news/nation/2018/07/05/theranos-elizabeth-holmes-lawsuits-patients-harm-arizona/742008002/; Carolyn Wang and Zachary Zinman, "An Adequate Warning, but Far from Reality," *Saratoga Falcon*, February 7, 2022, https://saratogafalcon.org/content/an-adequate-warning-but-far-from-reality-theranos-does-not-reflect-silicon-valley-startup-culture/.

43. Amanpour and Company, "The Whistleblower Who Exposed Theranos," PBS, August 2020, YouTube video, 3:29–3:37 and 5:19–5:27, https://www.youtube.com/watch?v=kuK57kt1oiI.

44. Tyler Shultz and Erika Cheung, "Spilling the Blood of a Silicon Valley Unicorn," McCoy Family Center for Ethics in Society, February 19, 2019, YouTube video, 18:55–19:20, https://www.youtube.com/watch?v=YJx-cU9CKLI.

45. The Healthcare Innovation Company (thINc), "WHCC TV 2019 Interview with Tyler Shultz, Theranos Whistleblower and Entrepreneur," May 28, 2019, YouTube video, 3:52–4:03, https://www.youtube.com/watch?v=nWf8ChqZkDc.
46. Erika Cheung, "Blowing the Whistle on Theranos," Inspirefest 2019, May 17, 2019, YouTube video, 5:48–6:19 and 7:19–7:26, https://www.youtube.com/watch?v=h7fAnxg7HZc.
47. Shultz and Cheung, "Spilling the Blood," 25:06–25:09.
48. Cheung, "Blowing the Whistle."
49. Yasmin Khorram, "Former Theranos Lab Director Says He Was Under 'Tremendous Pressure' to Show Technology Worked," *CNBC*, October 5, 2021, https://www.cnbc.com/2021/10/05/adam-rosendorff-ex-theranos-lab-director-testifies-about-pressure.html.
50. Tate Delloye, "Is Elizabeth Holmes' Ex Sunny Balwani Really a Villain—or a Victim? How Businessman Was Painted as Manipulative Mastermind by Theranos CEO as He Stands Trial for Fraud (While Their Rollercoaster Romance Is Laid Bare by 'Hulu' Show)," *Daily Mail*, March 15, 2022, https://www.dailymail.co.uk/news/article-10599973/Who-Sunny-Balwani-Inside-life-Theranos-COO-relationship-Elizabeth-Holmes.html.
51. Somerville, "Holmes Trial."
52. Yasmin Khorram, "Former Theranos Employees Are Still Shaken as Elizabeth Holmes Trial Looms," *CNBC*, August 27, 2021, https://www.cnbc.com/2021/08/27/former-theranos-employees-are-still-shaken-as-elizabeth-holmes-trial-looms.html.
53. Taylor Dunn et al., "Ex-Theranos CEO Elizabeth Holmes Says 'I Don't Know' 600-Plus Times in Never-Before-Broadcast Deposition Tapes," *ABC News*, January 24, 2019, https://abcnews.go.com/Business/theranos-ceo-elizabeth-holmes-600-times-broadcast-deposition/story?id=60576630.
54. Ethical Systems, "Can Evolutionary Thinking Help Companies Foster More Ethical Cultures?," October 16, 2019, YouTube video, 30:20–30:22, https://www.youtube.com/watch?v=e4BSi3EFiOs.
55. Dunn et al., "Holmes Says."
56. Yasmin Khorram, "Ex-Theranos Lab Director Testified That Company Cared More About 'Fundraising Than Patient Care,'" *CNBC*, September 24, 2021, https://www.cnbc.com/2021/09/24/ex-theranos-employee-says-company-cared-about-funding-over-patients.html; David Streitfeld, "The Epic Rise and Fall of Elizabeth Holmes," *New York Times*, January 3, 2022, https://www.nytimes.com/2022/01/03/technology/elizabeth-holmes-theranos.html.
57. CBS Mornings, "Tyler Shultz Reacts to Elizabeth Holmes Verdict," CBS, January 4, 2022, YouTube video, 2:28–2:55, https://www.youtube.com/watch?v=DCsB3Pv-J1Y.
58. Amanpour and Company, "The Whistleblower," YouTube video, 6:48–7:03, https://www.youtube.com/watch?v=kuK57kt1oiI.
59. Carreyrou, *Bad Blood*, 103, 173.
60. Fiegerman and O'Brian, "Theranos Employees Struggle."
61. John Carreyrou, "Hot Startup Theranos Has Struggled with Its Blood-Test Technology," *Wall Street Journal*, October 6, 2015, https://www.wsj.com/articles/theranos-has-struggled-with-blood-tests-1444881901.
62. Mad Money, "Theranos CEO Elizabeth Holmes: Firing Back at Doubters," CNBC, October 16, 2015, YouTube video, 1:38–1:47, https://www.youtube.com/watch?v=rGfaJZAdfNE.
63. Arielle Duhaime-Ross, "FDA Wants to Close the Loophole That Theranos Used, but Republicans Don't Understand Why," *Verge*, November 17, 2015, https://www.theverge.com/2015/11/17/9750048/ldt-loophole-fda-hearing-theranos-lab-tests.

64. Zaw Thiha Tun, "Theranos: A Fallen Unicorn," *Investopedia*, January 4, 2022, https://www.investopedia.com/articles/investing/020116/theranos-fallen-unicorn.asp.

65. Lydia Ramsey Pflanzer, "Walgreens Just Filed a $140 Million Lawsuit Against Theranos," *Business Insider*, November 8, 2016, https://www.businessinsider.com/walgreens-files-lawsuit-against-theranos-2016-11; Carreyrou, *Bad Blood*, 289.

66. US Securities and Exchange Commission, "Theranos, CEO Holmes, and Former President Balwani Charged with Massive Fraud," press release, March 14, 2018, https://www.sec.gov/news/press-release/2018-41.

67. Rishi Iyengar, "The Key Moments from Elizabeth Holmes' Trial," *CNN*, January 4, 2022, https://edition.cnn.com/2022/01/03/tech/theranos-trial-elizabeth-holmes-takeaways/index.html.

68. Yasmin Khorram, "Elizabeth Holmes Sentencing Proposed for September," *NBC*, January 11, 2022, https://www.nbcbayarea.com/news/business/money-report/elizabeth-holmes-sentencing-proposed-for-september/2775927/.

69. Kari Paul, "Ex-Theranos Executive Sunny Balwani Sentenced to Nearly 13 Years in Prison," *Guardian*, December 8, 2022, https://www.theguardian.com/technology/2022/dec/07/former-theranos-exec-sunny-balwani-prison-sentence.

70. Robert Trivers, "The Elements of a Scientific Theory of Self-Deception," *Annals of the New York Academy of Sciences* 907, no. 1 (2000): 114–131, https://doi.org/10.1111/j.1749-6632.2000.tb06619.x.

Chapter 5: Uber—an Embattled Unicorn

1. A taxi license was once so profitable in places like Manhattan that one could cost up to $1 million in the early 2000s; see Andy Kessler, "Travis Kalanick: The Transportation Trustbuster," *Wall Street Journal*, January 25, 2013, https://www.wsj.com/articles/SB10001424127887324235104578244231122376480.

2. Luke Vrkic, "A Very Short History of the Taxi," *Ingogo* (blog), March 7, 2017, https://www.ingogo.com.au/blog/a-very-short-history-of-the-taxi-cab.

3. A term inspired by Friedrich Nietzsche's concept of the *Übermensch*, or superman, which is typically portrayed as the underlying ideal of a human being.

4. Mike Isaac, *Super Pumped: The Battle for Uber* (Norton & Company, 2019), 60.

5. Isaac, *Super Pumped*, 58–59, 61.

6. Isaac, *Super Pumped*, 87.

7. Michael Wolff, "The Tech Company of the Year Is Uber," *USA Today*, December 22, 2013, https://web.archive.org/web/20170907081132/https://www.usatoday.com/story/money/columnist/wolff/2013/12/22/the-success-of-app-based-car-service-uber/4141669/; Matthew Panzarino and Alexia Tsotsis, "Uber Wins the 2014 Crunchie for Best Overall Startup," *TechCrunch*, February 6, 2015, https://techcrunch.com/2015/02/05/uber-wins-the-2014-crunchie-for-best-overall-startup/.

8. Michael Byhoff et al., "The Rise and Fall of Uber's Controversial CEO," Bloomberg Originals, June 21, 2017, YouTube video, 4:35, https://www.youtube.com/watch?v=61eTqB6ux_Q.

9. Mickey Rapkin, "Uber Cab Confessions," *GQ*, February 27, 2014, https://www.gq.com/story/uber-cab-confessions.

10. Isaac, *Super Pumped*, 115.

11. Kai-Uwe Schanz, *Gig Economy Work: Mind the Protection Gaps* (The Geneva Association, 2022), https://www.genevaassociation.org/sites/default/files/research-topics-document-type/pdf_public/ga_gig_economy_report_29_03_2022.pdf.

NOTES TO CHAPTER 5

12. *Cambridge English Dictionary*, s.v. "uberization," accessed September 16, 2024, https://dictionary.cambridge.org/dictionary/english/uberization.

13. Christopher Mims, "The Age of Tech Superheroes Must End," *Wall Street Journal*, June 7, 2018, https://www.wsj.com/articles/the-age-of-tech-superheroes-must-end-1528387420.

14. Isaac, *Super Pumped*, 9–10.

15. Maya Kosoff, "Everything You Need to Know About 'The Fountainhead,' a Book That Inspires Billionaire Uber CEO Travis Kalanick," *Business Insider*, June 1, 2015, https://www.businessinsider.com/how-ayn-rand-inspired-uber-ceo-travis-kalanick-2015-6.

16. Kosoff, "Everything You Need to Know."

17. Sarah Bahr, "In 'Super Pumped,' the Uber Founder Disrupts His Own Rise," *New York Times*, February 22, 2022, https://www.nytimes.com/2022/02/22/arts/television/super-pumped-uber-showtime.html.

18. Isaac, *Super Pumped*, 63.

19. Isaac, *Super Pumped*, 13, 15, 87.

20. Andrea Rungg and Philipp Alvares de Souza Soares, "More Than a Taxi Destroyer: UBERrolled," *Manager Magazin*, May 27, 2016, https://www.manager-magazin.de/magazin/artikel/uber-das-start-up-schreckt-auch-autokonzerne-ab-a-1103052.html.

21. Isaac, *Super Pumped*, 17, 114, 246.

22. Mike Isaac, "How Uber Deceives the Authorities Worldwide," *New York Times*, March 3, 2017, https://www.nytimes.com/2017/03/03/technology/uber-greyball-program-evade-authorities.html.

23. Kessler, "Travis Kalanick."

24. Interview with a former Uber top manager who wished to remain anonymous.

25. Isaac, *Super Pumped*, 18.

26. Interview with former Uber top manager.

27. Kessler, "Travis Kalanick."

28. Interview with former Uber top manager.

29. Sheelah Kolhatkar, "Uber's Opportunistic Ouster," *New Yorker*, July 3, 2017, https://www.newyorker.com/magazine/2017/07/10/ubers-opportunistic-ouster.

30. Davey Alba, "A Short History of the Many, Many Ways Uber Screwed Up," June 21, 2017, https://www.wired.com/story/timeline-uber-crises/.

31. Interview with former Uber top manager.

32. Isaac, *Super Pumped*, 11–12, 112.

33. Om Malik, "In Silicon Valley Now, It's Almost Always Winner Takes All," *New Yorker*, December 30, 2015, https://www.newyorker.com/tech/annals-of-technology/in-silicon-valley-now-its-almost-always-winner-takes-all.

34. Isaac, *Super Pumped*, 78, 82, 151, 185.

35. Casey Newton, "This Is Uber's Playbook for Sabotaging Lyft," *Verge*, August 26, 2014, https://www.theverge.com/2014/8/26/6067663/this-is-ubers-playbook-for-sabotaging-lyft.

36. Isaac, *Super Pumped*, 166.

37. Isaac, *Super Pumped*, 160.

38. As a side note, some people partied too hard. Uber employees ran into trouble with prostitutes who stole their company laptops; others consumed cocaine, and still others groped female colleagues or hijacked a shuttle bus to cruise through Vegas for a joy ride; Isaac, *Super Pumped*, 7.

39. Alison Griswold, "Uber Is Designed So That for One Employee to Get Ahead, Another Must Fail," *Quartz*, February 27, 2017, https://qz.com/918582/uber-is-designed-so-that-for-one-employee-to-succeed-another-must-fail.

40. Isaac, *Super Pumped*, 13.
41. Susan Fowler, *Whistleblower: My Journey to Silicon Valley and Fight for Justice at Uber* (Viking, 2020), 110.
42. Isaac, *Super Pumped*, 13.
43. C. William Thomas, "The Rise and Fall of Enron," *Journal of Accountancy* (March/April 2002): 42.
44. Griswold, "Uber Is Designed."
45. Mike Isaac, "Inside Uber's Aggressive, Unrestrained Workplace Culture," *New York Times*, February 22, 2017, https://www.nytimes.com/2017/02/22/technology/uber-workplace-culture.html.
46. Isaac, *Super Pumped*, 133.
47. Fowler, *Whistleblower*, 254.
48. Elizabeth Lopatto, "To Expose Sexism at Uber, Susan Fowler Blew Up Her Life," *Verge*, February 19, 2020, https://www.theverge.com/2020/2/19/21142081/susan-fowler-uber-whistleblower-interview-silicon-valley-discrimination-harassment.
49. Isaac, *Super Pumped*, 133.
50. Fowler, *Whistleblower*, 150.
51. Marco della Cava, Jessica Guynn, and Jon Swartz, "Uber's Kalanick Faces Crisis over 'Baller' Culture," *USA Today*, February 24, 2017, https://eu.usatoday.com/story/tech/news/2017/02/24/uber-travis-kalanick-/98328660/.
52. Della Cava, Guynn, and Swartz, "Uber's Kalanick Faces Crisis."
53. Rapkin, "Uber Cab Confessions."
54. Emily Peck, "Travis Kalanick's Ex Reveals New Details About Uber's Sexist Culture," *Huffington Post*, March 28, 2017, https://www.huffpost.com/entry/travis-kalanick-gabi-holzwarth-uber_n_58da7341e4b018c4606b8ec9.
55. Susan Fowler, "Reflecting on One Very, Very Strange Year at Uber," personal blog, February 19, 2017, https://www.susanjfowler.com/blog/2017/2/19/reflecting-on-one-very-strange-year-at-uber.
56. Fowler, *Whistleblower*, 4.
57. Fowler, *Whistleblower*, 118–119.
58. Fowler, *Whistleblower*, 138–139, 174.
59. Isaac, "Uber's Aggressive Culture."
60. Fowler, *Whistleblower*, 154.
61. Fowler, *Whistleblower*, 162.
62. Such a frat-house culture, in which women are marginalized and commodified, is not unusual for Silicon Valley tech startups. Only 25 percent of those working in the tech industry are women, and for startup funding, the situation is even grimmer. Only 2 percent of venture capital funding goes to female entrepreneurs (see Zoe Corbyn, "Why Sexism Is Rife in Silicon Valley," *Guardian*, March 17, 2018, https://www.theguardian.com/world/2018/mar/17/sexual-harassment-silicon-valley-emily-chang-brotopia-interview). In this overall frat-house atmosphere, it comes as no surprise that "six out of ten women working in Silicon Valley experience unwanted sexual advances" according to the Elephant in the Valley survey (see Jessica Guynn, "Sexism Charges Hit Technology Industry," *USA Today*, July 1, 2014, https://eu.usatoday.com/story/tech/2014/07/01/tinder-sexism-technology-snapchat-github/11903401/). As a result, tech companies have a retention problem, because women do not want to stay for long in such toxic macho environments (Corbyn, "Why Sexism Is Rife").
63. Sarah Lacy, "The Horrific Trickle Down of Asshole Culture: Why I've Just Deleted Uber from My Phone," *Internet Archive*, October 22, 2014, https://web.archive.org

NOTES TO CHAPTER 5

/web/20141202052906/https://pando.com/2014/10/22/the-horrific-trickle-down-of-asshole-culture-at-a-company-like-uber/.

64. Alyson Shonell, "All Hail the Uber Man! How Sharp-Elbowed Salesman Travis Kalanick Became Silicon Valley's Newest Star," *Business Insider*, January 11, 2014, https://www.businessinsider.com/uber-travis-kalanick-bio-2014-1.

65. Isaac, *Super Pumped*, 196.

66. Alba, "Short History."

67. Eric Newcomer, "In Video, Uber CEO Argues with Driver over Falling Fares," *Bloomberg*, February 28, 2017, https://www.bloomberg.com/news/articles/2017-02-28/in-video-uber-ceo-argues-with-driver-over-falling-fares; watch the video at https://www.youtube.com/watch?v=gTEDYCkNqns.

68. Isaac, "Uber Deceives Authorities."

69. Biz Carson, "Uber Fired More Than 20 Employees After Receiving 215 Claims in Probe of Sex Harassment and Other Incidents," *Business Insider*, June 6, 2017, https://www.businessinsider.com/uber-fired-more-than-20-employees-as-part-of-its-sex-harassment-probe-2017-6.

70. "Uber Special Committee Recommendations," https://fr.scribd.com/document/351186444/Uber-special-committee-recommendations.

71. Lopatto, "Expose Sexism at Uber."

72. Biz Carson, "Uber's Ex-CEO Travis Kalanick Has Dumped 90% of His Stock in Just Six Weeks," *Forbes*, December 18, 2019, https://www.forbes.com/sites/bizcarson/2019/12/18/uber-travis-kalanick-sells-most-of-his-shares/.

73. Isaac, "Inside Uber's Aggressive Culture."

74. Isaac, *Super Pumped*, 279.

75. Freya Pratty, "Travis Kalanick Is Building a Secretive Dark Kitchen Empire in Europe," *Sifted Reporters*, August 6, 2021, https://sifted.eu/articles/kalanick-dark-kitchens/.

76. Meghan Morris, "Travis Kalanick's Stealth $5 Billion Startup, CloudKitchens, Is Uber All Over Again, Ruled by a 'Temple of Bros,' Insiders Say," *Business Insider*, April 22, 2021, https://www.businessinsider.com/travis-kalanicks-cloudkitchens-repeats-uber-playbook-loses-staff-2121-4.

Chapter 6: Wells Fargo—Sell Like Hell

1. Gary Silverman, "The Anonymous Head of Wells Fargo Takes Centre Stage," *Financial Times*, November 20, 2015, https://www.ft.com/content/8f133540-8df5-11e5-8be4-3506bf20cc2b; Bharathy Premachandra and Azish Filabi, *Under Pressure: Fargo, Misconduct, Leadership, and Culture* (Ethical Systems, 2018), 5, https://www.ethicalsystems.org/wp-content/uploads/2013/07/files_WellsFargoCaseStudy_EthSystems_May2018FINAL.pdf.

2. Chris Arnold, "Former Wells Fargo Employees Describe Toxic Sales Culture, Even at HQ," *NPR*, October 4, 2016, https://www.npr.org/2016/10/04/496508361/former-wells-fargo-employees-describe-toxic-sales-culture-even-at-hq.

3. US Department of the Treasury, *Notice of Charges for Orders of Prohibition and Orders to Cease and Desist and Notice of Assessment of a Civil Money Penalty*, Office of the Comptroller of the Currency, 2020, https://www.occ.gov/static/enforcement-actions/eaN20-001.pdf (accessed June 7, 2024).

4. Claus Hulverscheidt, "US Financial House: 'Call and Earn Money!,'" *Süddeutsche Zeitung*, October 13, 2016, http://www.sueddeutsche.de/wirtschaft/us-finanzhaus-ruf-an-und-verdien-geld-1.3203735.

NOTES TO CHAPTER 6

5. Susan M. Ochs, "The Leadership Blind Spots at Wells Fargo," *Harvard Business Review*, October 6, 2016, https://hbr.org/2016/10/the-leadership-blind-spots-at-wells-fargo; Gallup, "Current and Previous Gallup Great Workplace Award Winners," accessed November 14, 2024, https://www.gallup.com/events/178865/gallup-great-workplace-award-current-previous-win-ners.aspx.

6. Marisa Aspan, "Q&A: Wells Fargo's John Stumpf on Regulation, Reputation, and Breaking Up the Banks," *American Banker*, November 21, 2013, https://www.americanbanker.com/news/q-amp-a-wells-fargos-john-stumpf-on-regulation-reputation-and-breaking-up-the-banks; Authenticated US Government Information GPO, *An Examination of Wells Fargo's Unauthorized Accounts and the Regulatory Response* (US Government Publishing Office, 2017), https://www.govinfo.gov/content/pkg/CHRG-114shrg23001/pdf/CHRG-114shrg23001.pdf (accessed June 7, 2024).

7. Michael Tanglis, *The "King of Cross-Sell" and the Race to Eight: An Analysis of Wells Fargo's Cross-Sell Numbers Since 1998* (Public Citizen, 2016), 4, https://www.citizen.org/wp-content/uploads/wells-fargo-king-of-cross-sell.pdf.

8. US Treasury, *Notice*, 16.

9. Independent Directors of the Board of Wells Fargo & Company, *Sales Practices Investigation Report*, April 10, 2017, 56–57, https://lowellmilkeninstitute.law.ucla.edu/wp-content/uploads/2018/01/WF-Board-Report.pdf.

10. E. Scott Reckard, "Wells Fargo's Pressure-Cooker Sales Culture Comes at a Cost," *Los Angeles Times*, December 21, 2013, https://www.latimes.com/business/la-fi-wells-fargo-sale-pressure-20131222-story.html.

11. Tanglis, *"King of Cross-Sell,"* 5.

12. Tanglis, *"King of Cross-Sell,"* 7.

13. US Treasury, *Notice*, 43–45.

14. "Most Powerful Women," *Fortune*, accessed November 14, 2024, https://fortune.com/most-powerful-women/2014/carrie-tolstedt/; "50 Most Powerful Women in Business," *Fortune*, in *CNN Money*, October 8, 2012, https://money.cnn.com/magazines/fortune/most-powerful-women/2012/snapshots/22.html; Wells Fargo, *Report*, 12–13.

15. Matt Egan, "$124 Million Payday for Wells Fargo Exec Who Led Fake Accounts Unit," *CNN Business*, September 13, 2016, http://money.cnn.com/2016/09/12/investing/wells-fargo-fake-accounts-exec-payday/index.html?iid=EL.

16. US Treasury, *Notice*, 26.

17. Reckard, "Wells Fargo's Sales Culture."

18. Emily Glazer and Christina Rexrode, "Wells Boss Says Staff at Fault for Scams," *Wall Street Journal*, September 14, 2016, https://www.wsj.com/articles/wells-fargo-ceo-defends-bank-culture-lays-blame-with-bad-employees-1473784452.

19. Stacy Cowley (compiled), "Voices from Wells Fargo: 'I Thought I Was Having a Heart Attack,'" *New York Times*, October 20, 2016, https://www.nytimes.com/2016/10/21/business/dealbook/voices-from-wells-fargo-i-thought-i-was-having-a-heart-attack.html.

20. Reckard, "Wells Fargo's Sales Culture."

21. Cowley, "Voices from Wells Fargo."

22. US Treasury, *Notice*, 21.

23. Arnold, "Wells Fargo Employees."

24. Reckard, "Wells Fargo's Sales Culture."

25. US Treasury, *Notice*, 4.

NOTES TO CHAPTER 6

26. Interview with a former Wells Fargo manager who wished to remain anonymous.
27. Wells Fargo, *Report*, 42.
28. Tanglis, *"King of Cross-Sell,"* 7.
29. Wells Fargo, *Report*, 22–23.
30. US Treasury, *Notice*, 19.
31. US Treasury, *Notice*, 22; Wells Fargo, *Report*, 30–31.
32. Wells Fargo, *Report*, 8, 43.
33. Arnold, "Wells Fargo Employees."
34. Interview with former Wells Fargo manager.
35. Matt Egan, "Ex-Wells Fargo Worker: Intimidation Included No Bathroom Breaks," *CNN Business*, October 12, 2016, https://money.cnn.com/2016/10/11/investing/wells-fargo-intimidation-bathroom-breaks/index.html.
36. Matt Egan, "Inside Wells Fargo, Workers Say the Mood Is Grim," *CNN Business*, November 3, 2016, https://money.cnn.com/2016/11/03/investing/wells-fargo-morale-problem/index.html.
37. Cowley, "Voices from Wells Fargo."
38. Arnold, "Wells Fargo Employees."
39. Cowley, "Voices from Wells Fargo."
40. US Treasury, *Notice*, 11–12.
41. Anastasia Christman, "Banking on the Hard Sell: Low Wages and Aggressive Sales Metrics Put Bank Workers and Customers at Risk," National Employment Law Project, June 10, 2016, https://www.nelp.org/insights-research/banking-on-the-hard-sell-low-wages-aggressive-sales-metrics-put-bank-workers-customers-at-risk/.
42. Christman, "Hard Sell," 11.
43. Christman, "Hard Sell," 11.
44. Matt Levine, "Wells Fargo Opened a Couple Million Fake Accounts," *Bloomberg*, September 9, 2016, https://www.bloomberg.com/opinion/articles/2016-09-09/wells-fargo-opened-a-couple-million-fake-accounts.
45. US Treasury, *Notice*, 5.
46. Christman, "Hard Sell," 9.
47. US Treasury, *Notice*, 5.
48. Christman, "Hard Sell," 9.
49. Kevin Wack, "Ghost Funding and Sandbagging: Wells Fargo's Sales Tactics on Trial," *American Banker*, November 20, 2019, https://www.americanbanker.com/news/ghost-funding-and-sandbagging-wells-fargos-sales-tactics-on-trial.
50. Christman, "Hard Sell," 11.
51. US Treasury, *Notice*, 5, 28–29.
52. Jim Hightower, "The Ethical Rot of Wells Fargo, from the Top Down," *Salon*, October 15, 2016, http://www.salon.com/2016/10/15/the-ethical-rot-of-wells-fargo-from-the-top-down.
53. Premachandra and Filabi, "Under Pressure," 7.
54. Reckard, "Wells Fargo's Sales Culture."
55. Stacy Cowley, "'Lions Hunting Zebras': Ex-Wells Fargo Bankers Describe Abuses," *New York Times*, October 20, 2016, http://www.nytimes.com/2016/10/21/business/dealbook/lions-hunting-zebras-ex-wells-fargo-bankers-describe-abuses.html.
56. Wells Fargo, *Report*, 34–36.
57. US Treasury, *Notice*, 39–40; Arnold, "Wells Fargo Employees."
58. Wells Fargo, *Report*, 34–36.

NOTES TO CHAPTER 7

59. US Treasury, *Notice*, 31.
60. Wells Fargo, *Report*, 19.
61. US Treasury, *Notice*, 22–23, 26.
62. Wells Fargo, *Report*, 16–17.
63. Matt Egan, "I Called the Wells Fargo Ethics Line and Was Fired," *CNN Business*, September 21, 2016, https://money.cnn.com/2016/09/21/investing/wells-fargo-fired-workers-retaliation-fake-accounts/index.html?iid=EL.
64. Matt Egan, "Wells Fargo Admits to Signs of Worker Retaliation," *CNN Business*, January 23, 2017, http://money.cnn.com/2017/01/23/investing/wells-fargo-retaliation-ethics-line/index.html.
65. James B. Stewart, "Wells Fargo Whistle-Blowers' Fate Becomes Just a Footnote," *New York Times*, May 4, 2017, https://www.nytimes.com/2017/05/04/business/wells-fargo-whistle-blowers.html.
66. Egan, "Ethics Line."
67. Laura J. Keller, Dakin Campbell, and Kartikay Mehrotra, "Wells Fargo's Stars Thrived While 5,000 Workers Got Fired," *Bloomberg*, November 3, 2016, https://www.bloomberg.com/news/articles/2016-11-03/wells-fargo-s-stars-climbed-while-abuses-flourished-beneath-them.
68. Wells Fargo, *Report*, 4.
69. Wells Fargo, *Report*, 14–15, 63.
70. Ochs, "Leadership Blind Spots."
71. Wells Fargo, *Report*, 56–57.
72. Keller, Campbell, and Mehrotra, "Wells Fargo's Stars Thrived."
73. Wells Fargo, *Report*, 11.
74. Wells Fargo, *Report*, 18.
75. Matt Kelly, "Wells Fargo's Staggering Compliance Costs," *Radical Compliance*, August 5, 2020, https://www.radicalcompliance.com/2020/08/05/wells-fargos-staggering-compliance-costs/.
76. Michael Hiltzik, "That Wells Fargo Accounts Scandal Was Even Worse Than You Can Imagine," column, *Los Angeles Times*, January 27, 2020, https://www.latimes.com/business/story/2020-01-27/wells-fargo-scandal; Julie DiMauro, "Former Wells Fargo Executive Carrie Tolstedt Settles SEC Fraud Charges," *GRIP*, June 2, 2023, https://www.grip.globalrelay.com/former-wells-fargo-executive-carrie-tolstedt-settles-sec-fraud-charges/.
77. Michael Hiltzik, "Even a $1-Billion Fine Won't Fix What's Broken at Wells Fargo," column, *Los Angeles Times*, April 20, 2018, https://www.latimes.com/business/hiltzik/la-fi-hiltzik-wells-fargo-20180420-story.html.
78. Emily Flitter, "The Price of Wells Fargo's Fake Account Scandal Grows by $3 Billion," *New York Times*, February 21, 2020, https://www.nytimes.com/2020/02/21/business/wells-fargo-settlement.html.
79. Emily Flitter and Stacy Cowley, "Wells Fargo Says Its Culture Has Changed. Some Employees Disagree," *New York Times*, March 9, 2019, https://www.nytimes.com/2019/03/09/business/wells-fargo-sales-culture.html.

Chapter 7: France Télécom—a Fatal Change Management

1. All cases are from the following sources: Court of Appeal of Paris, Paris High Court, Office of Brigitte Jolivet, Vice President Responsible for the Investigation, *Order of Partial Dismissal and Referral to the Criminal Court*, [in French] 2019, 90, 125–126, https://proceslombard.fr/wp-content/uploads/2019/04/ORDONNANCE-DE-RENVOI

-FRANCE-TELECOM.pdf (accessed June 8, 2024); The Public Prosecutor at the Paris High Court, *Final Indictment for Partial Dismissal and Referral to the Criminal Court*, [in French] 2019, 218, 295ff; Sophie Courageot, "Suicides at France Telecom: 'The Ex-Leaders Are Condemned, but That Will Not Bring My Brother Back,'" [in French] *franceinfo*, December 20, 2019, https://france3-regions.francetvinfo.fr/bourgogne-franche-comte/doubs/besancon/suicides-france-telecom-ex-dirigeants-sont-condamnes-cela-ne-ramenera-pas-mon-frere-1765267.html; Adam Nossiter, "35 Employees Committed Suicide: Will Their Bosses Go to Jail?," *New York Times*, July 9, 2019, https://www.nytimes.com/2019/07/09/world/europe/france-telecom-trial.html.

2. Christian Baudelot and Michel Gollac, "What Can Suicides at Work Say?," [in French] *Sociologie* 2, no. 6 (2015): 195–206, https://shs.cairn.info/revue-sociologie-2015-2-page-195?lang=fr; Nihel Chabrak, Russel Craig, and Nabyla Daidj, "Financialization and the Employee Suicide Crisis at France Telecom," *Journal of Business Ethics* 139, no. 3 (2016): 501–515.

3. "The Slow Death of a National Company," [in French] *Le Monde Diplomatique*, October 20, 2002, https://www.monde-diplomatique.fr/2002/10/A/9497.

4. Chabrak, Craig, and Daidj, "Suicide Crisis at France Telecom," 506; Florence Palpacuer and Amélie Seignour, "Resisting via Hybrid Spaces: The Cascade Effect of a Workplace Struggle Against Neoliberal Hegemony," *Journal of Management Inquiry* 29, no. 4 (2020): 418–432, 422.

5. Chabrak, Craig, and Daidj, "Suicide Crisis at France Telecom," 506; "Slow Death."

6. Paris Court of Appeal, *Order of Partial Dismissal*, 81.

7. Paris Court of Appeal, *Order of Partial Dismissal*, 47.

8. Odile Henry, "Unions and Expertise in Psychosocial Risks: Research Notes on the Dark Years of Management at France Telecom Orange," [in French] *Actes de la recherche en sciences sociales* 4, no. 194 (2012): 52–61; plea of Sylvie Topaloff, lawyer for the Sud PTT federation.

9. Henry, "Dark Years of Management," 56; Chabrak, Craig, and Daidj, "Suicide Crisis at France Telecom," 510.

10. Bernard Nicolas, "Humiliation, Depression, Resignation: France Télécom's Triple Play Offer," [in French] *Les Inrockuptibles*, September 25, 2010, https://www.lesinrocks.com/actu/humiliation-depression-demission-loffre-triple-play-de-france-telecom-8135-25-09-2010/.

11. Paris High Court Public Prosecutor, *Final Indictment for Partial Dismissal*, 65.

12. Palpacuer and Seignour, "Resisting via Hybrid Spaces," 423.

13. Paris High Court Public Prosecutor, *Final Indictment for Partial Dismissal*, 71.

14. Nicolas, "Humiliation, Depression, Resignation."

15. Paris Court of Appeal, *Order of Partial Dismissal*, 89.

16. Nicolas, "Humiliation, Depression, Resignation," 55–56.

17. Nicolas, "Humiliation, Depression, Resignation," 59.

18. Paris Court of Appeal, *Order of Partial Dismissal*, 281.

19. Paris Court of Appeal, *Order of Partial Dismissal*, 606.

20. Chabrak, Craig, and Daidj, "Suicide Crisis at France Telecom," 510.

21. Paris Court of Appeal, *Order of Partial Dismissal*, 204–206, 466–468.

22. Paris Court of Appeal, *Order of Partial Dismissal*, 219.

23. Baudelot and Gollac, "Suicides at Work."

24. Paris High Court Public Prosecutor, *Final Indictment for Partial Dismissal*, 67.

25. Corinne Audouin, "France Télécom Trial: 'I Was Bruised, Humiliated,'" [in French] *France Inter*, May 23, 2019, https://www.franceinter.fr/justice/proces-france

-telecom-j-ai-ete-meurtri-humilie; Paris High Court Public Prosecutor, *Final Indictment for Partial Dismissal*, 115.

26. Paris High Court Public Prosecutor, *Final Indictment for Partial Dismissal*, 115.
27. Paris High Court Public Prosecutor, *Final Indictment for Partial Dismissal*, 89.
28. Paris High Court Public Prosecutor, *Final Indictment for Partial Dismissal*, 32.
29. Paris High Court Public Prosecutor, *Final Indictment for Partial Dismissal*, 90.
30. Paris High Court Public Prosecutor, *Final Indictment for Partial Dismissal*, 87.
31. Paris Court of Appeal, *Order of Partial Dismissal*, 242–243.
32. Adam Nossiter, "35 Employees Committed Suicide. Will Their Bosses Go to Jail?," *New York Times*, July 9, 2019, https://www.nytimes.com/2019/07/09/world/europe/france-telecom-trial.html.
33. Baudelot and Gollac, "Suicides at Work."
34. Henry, "Trade Unions," 58.
35. Baudelot and Gollac, "Suicides at Work."
36. Paris Court of Appeal, *Order of Partial Dismissal*, 203.
37. Paris Court of Appeal, *Order of Partial Dismissal*, 446ff.
38. Paris Court of Appeal, *Order of Partial Dismissal*, 242–243.
39. Paris High Court Public Prosecutor, *Final Indictment for Partial Dismissal*, 96.
40. Louis-Pierre Wenès, interviewed by Jonathan Spragg (video recording), *Meet the Boss TV*, http://www.meettheboss.tv/video/looking-back-moving-forward; cited in Ulf Schäfer and Konstantin Korotov, *Suicides at France Telecom* (case study), May 19, 2014.
41. Henry, "Trade Unions," 55.
42. Palpacuer and Seignour, "Resisting via Hybrid Spaces," 426.
43. Paris High Court Public Prosecutor, *Final Indictment for Partial Dismissal*, 46, 60.
44. Sébastian Fosse, "France Telecom Verdict: A New 'Logic of Honor' in Business?," [in French] *The Conversation*, September 30, 2022, https://theconversation.com/verdict-france-telecom-une-nouvelle-logique-de-lhonneur-en-entreprise-191543.
45. Paris Court of Appeal, *Order of Partial Dismissal*, 589.
46. Ulf Schäfer and Konstantin Korotov, *Suicides at France Télécom*, ESMT Case 414-0149-1E (European School of Management & Technology, 2014), 9.

Chapter 8: Boeing—the Price of Cutting Costs

1. Hannah Beech and Muktita Suhartono, "'Spend the Minimum': After Crash, Lion Air's Safety Record Is Back in Spotlight," *New York Times*, November 22, 2018, https://www.nytimes.com/2018/11/22/world/asia/lion-air-crash-safety-failures.html.
2. House Committee on Transportation & Infrastructure, *The Design, Development & Certification of the Boeing 737 MAX*, September 2020, 135, https://democrats-transportation.house.gov/imo/media/doc/2020.09.15%20FINAL%20737%20MAX%20Report%20for%20Public%20Release.pdf.
3. Peter Robison, *Flying Blind: The 737 MAX Tragedy and the Fall of Boeing* (Random House, 2021), 275.
4. Julia Limitone, "Boeing CEO: 737 MAX Jets Are Safe," *Fox Business*, November 13, 2018, https://www.foxbusiness.com/business-leaders/boeing-ceo-our-airplanes-are-safe.
5. House Committee, *Design of the 737 MAX*, 37, 87.
6. Dominic Gates, "Will 787 Program Ever Show an Overall Profit? Analysts Grow More Skeptical," *Seattle Times*, October 17, 2015, https://www.seattletimes.com/business/boeing-aerospace/will-787-program-ever-show-an-overall-profit-analysts-grow-more-skeptical/.
7. House Committee, *Design of the 737 MAX*, 12–13, 40.

NOTES TO CHAPTER 8

8. Robison, *Flying Blind*, 79–82.
9. Robison, *Flying Blind*, 10–11, 90.
10. David Gelles, *The Man Who Broke Capitalism: How Jack Welch Gutted the Heartland and Crushed the Soul of Corporate America—and How to Undo His Legacy* (Simon & Schuster, 2022), 88.
11. Robison, *Flying Blind*, 97.
12. Robison, *Flying Blind*, 100.
13. House Committee, *Design of the 737 MAX*, 37.
14. Robison, *Flying Blind*, 100, 131.
15. Spyros Georgilidakis, "Boeing Rolling Back Controversial 'Partnering for Success' Deal?," *Mentour Pilot*, February 11, 2024, https://mentourpilot.com/boeing-rolling-back-controversial-partnering-for-success-deal/.
16. Patricia Callahan, "So Why Does Harry Stonecipher Think He Can Turn Around Boeing?," *Chicago Tribune*, updated August 22, 2019, available at https://www.chicagotribune.com/2004/02/29/.
17. Robison, *Flying Blind*, 205.
18. Robison, *Flying Blind*, 218.
19. Interview with a Boeing manager who wished to remain anonymous.
20. Interview with a Boeing coach who wished to remain anonymous.
21. Alec MacGillis, "The Case Against Boeing," *New Yorker*, November 11, 2019, https://www.newyorker.com/magazine/2019/11/18/the-case-against-boeing.
22. Robison, *Flying Blind*, 205.
23. Robison, *Flying Blind*, 220.
24. Will Jordan, "Exclusive: Safety Concerns Dog Boeing 787," Al Jazeera, September 8, 2014, https://www.aljazeera.com/economy/2014/9/8/exclusive-safety-concerns-dog-boeing-787.
25. Richard Aboulafia, "Boeing Will Pay a High Price for McNerney's Mistake of Treating Aviation Like It Was Any Other Industry," *Fortune*, June 24, 2015, https://www.forbes.com/sites/richardaboulafia/2015/06/24/boeing-mcnerney-and-the-high-price-of-treating-aircraft-like-it-was-any-other-industry/.
26. Robison, *Flying Blind*, 221.
27. Interview with Boeing manager.
28. Robison, *Flying Blind*, 226.
29. Robison, *Flying Blind*, 226.
30. William Lazonick and Mustafa E. Sakinç, "Make Passengers Safer? Boeing Just Made Shareholders Richer," *American Prospect*, May 31, 2019, https://prospect.org/environment/make-passengers-safer-boeing-just-made-shareholders-richer/.
31. Ricardo Landis, "Is The Boeing Company (NYSE:BA) a Smart Choice for Dividend Investors?," *Yahoo Finance*, December 20, 2018, https://finance.yahoo.com/news/boeing-company-nyse-ba-smart-110308246.html.
32. Lazonick and Sakinç, "Make Passengers Safer?"
33. Robison, *Flying Blind*, 11–12.
34. House Committee, *Design of the 737 MAX*, 42–43, 87.
35. Robison, *Flying Blind*, 213.
36. House Committee, *Design of the 737 MAX*, 89–90.
37. Julie Johnsson, Ryan Beene, and Mary Schlangenstein, "Boeing Held Off for Months on Disclosing Faulty Alert on 737 MAX," *Bloomberg*, May 5, 2019, https://

www.bloomberg.com/news/articles/2019-05-05/boeing-left-airlines-faa-in-dark-on-737-alert-linked-to-crash.

38. House Committee, *Design of the 737 MAX*, 100.

39. Dominic Gates, "Boeing Whistleblower Alleges Systemic Problems with 737 MAX," *Seattle Times*, June 18, 2020, https://www.seattletimes.com/business/boeing-aerospace/boeing-whistleblower-alleges-systemic-problems-with-737-max/.

40. Dominic Gates, Steve Miletich, and Lewis Kamb, "Boeing Whistleblower's Complaint Says 737 MAX Safety Upgrades Were Rejected over Cost," *Aviation Pros*, October 2, 2019, https://www.aviationpros.com/aircraft/commercial-airline/news/21108647/boeing-whistleblowers-complaint-says-737-max-safety-upgrades-were-rejected-over-cost.

41. House Committee, *Design of the 737 MAX*, 71, 86; Robison, *Flying Blind*, 167.

42. House Committee, *Design of the 737 MAX*, 100.

43. Robison, *Flying Blind*, 9.

44. House Committee, *Design of the 737 MAX*, 100.

45. Robison, *Flying Blind*, 243.

46. House Committee, *Design of the 737 MAX*, 73.

47. Robison, *Flying Blind*, 190–194.

48. Robison, *Flying Blind*, 193.

49. Natalie Kitroeff, David Gelles, and Jack Nicas, "The Roots of Boeing's 737 MAX Crisis: A Regulator Relaxes Its Oversight," *New York Times*, July 27, 2019, https://www.nytimes.com/2019/07/27/business/boeing-737-max-faa.html.

50. House Committee, *Design of the 737 MAX*, 66.

51. Robison, *Flying Blind*, 262–263.

52. House Committee, *Design of the 737 MAX*, 166–167, 173.

53. Interview with Boeing manager.

54. Robison, *Flying Blind*, 259.

55. Niraj Chokshi, Sydney Ember, and Santul Nerkar, "'Shortcuts Everywhere': How Boeing Favored Speed over Quality," *New York Times*, March 28, 2024, https://www.nytimes.com/2024/03/28/business/boeing-quality-problems-speed.html.

56. House Committee, *Design of the 737 MAX*, 185.

57. House Committee, *Design of the 737 MAX*, 135–136.

58. Robison, *Flying Blind*, 280.

59. House Committee, *Design of the 737 MAX*, 156.

60. House Committee, *Design of the 737 MAX*, 97, 110.

61. House Committee, *Design of the 737 MAX*, 9–10.

62. House Committee, *Design of the 737 MAX*, 20.

63. Ian Duncan and Lori Aratani, "Boeing's Manufacturing Woes Long Preceded Door-Panel Blowout," *Washington Post*, August 11, 2024, https://www.washingtonpost.com/transportation/2024/08/11/boeing-ntsb-faa-doorplug/; Luke Bodell, "Boeing's Broken Safety Culture: 5 Key Insights From Senate 787 Dreamliner & B777 Whistleblower Hearing," *Simple Flying*, April 17, 2024, https://simpleflying.com/boeing-whistleblower-senate-hearing-testimony/.

Chapter 9: Volkswagen—Cheating in the Name of Fairness

1. Nathan Bomey, "VW Surpasses Toyota as World's Largest Automaker in First Half of 2015," *USA Today*, July 28, 2015, https://eu.usatoday.com/story/money/2015/07/28/volkswagen-surpasses-toyota-worlds-largest-automaker-first-half-2015/30772509/.

NOTES TO CHAPTER 9

2. Letter of the California Environmental Protection Agency to Volkswagen, September 18, 2015, https://www.4cleanair.org/wp-content/uploads/2021/01/CARB_InUse ComplianceLetter_to_VW-09.18.15.pdf; a similar letter was sent to Volkswagen by the US Environmental Protection Agency (EPA) on the same day—see https://www.epa.gov /sites/default/files/2015-10/documents/vw-nov-caa-09-18-15.pdf.

3. Jack Ewing, "Volkswagen C.E.O. Martin Winterkorn Resigns amid Emissions Scandal," *New York Times*, September 23, 2015, https://www.nytimes.com/2015/09/24/business /international/volkswagen-chief-martin-winterkorn-resigns-amid-emissions-scandal.html.

4. Jan Schwartz and Victoria Bryan, "VW's Dieselgate Bill Hits $30 Billion After Another Charge," Reuters, September 29, 2017, https://www.reuters.com/article/uk -volkswagen-emissions-idUKKCN1C40RN; Sean O'Kane, "Volkswagen, BMW Fined $1 Billion for Colluding to Make Dirtier Cars," *Verge*, July 8, 2021, https://www.theverge .com/2021/7/8/22568356/volkswagen-bmw-daimler-emissions-cartel-fine-audi-porsche-eu.

5. US District Court, Eastern District of Michigan, *Plea Agreement: United States of America Versus Volkswagen AG*, 2:16-cr-20394-SFC-APP-10, ECF no. 138, January 18, 2019, 54, https://www.justice.gov/criminal-fraud/file/1145601/download; Jack Ewing, *Faster, Higher, Farther: The Volkswagen Scandal* (Norton, 2017), 119.

6. Georg Mascolo and Klaus Ott, "The Story of the VW Fraud," [in German] *Süddeutsche Zeitung*, April 25, 2016, http://www.sueddeutsche.de/wirtschaft/volkswagen -die-geschichte-des-vw-betrugs-1.2965786-3.

7. Chris Perkins, "VW's Emissions-Cheating Defeat Device Was Developed by Audi in 1999 to Reduce Noise," *Road and Track*, July 19, 2016, https://www.roadandtrack.com /new-cars/car-technology/news/a30029/vw-acoustic-function-defeat-device/.

8. James Grimmelmann, "The VW Scandal Is Just the Beginning," *Mother Jones*, September 24, 2015, https://www.motherjones.com/environment/2015/09/volkswagen -defeat-device-copyright-harry-potter/.

9. US District Court, Michigan, *Plea Agreement*.

10. Ewing, *Faster, Higher, Farther*, 169–171.

11. Ewing, *Faster, Higher, Farther*, 169–171.

12. US District Court, Northern District of California, San Francisco Division, *Plaintiffs' Notice of Motion, Motion, and Memorandum in Support of Preliminary Approval of the Bosch Class Action Settlement Agreement and Release and Approval of Class Notice*, 2672 CRB, ECF no. 2838, January 31, 2017, 10, https://www.cand.uscourts.gov /filelibrary/2952/2838-Motion-for-Preliminary-Approval-of-Bosch.pdf.

13. Ewing, *Faster, Higher, Farther*, 172–174.

14. US District Court, Michigan, *Plea Agreement*.

15. Max Hägler and Volkmar Kabisch, "VW Emissions Scandal: Fear and Arrogance," [in German] *Süddeutsche Zeitung*, October 3, 2015, http://www.sueddeutsche.de /wirtschaft/vw-abgas-skandal-angst-und-arroganz-1.2675660; conversation on September 19, 2021, with a Volkswagen manager who wished to remain anonymous.

16. Conversation with Volkswagen manager.

17. Dietmar Hawranek and Dirk Kurbjuweit, "Wolfsburger Empire," [in German] *Der Spiegel*, August 18, 2013, http://www.spiegel.de/spiegel/print/d-107728908.html.

18. Ewing, *Faster, Higher, Farther*, 89.

19. Geoffrey Smith and Roger Parloff, "Hoaxwagen," *Fortune*, March 7, 2016, https:// fortune.com/longform/inside-volkswagen-emissions-scandal/.

20. Conversation with Volkswagen manager.

21. Ewing, *Faster, Higher, Farther*, 90.

22. Conversation with Volkswagen manager.

23. Andreas Cremer and Tom Bergin, "Fear and Respect: VW's Culture Under Winterkorn," Reuters, October 10, 2015, https://www.reuters.com/article/us-volkswagen-emissions-culture-idUSKCN0S40MT20151010.

24. Hägler and Kabisch, "VW Emissions Scandal."

25. Antonia Schäfer, "Behind the Scenes at VW: This Is How Winterkorn Drove the Car Giant into the Abyss," [in German] *Focus*, September 29, 2015, https://www.focus.de/finanzen/boerse/cholerische-anfaelle-und-angstkultur-hinter-den-kulissen-von-vw-so-trieb-winterkorn-den-autoriesen-in-den-abgrund_id_4979738.html.

26. Danny Hakim, Aaron M. Kessler, and Jack Ewing, "As Volkswagen Pushed to Be No. 1, Ambitions Fueled a Scandal," *New York Times*, September 26, 2015, http://www.nytimes.com/2015/09/27/business/as-vw-pushed-to-be-no-1-ambitions-fueled-a-scandal.html?_r=1.

27. Smith and Parloff, "Hoaxwagen."

28. David Michaels, *The Triumph of Doubt: Dark Money and the Science of Deception* (Oxford University Press, 2020), 164.

29. Brad Tuttle, "This Company Just Overtook Toyota to Become the World's Top Automaker," *Fortune*, July 28, 2015, https://fortune.com/2015/07/28/toyota-volkswagon-most-sales-globally/.

30. Ewing, *Faster, Higher, Farther*.

31. Ewing, *Faster, Higher, Farther*, 121.

32. Hakim, Kessler, and Ewing, "Volkswagen Pushed."

33. Paul Kilby, "Fraudsters, Fakes, and Flaws," *Fraud Magazine*, May/June 2022, https://www.fraud-magazine.com/article.aspx?id=4295017580.

34. Sönke Iwersen et al., "How Control Failed at VW," [in German] *Handelsblatt*, February 7, 2019, https://www.handelsblatt.com/unternehmen/industrie/dieselskandal-wie-die-kontrolle-bei-vw-versagte/23955944.html?ticket=ST-28402633-MumPc0wjYbvbeAFeXbCV-ap3.

35. Mengqi Sun and Jack Hagel, "Volkswagen Tries to Change Workplace Culture That Fueled Emissions Scandal," *Wall Street Journal*, September 30, 2020, https://www.wsj.com/articles/volkswagen-tries-to-change-workplace-culture-that-fueled-emissions-scandal-11601425486.

36. Smith and Parloff, "Hoaxwagen."

37. Gerhard Prätorius, "Sustainability Management in the Automotive Sector," in *Responsible Business: How to Manage a CSR Strategy Successfully*, ed. Manfred Pohl and Nick Tolhurst (Wiley, 2012), 193–208.

38. Ewing, *Faster, Higher, Farther*, 126.

39. Luc Bovens, "The Ethics of Dieselgate," *Midwest Studies in Philosophy* XL (2016): 262–283, 264.

40. Michaels, *Triumph of Doubt*, 162.

41. Smith and Parloff, "Hoaxwagen."

42. Bovens, "Ethics of Dieselgate," 264.

43. Smith and Parloff, "Hoaxwagen."

44. "Dirty Secrets: A Scandal in the Motor Industry," Leaders, *Economist*, September 26, 2015, http://www.economist.com/news/leaders/21666226-volkswagens-falsification-pollution-tests-opens-door-very-different-car.

45. Alexander Stoklosa, "VW CEO Characterizes Diesel Scandal as a 'Technical Problem,' Says Company Didn't Lie," *Car and Driver*, January 12, 2016, https://www

.caranddriver.com/news/a15350329/vw-ceo-characterizes-diesel-scandal-as-a-technical-problem-says-company-didnt-lie/.

46. Ewing, *Faster, Higher, Farther*, 123.

47. Jeff Plungis, "Carmaker Cheating on Emissions Almost as Old as Pollution Tests," *Bloomberg*, September 23, 2015, http://www.bloomberg.com/news/articles/2015-09-23/carmaker-cheating-on-emissions-almost-as-old-as-pollution-tests.

48. Plungis, "Carmaker Cheating."

49. Ben Knight, "Most EU Carmakers Fake Emissions," *DW*, November 5, 2016, https://www.dw.com/en/study-most-eu-carmakers-report-false-co2-emissions/a-19250251.

50. "The Volkswagen Scandal: A Mucky Business," Briefing, *The Economist*, September 26, 2015, http://www.economist.com/news/briefing/21667918-systematic-fraud-worlds-biggest-carmaker-threatens-engulf-entire-industry-and; conversation with Volkswagen manager.

51. Ewing, *Faster, Higher, Farther*, 368f.

52. Editorial Board, "What Was Volkswagen Thinking?" Opinion, *New York Times*, September 23, 2015, http://www.nytimes.com/2015/09/23/opinion/what-was-volkswagen-thinking.html.

Chapter 10: Foxconn—Welcome to the Machine

1. Xu Lizhi, "I Just Fall Asleep on My Feet," from *A New Day: Selected Poems by Xu Lizhi*, translated by Eleanor Goodman (Zephyr Press, forthcoming 2026), reprinted with her permission; for original Chinese, see https://zhuanlan.zhihu.com/p/464511443.

2. Ishaan Tharoor, "The Haunting Poetry of a Chinese Factory Worker Who Committed Suicide," *Washington Post*, November 12, 2014, https://www.washingtonpost.com/news/worldviews/wp/2014/11/12/the-haunting-poetry-of-a-chinese-factory-worker-who-committed-suicide/.

3. Pun Ngai, "Deconstructing Foxconn," [in Chinese] *Chinese Workers* 1 (2011): 22–24 (Chinese source: 解构富士康).

4. Terry Cheng, "Let Me Be Fair," [in Chinese] Facebook post, May 19, 2019, https://www.facebook.com/100080633499772/posts/1044067319134521/ (Chinese source: 我來說說公道話).

5. Working on this case was challenging, as there are fewer critical sources available compared to the other scandals we cover in this book. Furthermore, we cannot read Chinese, which makes it more difficult to interpret the situation at Foxconn. We could not, for instance, get deep enough into the case to sufficiently understand linguistic patterns for our *manipulative language* building block. We relied on a native speaker, Yue Wu, to find and translate Chinese sources and would like to thank her for her tremendous help with this case. We also thank Eleanor Goodman, Tanzhou Liu, Qi Yi, and Jinfeng Xu for their feedback and some additional fact-checking.

6. Kabir Chibber, "Foxconn: 'Hidden Dragon' Out in the Open" *BBC News*, September 24, 2012, https://www.bbc.com/news/business-19699156.

7. Pun Ngai, "The Foxconn Way of Production Is Undesirable," [in Chinese] *New York Times*, Chinese edition, November 6, 2012, https://cn.nytimes.com/business/20121106/cc06foxconn/ (Chinese source: 富士康生產方式不可取); Jenny Chan and Ngai Pun, "Suicide as Protest for the New Generation of Chinese Migrant Workers: Foxconn, Global Capital, and the State," *Asia-Pacific Journal* 37, no. 2 (2010) 1–50, https://apjjf.org/jenny-chan/3408/article.

NOTES TO CHAPTER 10

8. Chan and Pun, "Suicide as Protest"; Foxconn Research Group of Universities Across the Taiwan Strait and in Three Places, *Foxconn Research Report*, reposted on *Coolloud*, October 15, 2010, https://www.coolloud.org.tw/node/55067 (Chinese source: 兩岸三地高校富士康調查報告).

9. Ru Fang, "Terry Gou's Purgatory," [in Chinese] *IFENG.com*, June 22, 2010, https://finance.ifeng.com/a/20100622/2332982_0.shtml (Chinese source: 郭台銘的煉獄).

10. Ngai, "Foxconn Production."

11. "About Foxconn," Foxconn, accessed September 13, 2024, https://www.foxconn.com.cn/about.

12. Foxconn Research Group of Universities Across the Taiwan Strait and in Three Places, *Foxconn, Have You Mended Your Ways?—2012 Foxconn Research Report on Universities in Two Sides of the Taiwan Strait and Three Places*, reposted on *Coolloud*, April 6, 2012, https://www.coolloud.org.tw/node/67639 (Chinese source: 富士康, 你改过自新了吗？—2012 年度"两岸三地"高校富士康调研报告).

13. Wieland Wagner, "Life Inside the Foxconn 'Suicide Factory,'" *The Week*, January 9, 2015, https://theweek.com/articles/493939/life-inside-foxconn-suicide-factory.

14. Wagner, "Life Inside Foxconn."

15. Wen-lung Hsu, the founder of the Chi Mei Corporation, cited in Fang, "Terry Gou's Purgatory." Notwithstanding the fact that Gou handed over his role as CEO to his special assistant Young Liu as of July 1, 2019, our narrative of this case takes us back to 2010, when he was still CEO.

16. Terry Gou, interviewed by Yu Ying, cited in Xuedi Huang, Aimeili [pseud.], and Mengxiaodu [pseud.], eds., "Terry Gou: There Is No High-Tech Out of the Lab, Only the Discipline of Execution," [in Chinese] *SOHU*, July 17, 2018, https://www.sohu.com/a/241711101_516458#google_vignette (Chinese source: 郭台铭: 走出实验室没有高科技, 只有执行的纪律); see also "Visionaries: Terry Guo (II); The Discipline of Execution in the Manufacturing Industry," [in Chinese] YouTube video posted by Phoenix TV, https://www.youtube.com/watch?v=GdKwDdDeVFM (Chinese source: 《領航者 Visionaries》郭台銘 Terry Guo (II): 製造業只能靠執行的紀律).

17. Huang, Aimeli, and Mengxiaodu, "Terry Gou."

18. Cheng, "Let Me Be Fair."

19. Fang, "Terry Gou's Purgatory."

20. Cheng, "Let Me Be Fair."

21. Terry Cheng, "The Past Is Not Like Smoke," Facebook post, May 21, 2019, https://www.facebook.com/permalink.php?story_fbid=1182719771908167&id=100005104664045 (Chinese source: 往事並不如煙).

22. Cheng, "The Past."

23. Note that our ordering of the categories is different than that in Cheng's list.

24. Cheng, "The Past."

25. Such hopes were fueled by the fact that Terry Gou had granted a very generous compensation to the family of Danyong Sun, an engineer who had died by suicide (Cheng, "Let Me Be Fair"). Sun's suicide was broadly reported in the media, and Gou's reaction became widely known. Many employees called Foxconn's care center directly to inquire about the amount of compensation after a suicide (Fang, "Terry Gou's Purgatory"). At Hong Hai's annual shareholders' meeting in Taipei on June 8, 2010, Gou showed a slide of a letter that read, "I am about to jump from a Foxconn building. Don't be sad, as Foxconn will compensate you. This is the only way your son can repay you" (Fang, "Terry Gou's Purgatory").

26. Cheng, "The Past."

27. Fei Wang, Di Han, and Chunwei Zhang, "Why Is It Always Foxconn That Gets Shot?," [in Chinese] *IFENG*, October 21, 2013, https://tech.ifeng.com/it/special/foxconn-zq (Chinese source: 为什么中枪的总是富士康?).

28. Fang, "Terry Gou's Purgatory"; Wang, Han, and Zhang, "Foxconn Gets Shot."

29. Cheng, "The Past."

30. Cheng, "Let Me Be Fair"; Fang, "Terry Gou's Purgatory"; it was some 3 million square kilometers, according to Jing Xu, "Foxconn Will Uniformly Remove 3 Million Square Meters of Protective Netting from Its Factories," Caixin Web, August 17, 2010, https://finance.sina.cn/sa/2010-08-17/detail-ikftssan9146157.d.html (Chinese source: 富士康将统一拆除厂区300万平米防护网).

31. Fang, "Terry Gou's Purgatory"; Su Wang, "Foxconn's 'Letter to Foxconn Colleagues' Exposed," [in Chinese] Caixin Media, May 25, 2021, https://finance.sina.cn/sa/2010-05-26/detail-ikftpnny0317413.d.html (Chinese source: 富士康《致富士康同仁的一封信》曝光); see also Jenny Chan, "A Suicide Survivor: The Life of a Chinese Worker," *New Technology, Work, and Employment* 28, no. 2 (2013): 84–99.

32. According to Cheng, "Let Me Be Fair," the suicide mortality rate in mainland China was 7.8 people per 100,000 in 2012, and according to Sina Finance, the rate in China in 2008 was about 12 suicides per 100,000, https://finance.sina.cn/sa/2010-05-13/detail-ikftpnny0339167.d.html (Chinese source: 富士康八连跳自杀之谜). In Taiwan, where Foxconn was founded, this figure was 16.4 in 2017, and 11.3 in all OECD countries in 2009 ("Health at a Glance 2011, OECD Indicators," OECD, 2011, https://www.oecd-ilibrary.org/docserver/health_glance-2011-en.pdf). Putting the 12 suicides that occurred on the Foxconn site in relation to the over 1 million people the company employed in mainland China in 2010 gives a ratio of 1.2 per 100,000; dividing it by the 300,000 employees in Shenzhen gives a ratio of 4 per 100,000.

33. Cheng, "Let Me Be Fair." In his defense, an article examining this relationship later concluded that "strikingly, the coverage of the Foxconn suicides in the Beijing-based newspapers did have a significant influence on future occurrences"; see Qijin Cheng, Feng Chen, and Paul SF Yip, "The Foxconn Suicides and Their Media Prominence: Is the Werther Effect Applicable in China?," *BMC Public Health* 11 (2011): 1–11.

34. You Wang, "Employee Reveals Foxconn Sweatshop Shady Practices: Machines Penalize You for Standing for 12 Hours," *China Business News*, June 15, 2006, http://www.coolloud.org.tw/node/52284 (Chinese source: 员工揭富士康血汗工厂黑幕: 机器罚你站12小时).

35. Cheng, "Let Me Be Fair"; the detailed contents remained unpublished; see "Terry Gou: Chinese Central Government Sent a Delegation to Investigate the Longhua Factory in Shenzhen," [in Chinese] *Chinese Wall Street Journal*, June 8, 2010, https://web.archive.org/web/20100614063230/http://chinese.wsj.com/gb/20100608/bch121409.asp (Chinese source: 郭台铭: 中央政府曾派团调查深圳龙华工厂).

36. Cheng, "Let Me Be Fair"; Foxconn Research Group, *Foxconn Research Report*.

37. Zhiyi Liu, "Youth and Destiny with Machines: Undercover at Foxconn for 28 Days Journal," [in Chinese] *Southern Weekend*, May 12, 2010, https://www.infzm.com/contents/44881?source=131 (Chinese source: 与机器相伴的青春和命运: 潜伏富士康28天手记).

38. Fang, "Terry Gou's Purgatory."

39. Ma Xiaoyuan, Huang Xiao, and Shuang Rui, "Foxconn Caught in Another Overtime Scandal: Employees Say They Feel Like Machines, Walking Corpses," Xinhua News

Agency, February 5, 2015, https://finance.sina.cn/chanjing/gsxw/2015-02-05/detail-icczm vun5849453.d.html (Chinese source: 富士康再陷加班门: 员工说像是个机器行尸走肉).

40. Frederick Winslow Taylor (1856–1915) was an American mechanical engineer and the founding father of scientific management.

41. Foxconn Research Group, *Foxconn Research Report*.

42. Foxconn Research Group, *Foxconn Research Report*.

43. Foxconn Research Group, *Foxconn Research Report*.

44. Foxconn Research Group, *Foxconn Research Report*; George Orwell, *Nineteen Eighty-Four* (Penguin, 2000).

45. Foxconn Research Group, *Foxconn Research Report*.

46. Xiao Lu, "Silence Mode Reveals Foxconn's Management Conflicts: Mandatory Quality Inspection Led to Grievances," [in Chinese] *China Times*, May 4, 2013, https://tech.sina.com.cn/it/2013-05-04/09488304636.shtml (Chinese source: 静音模式曝富士康管理冲突: 强制质检引怨气).

47. Wagner, "Life Inside Foxconn."

48. Foxconn Research Group, *Foxconn, Have You Mended Your Ways?*

49. Foxconn Research Group, *Foxconn, Have You Mended Your Ways?*

50. Foxconn Research Group, *Foxconn, Have You Mended Your Ways?*

51. Foxconn Research Group, *Foxconn, Have You Mended Your Ways?*

52. Foxconn Research Group, *Foxconn, Have You Mended Your Ways?*

53. Zhiyi Liu, "The Mystery of Foxconn's Eight Consecutive Suicide Jumps," [in Chinese] *Southern Weekend*, May 13, 2010, https://finance.sina.cn/sa/2010-05-13/detail-ikftpnny0339167.d.html (Chinese source: 富士康八连跳自杀之谜).

54. Liu, "Undercover at Foxconn."

55. Foxconn Research Group, *Foxconn Research Report*.

56. Foxconn Research Group, *Foxconn Research Report*.

57. Jenny Chan, Mark Selden, and Ngai Pun, *Dying for an iPhone: Apple, Foxconn, and the Lives of China's Workers* (Haymarket Books, 2020), 8.

58. Liu, "Foxconn's Suicide Jumps."

59. Fang, "Terry Gou's Purgatory."

60. Fang, "Terry Gou's Purgatory"; Liu, "Foxconn's Suicide Jumps."

61. Foxconn Research Group, *Foxconn Research Report*.

62. Hannah Arendt, *Eichmann in Jerusalem: A Report on the Banality of Evil* (Viking Press, 1963).

63. Émile Durkheim, *Le Suicide: Étude de Sociologie* (Félix Alcan, 1897).

64. Chan, "Suicide Survivor."

65. CCTV, "Old News: Ten Consecutive Jumps Are Unbearable Weight, Foxconn Responds to Questions," [in Chinese] *CCTV News*, January 13, 2011, https://tv.cctv.com/2011/01/13/VIDEFMVsqOFfSOV9BbeOwony110111.shtml (Chinese source: 十连跳不堪之重 富士康回应质疑).

66. Liu, "Foxconn's Suicide Jumps."

67. Liu, "Foxconn's Suicide Jumps"; Foxconn Research Group, *Foxconn, Have You Mended Your Ways?*

68. Program on Negotiation staff, "When Armed with Power in Negotiation, Use It Wisely," *Business Negotiations* (blog), Harvard Law School, June 20, 2023, https://www.pon.harvard.edu/daily/business-negotiations/when-armed-with-negotiating-power-use-it-wisely-nb/.

69. Foxconn Research Group, *Foxconn, Have You Mended Your Ways?*

70. Foxconn Research Group, *Foxconn Research Report.*
71. Fang, "Terry Gou's Purgatory."
72. Foxconn Research Group, *Foxconn, Have You Mended Your Ways?*
73. Foxconn Research Group, *Foxconn, Have You Mended Your Ways?*
74. Xu Lizhi, "I Just Fall Asleep on My Feet."
75. Ai Lun, "Apple and Foxconn: A Distorted Profit Chain," [in Chinese] *China Youth Online*, February 2, 2012, https://zqb.cyol.com/html/2012-02/02/nw.D110000zgqnb_2012 0202_3-12.htm (Chinese source: 苹果与富士康: 畸形的利益链).
76. Leander Kahney, *Tim Cook: The Genius Who Took Apple to the Next Level* (Portfolio, 2019).
77. Kahney, *Tim Cook.*
78. Robert Hunter Wade, "Is Globalization Reducing Poverty and Inequality?," in *Neoliberalism, Globalization, and Inequalities: Consequences for Health and Quality of Life*, ed. Vincente Navarro (Routledge, 2020): 143–176; Joseph E. Stiglitz, *Making Globalization Work* (W. W. Norton & Company, 2007), xiv.

Chapter 11: The Bright Pattern

1. Francis Fukuyama, "The End of History?," *The National Interest* 16 (1989): 3–18, 3.
2. Thomas L. Friedman, "Foreign Affairs Big Mac I," *New York Times*, December 8, 1996, https://www.nytimes.com/1996/12/08/opinion/foreign-affairs-big-mac-i.html.
3. Pippa Stevens, "Stakeholder Capitalism Has Reached a 'Tipping Point,' Says Salesforce CEO Benioff," *CNBC*, January 21, 2020, https://www.cnbc.com/2020/01/21/stakeholder-capitalism-has-reached-a-tipping-point-says-salesforce-ceo-benioff.html.
4. Briony Harris, "Angela Merkel Wants Us to Overcome Our Differences and Focus on Better Communication," World Economic Forum, January 23, 2020, https://www.weforum.org/agenda/2020/01/merkel-at-davos-2020/.
5. Staffan I. Lindberg, ed., *Democracy Report 2024: Democracy Winning and Losing at the Ballot* (V-Dem Institute, 2024), https://v-dem.net/documents/43/v-dem_dr2024_lowres.pdf.
6. Andreas Georg Scherer and Guido Palazzo, "Toward a Political Conception of Corporate Responsibility: Business and Society Seen from a Habermasian Perspective," *Academy of Management Review* 32, no. 4 (2007): 1096–1120.
7. Alison Taylor, *Higher Ground: How Business Can Do the Right Thing in a Turbulent World* (Harvard Business Press, 2024).
8. Charles Brenner, "Brief Communication: Evenly Hovering Attention," *Psychoanalytic Quarterly* 69, no. 3 (2000): 545–549, https://pubmed.ncbi.nlm.nih.gov/10955287/.
9. Taylor, *Higher Ground.*
10. Albert O. Hirschman, *Exit, Voice, and Loyalty: Responses to Decline in Firms, Organizations, and States* (Harvard University Press, 1970). Note that these three strategies essentially correspond to the reactions of animals to danger: flight, fight, and freeze.
11. Edgar H. Schein, *The Corporate Culture Survival Guide* (Jossey-Bass, 1999), 27.
12. Ethan R. Burris, "The Risks and Rewards of Speaking Up: Managerial Responses to Employee Voice," *The Academy of Management Journal* 55, no. 4 (2012): 851–875, https://doi.org/10.5465/amj.2010.0562.
13. Amy C. Edmondson, *The Fearless Organization: Creating Psychological Safety in the Workplace for Learning, Innovation, and Growth* (Wiley, 2019).
14. Megan Reitz and John Higgins, "The Problem with Saying My Door Is Always Open," *Harvard Business Review*, March 9, 2017, https://hbr.org/2017/03/the-problem-with-saying-my-door-is-always-open.

15. David M. Schweiger, William R. Sandberg, and James W. Ragan, "Group Approaches for Improving Strategic Decision Making: A Comparative Analysis of Dialectical Inquiry, Devil's Advocacy, and Consensus," *Academy of Management Journal* 29, no. 1 (1986): 51–71.

16. Frederick B. Bird and James A. Waters, "The Moral Muteness of Managers," *California Management Review* 32, no. 1 (1989): 73–88.

17. Jonathan Haidt, "The Emotional Dog and Its Rational Tail: A Social Intuitionist Approach to Moral Judgment," *Psychological Review* 108 (2001): 814–834.

18. Daryl C. Cameron et al., "Implicit Moral Evaluations: A Multinomial Modeling Approach," *Cognition* 158 (2017): 224–241; Julian De Freitas and Alon Hafri, "Moral Thin-Slicing: Forming Moral Impressions from a Brief Glance," *Journal of Experimental Social Psychology* 112 (2024): 1–18.

19. Antoine Ferrère et al., "Fostering Ethical Conduct Through Psychological Safety," *MIT Sloan Management Review* 63, no. 4 (2022): 39–43.

20. David Welsh et al., "Reconceptualizing Goal Setting's Dark Side: The Ethical Consequences of Learning Versus Outcome Goals," *Organizational Behavior and Human Decision Processes* 150 (2019): 14–27, 17.

21. Lisa D. Ordonez et al., "Goals Gone Wild: The Systematic Side Effects of Overprescribing Goal Setting," *Academy of Management Perspectives* 23 (2009): 6–16.

22. Dina Denham Smith, "When Your Boss Gives You a Totally Unrealistic Goal," *Harvard Business Review*, January 9, 2024, https://hbr.org/2024/01/when-your-boss-gives-you-a-totally-unrealistic-goal.

23. Sim B. Sitkin et al., "The Paradox of Stretch Goals: Organizations in Pursuit of the Seemingly Impossible," *Academy of Management Review* 36, no. 3 (2011): 544–566.

24. Siri Schubert and Christian T. Miller, "At Siemens, Bribery Was Just a Line Item," *New York Times*, December 20, 2008, https://www.nytimes.com/2008/12/21/business/worldbusiness/21siemens.html.

25. "Für augenblicklichen Gewinn verkaufe ich die Zukunft nicht."

26. Peter Vanham and Nicholas Gordon, "This Bank Doesn't Believe in Bonuses: 'Human Nature Is What Drives People,'" *Fortune*, December 19, 2023, https://fortune.com/europe/2023/12/19/handelsbanken-no-bonus-uk-ceo-mikael-sorensen-europe-economy/.

27. Kevin R. Murphy, "Performance Evaluation Will Not Die, but It Should," *Human Resource Management Journal* (2019): 1–19, https://doi.org/10.1111/1748-8583.12259.

28. Jan K. Woike and Sebastian Hafenbrädl, "Rivals Without a Cause? Relative Performance Feedback Creates Destructive Competition Despite Aligned Incentives," *Journal of Behavioral Decision Making* 33, no. 4 (2020): 523–537.

29. Herman Aguinis and Kyle J. Bradley, "The Secret Sauce for Organizational Success: Managing and Producing Star Performers," *Organizational Dynamics* 44, no. 3 (2015): 161–168.

30. Jane B. Gregory and Paul E. Levy, "It's Not Me, It's You: A Multilevel Examination of Variables That Impact Employee Coaching Relationships," *Consulting Psychology Journal: Practice and Research* 63 (2011): 67–88, https://doi.org/10.1037/a0024152.

31. Murphy, "Performance Evaluation."

32. Kelly Cheng, "Zappos: A Case Study in Work Environment Redesign," *Deloitte Insights*, June 13, 2013, https://www2.deloitte.com/us/en/insights/topics/talent/zappos.html; Lorelei Trisca, "Performance Reviews and Feedback at Zappos: Pursuing Growth

and Learning," accessed November 14, 2024, https://www.zavvy.io/hr-examples/employee-performance-reviews-at-zappos.

33. Carmine Gallo, "America's Happiest Employee," *Forbes*, December 26, 2012, https://www.forbes.com/sites/carminegallo/2012/12/26/americas-happiest-employee/.

34. Jodi Kantor and David Streitfeld, "Inside Amazon: Wrestling Big Ideas in a Bruising Workplace," *New York Times*, August 15, 2015, http://www.nytimes.com/2015/08/16/technology/inside-amazon-wrestling-big-ideas-in-a-bruising-workplace.html.

35. Kirsten Grind, "Amazon Changes at Zappos Slowly Dismantle Tony Hsieh's Legacy," *Wall Street Journal*, February 11, 2023, https://www.wsj.com/articles/amazon-changes-at-zappos-slowly-dismantle-tony-hsiehs-legacy-5d393647.

36. Joseph L. Badaracco, *Defining Moments: When Managers Must Choose Between Right and Right* (Harvard Business School Press, 1997).

37. The four steps are from an internal document in possession of the authors; the rest of the framework is in Siemens, *Business Conduct Guidelines: Transform the Everyday*, accessed November 5, 2024, https://assets.new.siemens.com/siemens/assets/api/uuid:5c242542-e991-4b97-af63-090ad509be74/sag-bcg-en.pdf.

38. Takeda, *Living Our Values Every Day: Global Code of Conduct*, accessed November 14, 2024, https://assets-dam.takeda.com/raw/upload/v1675193384/legacy-dotcom/siteassets/system/who-we-are/corporate-governance/compliance/coc_digital-booklet_external.pdf.

39. Jane Croft, "Citibank Analyst Dismissed for Lying About Meals Expenses Claim Under €100 Limit," *Financial Times*, October 16, 2023, https://www.ft.com/content/a7934111-fd57-4bbd-bd39-6c295236175d.

40. Guillermina Jasso, Kjell Y. Törnblom, and Clara Sabbagh, "Distributive Justice," in *Handbook of Social Justice Theory and Research*, ed. Clara Sabbagh and Manfred Schmitt (Springer, 2016), https://doi.org/10.1007/978-1-4939-3216-0_1.

41. Brian Harward, Alison Taylor, and Shayne Kavanagh, *What's Fair? Exploring the Behavioral Science of Justice and Fairness, Part 1: The Three Forms of Fairness* (Government Finance Officers Association, 2021), https://www.gfoa.org/materials/whats-fair-1.

42. Morton Deutsch, "Equity, Equality, and Need: What Determines Which Value Will Be Used as the Basis of Distributive Justice?," *Journal of Social Issues* 31, no. 3 (1975): 137–149, https://spssi.onlinelibrary.wiley.com/doi/abs/10.1111/j.1540-4560.1975.tb01000.x.

43. Edith Barrett-Howard and Tom R. Tyler, "Procedural Justice as a Criterion in Allocation Decisions," *Journal of Personality and Social Psychology* 50, no. 2 (1986): 296–304; John Thibaut and Laurens Walker, "A Theory of Procedure," *California Law Review* 66 (1978): 541–546; Jerald Greenberg, "Determinants of Perceived Fairness of Performance Evaluations," *Journal of Applied Psychology* 71, no. 2 (1986): 340–342.

44. Gerald S. Leventhal, "What Should Be Done with Equity Theory?" in *Social Exchange*, ed. Kenneth J. Gergen, Martin S. Greenberg, and Richard H. Willis (Springer, 1980), https://doi.org/10.1007/978-1-4613-3087-5_2.

45. Gerold Mikula, Birgit Petri, and Norbert Tanzer, "What People Regard as Unjust: Types and Structures of Everyday Experiences of Injustice," *European Journal of Social Psychology* 20, no. 2 (1990): 133–149, 133.

46. Günter Gaus, "Hannah Arendt on the Year 1933: 'The Problem Was What Our Friends Were Doing!,'" October 28, 1964, 4:21, video interview in German posted on YouTube, https://www.youtube.com/watch?v=CdCVs376q0U.

47. Nicholas A. Christakis, *Blueprint: The Evolutionary Origin of a Good Society* (Little, Brown Spark, 2019); Rutger Bregman, *Humankind: A Hopeful History* (Bloomsbury, 2019).

48. Ernst Fehr and Urs Fischbacher, "The Nature of Human Altruism," *Nature* 425, no. 6960 (2019): 785–791; Simon Gächter and Ernst Fehr, "Collective Action as a Social Exchange," *Journal of Economic Behavior & Organization* 39, no. 4 (1999): 341–369; Martin A. Nowak and Karl Sigmund, "Tit for Tat in Heterogeneous Populations," *Nature* 355, no. 6357 (1992): 250–253.

49. Steven J. Gilbert, "Another Look at the Milgram Obedience Studies: The Role of the Gradated Series of Shocks," *Personality and Social Psychology Bulletin* 7, no. 4 (1981): 690–695.

50. Dennis Gioia, "Pinto Fires and Personal Ethics: A Script of Missed Opportunities," *Journal of Business Ethics* 11, no. 5/6 (1992): 379–389.

51. Gabriela N. Mujal et al., "A Systematic Review of Bystander Interventions for the Prevention of Sexual Violence," *Trauma, Violence & Abuse* 22, no. 2 (2021): 381–396.

52. Neil Garrett et al., "The Brain Adapts to Dishonesty," *Nature Neuroscience* 19, no. 12 (2016): 1727–1732.

53. Gilbert, "Milgram Obedience Studies."

54. Clayton Christensen, "How Will You Measure Your Life?" *Harvard Business School Working Knowledge*, May 9, 2012, https://hbswk.hbs.edu/item/clayton-christensens-how-will-you-measure-your-life.

55. Oliver J. Sheldon and Ayelet Fishbach, "Anticipating and Resisting the Temptation to Behave Unethically," *Personality and Social Psychology Bulletin* 41, no. 7 (2015): 962–975.

56. Edward E. Evans-Pritchard, *Witchcraft, Oracles, and Magic Among the Azande* (Clarendon Press, 1937; repr. 1967), 244.

Chapter 12: After the Fall

1. Ian Duncan and Lori Aratani, "Boeing's Manufacturing Woes Long Preceded Door-Panel Blowout," *Washington Post*, August 11, 2024, https://www.washingtonpost.com/transportation/2024/08/11/boeing-ntsb-faa-doorplug/; Luke Bodell, "Boeing's Broken Safety Culture: 5 Key Insights From Senate 787 Dreamliner & B777 Whistleblower Hearing," *Simple Flying*, April 17, 2024, https://simpleflying.com/boeing-whistleblower-senate-hearing-testimony/.

2. Emily Flitter, "Elizabeth Warren Asks the Fed to Break Up Wells Fargo," *New York Times*, September 14, 2021, https://www.nytimes.com/2021/09/14/business/wells-fargo-elizabeth-warren.html.

3. Boeing, "Boeing Statement on the Senate Commerce Committee Report on Aviation Safety Oversight," news release, December 18, 2020, https://boeing.mediaroom.com/news-releases-statements?item=130790.

4. Olivier Boiral et al., "Through the Smokescreen of the Dieselgate Disclosure: Neutralizing the Impacts of a Major Sustainability Scandal," *Organization & Environment* 35, no. 2 (2022): 184.

5. William Faulkner, *Requiem for a Nun* (Chatto & Windus, 1919), 85, available from the Internet Archive at https://archive.org/details/in.ernet.dli.2015.149792/page/n85/mode/2up.

6. Syracuse University, "What Is Moral Injury?," Moral Injury Project, accessed June 6, 2024, https://moralinjuryproject.syr.edu/about-moral-injury/.

7. Brett T. Litz et al., "Moral Injury and Moral Repair in War Veterans: A Preliminary Model and Intervention Strategy," *Clinical Psychology Review* 29 (2009): 695–706, 705.

8. Angus Liu, "With New Settlement, Novartis Has Shelled Out $1.3B for Kickbacks, Bribery, and Price Fixing This Year," *Fierce Pharma*, July 2, 2020, https://www.fiercepharma.com/pharma/novartis-shells-out-729m-to-settle-dragged-out-u-s-kickback-charges-limits-speaker-programs.

9. Klaus Moosmayer, "Ethics and Integrated Assurance: The Challenge of Building Trust," *Risk and Compliance Magazine*, April/June 2024, https://riskandcompliancemagazine.com/ethics-and-integrated-assurance-the-challenge-of-building-trust.

10. Antoine Ferrère, "Reimagining Ethics, Risks & Compliance with Behavioral Science at Novartis," *Starling Insights*, May 15, 2022, https://insights.starlingtrust.com/content/compendium/reimagining-ethics-risks-and-compliance-with-behavioral-science-at-novartis.

11. Ferrère, "Reimagining Ethics."

12. Guido Palazzo and Ulrich Hoffrage, "Unethical Decision Making in Organizations," Coursera course, https://www.coursera.org/learn/unethical-decision-making.

Epilogue

1. Sharon Lerner, "How 3M Discovered, Then Concealed, the Dangers of Forever Chemicals: The Company Found Its Own Toxic Compounds in Human Blood—and Kept Selling Them," *New Yorker*, May 20, 2024, https://www.newyorker.com/magazine/2024/05/27/3m-forever-chemicals-pfas-pfos-toxic.

2. Jean-Philippe de Saint Martin et al., *Mission on the Management of Accommodation Establishments for Dependent Elderly People (EHPAD) of the Orpea Group*, [in French] March 2022, report from the General Inspectorate of Finance and the General Inspectorate of Social Affairs, https://solidarites.gouv.fr/ehpad-du-groupe-orpea-publication-du-rapport-igas-igf.

3. Peter Eavis, Mark Walker, and Niraj Chokshi, "Norfolk Southern's Push for Profits Compromised Safety, Workers Say," *New York Times*, April 2, 2023, https://www.nytimes.com/2023/04/02/business/norfolk-southern-railroad-safety.html.

4. Nick Wallis, *The Great Post Office Scandal: The Fight to Expose a Multimillion Pound IT Disaster Which Put Innocent People in Jail* (Goodmi, 2021).

5. For Tesla, there's even a Wikipedia entry just on their lawsuits: Wikipedia, s.v. "List of Lawsuits Involving Tesla, Inc.," https://en.m.wikipedia.org/wiki/List_of_lawsuits_involving_Tesla,_Inc. As we access it, on May 29, 2024, Tesla had been involved in 1,750 lawsuits worldwide.

6. Philip Zimbardo, *The Lucifer Effect: How Good People Turn Evil* (Random House, 2007), 230–231.

INDEX

3M, 166, 265
60 Minutes (TV show), 27
737 MAX, 161–163, 169–179, 250

accountability, 41, 255–259, 267–268.
 See also transparency
ACT plan, 148–153
Addis Ababa Bole International
 Airport, 162
"after the fall," 2–3, 6, 83–84, 120–126,
 249–263
Airbus, 162–163
Al Jazeera (news website), 169
Alaska Airlines, 179, 250
Alighieri, Dante, 49–50, 83–84
Amazon, 115–116, 236, 266
ambiguous rules
 antidote to, 220, 236–239
 examples of, 69–72, 90–91, 111, 120,
  138, 151, 168–169, 191, 194, 197–198,
  215–216
 explanation of, 5, 52, 69–72
 moral clarity and, 220, 236–239

Andersen, Hans Christian, 35, 39,
 47–49, 102
angle of attack (AOA) sensor, 172–173, 177
AOA Disagree Alert, 173
Apple, 99, 200, 214–215
Arendt, Hannah, 17–18, 32, 211, 243, 268
Armstrong, Lance, 72–73
Arriola, Ana, 98–99
Arthur Andersen, 2, 10
Asch, Solomon, 77–78
AtkinsRéalis, 229
Audi, 182–184, 186
Austin, John L., 61

Bacon, Francis, 23
bad apples
 bad apple theory, 261, 267
 examples of, 3–21, 128–129, 136–142,
  197–198, 249–252, 261–263, 265–269
 explanation of, 3–14, 48, 102, 217
Bado, Bill, 137
Balwani, Ramesh "Sunny," 93–94, 97–102
banality of evil, 18, 32

INDEX

Bandura, Albert, 30, 65
bank scandals, 1–4, 6, 49, 60, 62, 125–142, 224, 250
Barberot, Olivier, 146, 158–159
Barnwell, Del, 89
Barron's (magazine), 125
Bateson, Gregory, 70
Beckman Coulter, 90
behavioral change, 235, 262
behavioral principles, 238–239
behavioral sciences, 257–263, 268
Benioff, Marc, 221
Berlin Wall, 214, 220
Berry, Freya, 89
Beth Israel Medical Center, 27
biodiversity, 81, 221, 224
biotech industry, 13, 86, 89
Bird, Frederick, 228
blindness
  blind spots, 8, 23
  ethical blindness, 5, 7–33, 35, 40, 83, 102–103, 219, 224–225, 239, 245–246, 249, 266–267
  seeing own blindness, 8, 23
  theory-induced blindness, 54
blood tests, 85–103, 237
Bloomberg (news website), 121, 134, 172
Blueprint (Christakis), 243
BMW, 183
Boeing
  analysis of, 6, 49, 161–180, 224, 250–252
  certification processes, 174–176, 178
  crashes and, 161–163, 169–179, 250
  downfall of, 2, 250–251
  malfunctions and, 161–180, 250–252
  merger of, 162–165
  pilots and, 161–180, 250
  pressure and, 162–167, 180
  training programs at, 174, 177–178
Boiral, Olivier, 252
Bonanni, Fabrizio, 86
Bosch, 190

Bouygues, 148
Bower, Joseph, 54–55
Bregman, Rutger, 243
bright pattern
  as antidote to the dark pattern, 84, 219–248, 267
  building blocks of, 219–248
  constructive incentives, 220, 234–236
  courageous upstanders, 220, 242–245
  explanation of, 219–248
  holistic responsibility, 219–224
  integrity goals, 220, 231–233
  moral clarity, 220, 236–239
  moral conversations, 220, 228–230
  organizational fairness, 220, 240–242
  speak-up culture, 220, 224–227
  virtuous circle, 220, 245–248
Brock, Heather, 137
Browning, Christopher, 18, 76
building blocks, of the bright pattern, 84, 219–248, 267. *See also* bright pattern
building blocks, of the dark pattern
  ambiguous rules, 5, 52, 69–72, 90–91, 111, 120, 138, 151, 168–169, 191, 194, 197–198, 215–216
  antidotes to, 219–248
  corrupting goals, 5, 52, 63–66, 94, 113, 123, 131, 147, 156, 188–189, 208–209, 220, 231–233
  dangerous groups, 5, 52, 75–79, 91–93, 113, 120, 138, 156, 174, 176, 193, 211, 220, 242–245
  destructive incentives, 5, 52, 66–69, 95, 117, 123, 131, 152, 164, 167, 170, 178–179, 187, 189, 212, 220, 234–236
  explanation of, 5–7, 51–84
  manipulative language, 5, 52, 60–63, 96, 109–112, 114, 132, 149, 153, 164–167, 175, 187, 208, 245
  perceived unfairness, 5, 52, 72–75, 91, 112, 134, 156–157, 170–171, 192–196, 213–214, 220, 240–242

INDEX

rigid ideology, 5, 52–56, 87–88, 107–108, 128, 147, 163, 166, 176, 206, 216, 219–224, 269
slippery slope, 5, 8, 21–22, 52–53, 79–83, 100–102, 114–115, 139–140, 157, 169, 187, 190, 209, 220, 245–249
toxic leadership, 5, 52, 56–59, 94, 99, 117, 120, 123, 130–131, 138–139, 151, 168, 174, 187, 198, 208, 220, 224–227, 257, 267
see also dark pattern
Burris, Ethan, 225
Business Insider (news website), 88, 122
bystander effect, 78–79, 138, 156, 174, 243, 245

Cadillac, 195
California Air Resources Board (CARB), 181–184, 194, 197
Camp, Garrett, 105
capitalism, 14, 21, 68, 87–91, 221–222
Carreyrou, John, 100
CBS, 27
Centers for Disease Control and Prevention, 86
Centers for Medicare & Medicaid Services (CMS), 90, 101
certification, 90, 174–178
CFO (magazine), 4
channelized attention, 65–66
cheating, 1, 4, 64–75, 88–103, 128, 181–198, 237, 260
Cheng, Terry (Tianzong), 203
Cheung, Erika, 97–100
Chicago Tribune (newspaper), 166
Christakis, Nicholas, 243–244
Christensen, Clayton, 55, 247
Ciroux, Christel, 143–144
Citibank, 240
Clean Air Act, 184
CloudKitchens, 121–122
CNBC, 100

code of conduct, 137, 250–253
cognitive dissonance, 25, 30, 165, 230, 253
collaboration, 26, 92, 187, 234–235, 244–245
commitment, escalation of, 45–48, 82–83, 248
communist regimes, 31, 107
compared individual performance, 151–152, 158. *See also* performance
comparisons, advantageous, 31
competition
  aggressive competition, 15, 66–69, 113, 120, 141, 145–146, 148–149, 164, 180, 186, 232
  creative destruction of, 54–55
  fierce competition, 54, 120, 148–149, 164, 180, 186, 232
  internal competition, 69, 141, 151–152, 164, 180, 186
  international competition, 15, 146, 194, 232
  pressure of, 52, 54, 131, 215, 232
  unhealthy competition, 52, 54–55, 66–68
compliance
  developing system of, 222, 226–233, 254–258
  effective compliance, 254–258
  ethics and, 222–233, 239, 258–263
  legal compliance, 72, 183–184, 238
  light tower of, 190–191
  risk management and, 222–225, 230–233, 258–263
  rule violations and, 4, 231, 237
  systemic compliance problems, 250–263
Complicit (film), 216
Condit, Philip M., 164
confabulation, 24, 33
conflict resolution, 24, 30–33, 241
consequences
  anticipating, 246–247
  minimizing, 30–31, 58, 62–65, 103, 233, 236
  moral consequences, 30
  negative consequences, 151, 156

INDEX

construction of reality, 22–31, 33, 41–42, 49, 61, 79, 193. *See also* reality-distortion field, 99
constructive incentives, 220, 234–236
context
  building blocks of, 5
  inside perspectives and, 43–49
  outside perspectives and, 43–49
  pathological contexts, 43, 47–48
  power of, 5–8, 35–50
  role of, 5, 18–22
  strength of, 19–20
  tunnel vision and, 42–44, 52, 170
contradictory injunctions, 70–72
Cook, Tim, 216
cooperation, 61–63, 68–69, 242–244
corporate failure, 7, 216
corporate hell, 47–51, 62–63, 83–84, 114, 147–157
corporate psychopaths, 57–58
corrupting goals
  antidote to, 220, 231–233
  examples of, 63–66, 94, 113, 123, 131, 147, 156, 188–189, 208–209
  explanation of, 5, 52, 63–66
  integrity goals and, 220, 231–233
  see also goals
courageous upstanders, 220, 242–245
Courrier, Andrée, 152
Coursera: Unethical Decision Making in Organizations, 262
Cramer, Jim, 100
creative destruction, 13, 54
cross-selling, 1, 126–128, 141
cultish language, 62–63

dangerous groups
  antidote to, 220, 242–245
  courageous upstanders and, 220, 242–245
  examples of, 75–79, 91–93, 113, 120, 138, 156, 174, 176, 193, 211

explanation of, 5, 52, 75–79
Dante, 49–50, 83–84
dark pattern
  ambiguous rules, 5, 52, 69–72, 90–91, 111, 120, 138, 151, 168–169, 191, 194, 197–198, 215–216
  antidotes for, 219–248
  bright pattern and, 84, 219–248, 267
  building blocks of, 5–7, 51–84
  corporate hell and, 47–51, 62–63, 83–84, 114, 147–157
  corrupting goals, 5, 52, 63–66, 94, 113, 123, 131, 147, 156, 188–189, 208–209, 220, 231–233
  dangerous groups, 5, 52, 75–79, 91–93, 113, 120, 138, 156, 174, 176, 193, 211, 220, 242–245
  destructive incentives, 5, 52, 66–69, 95, 117, 123, 131, 152, 164, 167, 170, 178–179, 187, 189, 212, 220, 234–236
  explanation of, 5, 49, 51–84
  manipulative language, 5, 52, 60–63, 96, 109–112, 114, 132, 149, 153, 164–167, 175, 187, 208, 245
  perceived unfairness, 5, 52, 72–75, 91, 112, 134, 156–157, 170–171, 192–196, 213–214, 220, 240–242
  power of, 7–8
  rigid ideology, 5, 52–56, 87–88, 107–108, 128, 147, 163, 166, 176, 206, 216, 219–224, 269
  slippery slope, 5, 8, 21–22, 52–53, 79–83, 100–102, 114–115, 139–140, 157, 169, 187, 190, 209, 220, 245–249
  toxic leadership, 5, 52, 56–59, 94, 99, 117, 120, 123, 130–131, 138–139, 151, 168, 174, 187, 198, 208, 220, 224–227, 257, 267
  warning signs of, 245–246, 249, 266–267
dark triad of personality, 57–59, 99–100
Darwinism, 68, 117, 122, 236, 267
data, fake, 88–103, 183–197

INDEX

data science, 260–266
decision-makers
  ethical dimensions of, 5, 22–26, 235–239, 260–262
  individual decision-makers, 14–32, 35
  power of, 35–50
  role of, 5, 22–26, 35–50
decision-making
  behavioral principles for, 238–239
  defensive decision-making, 40–41
  ethical blindness and, 5, 7, 16
  ethical decision-making, 5, 22–26, 235–239, 260–262
  ethical principles for, 235, 238–239
  fear and, 40–43, 248
  frames and, 22–24, 29–30, 33, 42
  process of, 237–239
  steps for, 238–239
  unethical decision-making, 6–7, 20–24, 33, 62, 82–83, 249–250, 260–262
  values and, 42, 235, 238–239
dehumanization, 32, 132, 207–217
deliberate ignorance, 71–72
DeLorenzo, Matt, 190
Deparis, Michel, 157–158
Der Spiegel (magazine), 185
deregulation, 13–14, 55, 72, 107, 122, 175–176
destructive incentives
  antidote to, 220, 234–236
  constructive incentives and, 220, 234–236
  examples of, 66–69, 95, 117, 123, 131, 152, 164, 167, 170, 178–179, 187, 189, 212
  explanation of, 5, 52, 66–69
Deutsche Umwelthilfe, 194
The Devil's Advocate (film), 246–247
Dieselgate, 182, 185–193, 198, 252, 258.
  See also Volkswagen
Dirty Money (documentary), 190
discrimination, 62, 79, 118

disengagement
  advantageous comparisons, 31
  diffusion of responsibility, 32
  displacement of responsibility, 31–32
  effects of, 30–33, 122–123, 261
  euphemistic labeling, 31
  examples of, 30–32
  mechanisms of, 30–32
  minimizing consequences, 30–31
  moral disengagement, 30–33, 122–123, 261
  moral justification, 31–32, 122
  victim dehumanization, 32
disruption, 55–56, 63, 66, 86–88, 90–92, 95, 102, 108, 111, 114
distortion
  of action, 78–79
  of judgment, 78
  of reality, 5, 25–33, 35, 79, 99, 226, 249, 268
  reality-distortion field, 99
The Divine Comedy (Dante), 49–50
dot-com bubble, 13, 145
double bind, 70–72, 138, 142, 168–169, 180, 261
Doublet, Daniel, 153
Dow Jones Sustainability Index, 191
Durkheim, Émile, 211

École de management France, 147–148
ecological crisis, 221–223
The Economist (newspaper), 3, 194
Edison, Thomas, 88
Edison blood analyzer, 88–98
Eichmann, Adolf, 17–19, 32, 48
"Eight Is Great" strategy, 126–129, 131–132
Electronics TakeBack Coalition, 216
emissions tests, 181–198
"The Emperor's New Clothes" (Andersen), 35–49, 187
Enlightenment, 8, 25

INDEX

Enron
 accounting and, 14, 62
 analysis of, 10–14, 17, 56, 62, 67–68, 83, 116
 downfall of, 2–3, 10
 fraud and, 10–14, 56, 62, 67–68
 meritocracy and, 68, 116
Environmental, Social, and Governance (ESG), 222
Environmental Protection Agency (EPA), 195
EPO drug, 72–74, 79–80
equality/equity, 241
escalation of commitment, 45–48, 53, 82–83, 248
ethical behavior, 238–239, 261–262. *See also* unethical behavior
ethical blindness
 corporate failure and, 7
 dark pattern and, 219, 224–225
 decision-making and, 35, 40, 83, 239, 266–267
 explanation of, 5, 7–33
 intentions and, 102–103
 reducing, 225
 seeing own blindness, 8, 23
 theory-induced blindness, 54
 unethical behavior and, 7, 19–22, 33
 warning signs of, 245–246, 249, 266–267
ethical code of conduct, 137, 250–253
ethical concerns, 62, 238, 248
ethical decision-making, 5, 22–26, 235–239, 260–262
ethical dilemma situations, 151–152, 223, 236–239, 246
ethical dimensions, 5, 22–26, 235–239, 260–262
ethical drift, 82
ethical fading, 21, 33, 245
ethical judgment, 82–83
ethical leadership, 262, 268–269

ethical principles, 131, 228–232, 235, 238–239, 267
ethics, risk, and compliance (ERC), 230, 258–263
ethics training, 69–72, 137–138, 223, 239, 257–258, 262–263
Ethiopian Airlines, 162, 179
euphemistic language, 31, 62, 114, 142, 153, 165
European Commission, 144–145, 193
European Federation for Transport and Environment, 193
evaluation apprehension, 78
Evans-Pritchard, Edward E., 248
evil
 banality of, 18, 32
 examples of, 3, 11–12, 18–22, 32, 48, 52–53
 organizational evil, 21–22
Ewbank, Curtis, 172–173
Excellence Award for CFOs, 4

Facebook, 55, 266
Faculty of Business and Economics, 6
failure
 corporate failure, 7, 216
 fear of, 41, 64, 156
 human failure, 162
 moral failure, 2, 5–7, 17, 219, 228
 personal failure, 64, 131, 155, 253–254
 professional failure, 155
Fair Labor Association, 216
fairness
 cheating and, 181–198
 distributive fairness, 241
 interactional fairness, 241–242
 organizational fairness, 220, 240–242
 procedural fairness, 241–242
 restoring, 73–75, 220, 240–242, 261–262
 see also perceived unfairness
fairy tales, 35–49, 89, 102, 187
fake it till you make it, 88–89, 103, 190

INDEX

fake accounts, 114–115, 128–135, 139–140
fake data, 88–103, 183–197
Fargo, William, 125
Fastow, Andrew, 10, 19
Faulkner, William, 252
FBI, 197
fear
   creation of, 41
   culture of, 45, 59–60, 131, 151, 186–187, 247, 256–258, 267–268
   decision-making and, 40–43, 248
   of being judged, 78
   of failure, 41, 64, 156
   or retaliation, 225
   state of, 41, 49, 103
Federal Aviation Administration (FAA), 174–176, 179
Federal Reserve, 54
Ferrère, Antoine, 260
Festinger, Leon, 25, 30
financial crisis, 1–2, 21, 60, 125–126, 139, 234
Financial Times (newspaper), 125
Foege, William, 86
Food and Drug Administration (FDA), 27–28, 90, 95, 101
Forbes (magazine), 169, 235
Ford, 10–12, 14–17, 22, 195, 244
Ford Pinto, 10–12, 14–17, 244
Fortune (magazine), 13, 86, 90, 127, 200
The Fountainhead (Rand), 107
Fowler, Susan, 118–119, 121
Foxconn
   analysis of, 49, 199–218
   global supply chains and, 214–217
   machines and, 205–218
   suicides at, 200, 202–205, 210, 214, 217
frames, 22–24, 29–30, 33, 42. *See also* reality
France Management School, 147–148
France Télécom (FT)
   analysis of, 49, 143–160, 224, 243

corporate hell and, 147–157
downfall of, 145–160
pressure and, 144–155, 159–160
suicides at, 143–144, 150, 152–160
Frankenstein (Shelley), 41
fraud
   AtkinsRéalis and, 229
   at Enron, 10–14, 56, 62, 67–68
   at Theranos, 89, 100–103
   at Uber, 115–121
   at Volkswagen, 184–198
   at Wells Fargo, 3–4, 125–142, 159
Free, 148
Freud, Sigmund, 223
Friedman, Milton, 14, 53–54, 128, 221–222
Friedman, Thomas, 221
Frist, Bill, 86
Frontiers (magazine), 176
Fukuyama, Francis, 220–221
Fuld, Richard, 60
fundamental attribution error, 9

Gallup Great Workplace Award, 126
game theory, 244
Gaussian distribution curve, 67, 167, 234–235
General Electric (GE), 63–68, 163–164
General Motors, 195
Gibney, Alex, 190
gig economy, 105–108
Gilbert, Steven, 244
Gioia, Dennis, 14–16, 19, 22, 48, 244
Glassdoor, 61–62
global markets, 147, 165, 188–194, 200–202, 214–233
goals
   corrupting goals, 5, 52, 63–66, 94, 113, 123, 131, 147, 156, 188–189, 208–209, 220
   demanding goals, 63–64
   goal sickness, 65
   integrity goals, 220, 231–233, 238

315

INDEX

goals (*Cont.*)
  learning goals, 231–233
  outcome goals, 231–233, 236
  specific goals, 63–64
  stretch goals, 63, 67
  unrealistic goals, 48, 52, 63–66, 69, 90, 130–142, 147, 177, 188–189, 217–218
"Golden Arches Theory of Conflict Prevention," 221
Goldhagen, Daniel, 18
Golding, William, 242–243
Goldman Sachs, 21, 159
good people, 3–21, 26, 33, 113, 146, 249–253, 262, 267
Goodman, Eleanor, 200
Google, 121
Gou, Terry (Taiming), 200, 202–203, 213, 216
GQ (magazine), 117
Great Depression, 125
greed, 13–14, 54–55
Greenberg, Jerald, 73–74
Greenspan, Alan, 54
Gr-Eight strategy, 126–129, 131–132
Greiner, Friedrich, 105
Grenoville, Nicolas, 144
Greyball tool, 109–110, 121
groupthink, 42–43, 79, 91–93
Guardians, 24–26
Guitron, Yesenia, 137
Gulf War, 133

Hafenbrädl, Sebastian, 234
Haidt, Jonathan, 229–230
Hamilton, Tyler, 73, 79
Handelsbanken, 234–235
Hansen, Ricky, 137
harassment, 118, 154, 158, 224, 243–244
Harvard Business School, 54–55
Harvard University, 13, 56, 247
Harvino (copilot), 161, 179
Hatz, Wolfgang, 192

health care, 85–103, 106, 258
hell, corporate, 47–51, 62–63, 83–84, 114, 147–157
Hirschman, Albert O., 224
Hitler, Adolf, 11, 17–19, 56
Hitler's Willing Executioners (Goldhagen), 18
Hobbes, Thomas, 242
Hoffman, Captain, 76
Holden, Jeff, 115
Holder, Eric, 121
Hölderlin, Friedrich, 219
holistic responsibility, 219–224
Holmes, Elizabeth, 3, 60–63, 85–89, 93–102
Holocaust, 17–18, 243
Holzwarth, Gabi, 118
Homo economicus, 21
Hon Hai Precision Industry, 200
Honda, 195
HP, 200
Hsieh, Tony, 236
Huffington, Arianna, 121
human failure, 162
human resources (HR), 118–119, 121, 137–139, 148, 150, 152–153, 156, 159
human rights, 215, 222–224, 238
Humankind (Bregman), 243
hyperaggressive behavior, 120
hyperaggressive language, 114
hyper-alpha culture, 117, 119–120

"I Just Fall Asleep on My Feet" (Lizhi), 199–200
ignorance, deliberate, 71–72
ignorance, pluralistic, 78
illusion of superiority, 9
industrialization, 54, 207
inhumane actions, 32, 132, 207–217
injunctions, 70–72
innovation, 13, 53–54, 85–86, 88, 108, 145–146

INDEX

integrity goals, 220, 231–233, 238. *See also* goals
intentions
  bad intentions, 4–21, 33, 48, 102–103, 128–142, 197–198, 217, 249–252, 261–263, 265–269
  best of, 20, 81, 103
  good intentions, 4–12, 18–21, 26, 33, 45, 81, 103, 249–253, 262, 267
International Council on Clean Transportation (ICCT), 183, 195
iPads, 213–214
iPhones, 106, 114, 213–214

Janis, Irving, 79
Jobs, Steve, 3, 85, 87, 99, 102, 216
Joint Research Centre (JRC), 193–194
Jomo Kenyatta International Airport, 162
Jones, Jim, 26
judgment
  distortion of, 78
  ethical judgment, 82–83
  fear of, 78
  mistrusting, 42–47
justifications, 31–32, 57, 82, 91, 122, 253
just-noticeable difference, 81

Kahneman, Daniel, 54
Kalanick, Travis, 105–122
Kant, Immanuel, 17, 19
Karolinska Hospital, 59
Khan, Genghis, 202
Kissinger, Henry, 86
Kleinman, Carol, 82
"Know Thyself," 247–248
Kovacevich, Richard, 86, 126–127
Krebs, Rudolf, 189
Krings, Franciska, 7, 21, 271
Kroc, Ray, 53
Ku, Edmond, 88
Kyoto Protocol, 192

La Divina Commedia (Dante), 49–50
Labor Law, 213
Lacy, Sarah, 119
language
  cultish language, 62–63
  euphemistic language, 31, 62, 114, 142, 153, 165
  hyperaggressive language, 114
  manipulative language, 5, 52, 60–63, 96, 109–112, 114, 132, 149, 153, 164–167, 175, 187, 208, 220
  power of, 96, 230
  types of, 60–63
  war language, 60, 62, 160
Lasselin, Thierry, 148
Laurent, Jean-Michel, 143
Lay, Kenneth, 3
leadership, ethical, 262, 268–269
leadership training, 226–227, 233, 262–263. *See also* toxic leadership
legal compliance, 72, 183–184, 238. *See also* compliance
legal rules, 55, 224, 237, 269
Lehman Brothers, 2, 60, 62
Lion Air, 161–162, 172–174, 177–179
Litz, Brett, 253
Liu Zhiyi, 206, 209–210
Lombard, Didier, 146–148, 157–159
Lord of the Flies (Golding), 242–243
Los Angeles Times (newspaper), 128, 136
Loving Heart Safety Project, 203, 205
Lyft, 106, 112–114

Ma Xiangqian, 210
Macchiarini, Paolo, 59
Machiavellianism, 52, 57, 100
Mad Money (TV show), 100
management training, 147–151, 226–227, 233, 262–263
Manager Magazin (magazine), 108–109
Maneuvering Characteristics Augmentation System (MCAS), 172–175, 177–179

INDEX

manipulative language
  antidote to, 220, 228–230
  examples of, 60–63, 96, 109–112, 114, 132, 149, 153, 164–167, 175, 187, 208
  explanation of, 5, 52, 60–63
  moral conversations and, 220, 228–230, 245
Martin, Dorothy, 24–26
Marx, Karl, 207
mass suicide, 26. *See also* suicide
Mattis, James, 86
MAX airplanes, 161–163, 169–179, 250
McDonald, Lawrence, 60
McDonald's, 53, 129, 221
McDonnell Douglas, 163–165
McKinsey, 26, 29–30
McNerney, James, 166–171
Medicaid, 90, 101, 133
Medicare, 90, 101
medtech industry, 86, 90, 95–96, 250
memory
  autobiographical, 24
  environmental generational amnesia, 80
  politics of, 257
meritocracy, 68, 107, 116–117
Merkel, Angela, 221
Miami International Airport, 197
Milgram, Stanley, 246
Millar, David, 80
miniLab, 88, 99
MIT, 225
MOOC (massive open online course), 7, 262
Moosmayer, Klaus, 258–259
moral clarity, 220, 236–239
moral cliff, 5, 266
moral collapse, 57, 142, 251, 255–257, 263
moral conflicts, 30–33
moral consequences, 30
moral conversations, 220, 228–230, 245
moral decay, 81–82
moral decisions, 19

moral disengagement
  advantageous comparisons, 31
  blaming the victim, 32
  dehumanizing the victim, 32
  diffusion of responsibility, 32
  displacement of responsibility, 31–32
  effects of, 30–33, 122–123, 261
  euphemistic labeling, 31
  examples of, 30–33
  mechanisms of, 30–32
  minimizing consequences, 30–31
  moral justification, 31–32, 122
moral failure, 2–3, 5–7, 17, 219, 228
moral healing, 253–257
moral injury, 253
moral justification, 31–32, 122
moral reference point, 83
moral responsibility, 223
moral rules, 55–58, 237, 269
moral standards, 9, 30, 33, 81–82
moral vocabulary, 228–229
Morrison, Zack, 93
Motivator reports, 130, 132
MS Contin, 27
Muilenburg, Dennis, 162, 170–171, 176
Müller, Matthias, 191, 194

narcissism, 52, 57–58, 79, 100
National Highway Traffic Safety Administration, 16
National Socialist Party (NSDAP), 11, 56–57
Nazis, 10–12, 17–18, 32, 56
negative injunctions, 70–72
neoliberalism, 13–14, 19, 54–56, 87–88, 147, 216
Netflix, 3, 257
new economy, 12–14
New England Journal of Medicine (journal), 27
New Experiences in Telecom (NExT), 146, 150, 153, 155

INDEX

New York (magazine), 60
New York Times (newspaper), 28, 53, 121, 141, 161, 190, 197, 236
New Yorker (magazine), 17, 88
Nies, Micah, 98
Nineteen Eighty-Four (Orwell), 207
Nobel Prize, 14, 59
Nokia, 148, 200
Norfolk Southern Corporation, 265–266
Novartis, 89, 230, 258–263
Nunn, Sam, 86
Nuremberg trials, 10–12, 17, 32
nursing, 81–82

occupational safety, 216, 227–229, 238, 261–262
opioids, 27–29
The Oprah Winfrey Show (TV show), 72–73
Orange S.A., 49. *See also* France Télécom
Ordinary Men (Browning), 18
organizational fairness, 220, 240–242
Orpea, 265
Orwell, George, 207
OxyContin, 27–29

Palazzo, Bettina, 69–70
"Partnering for Success," 165
Paulhus, Delroy, 57
Pauly, Daniel, 80–81
Payden, Angie, 132
Peoples Temple Agricultural Project, 26
perceived unfairness
  antidote to, 220, 240–242
  examples of, 72–75, 91, 112, 134, 156–157, 170–171, 192–196, 213–214
  explanation of, 5, 52, 72–75
  organizational fairness and, 220, 240–242
performance
  compared individual performance, 151–152, 158

performance-enhancing drugs, 72–74, 79–80
performance-evaluation process, 120–122, 170, 233–236, 240–241
Performance Individuelle Comparée (PIC), 151–152, 158
personal failure, 64, 131, 155, 253–254
personality, dark triad of, 57–59, 99–100
Pham, Kevin, 136
pharmaceutical industry, 2, 26–30, 72–74, 79–80, 86–89, 98–101, 230–231, 237–239, 250, 258–263
Piëch, Ferdinand, 185–186
pluralistic ignorance, 78
Poetsch, Hans Dieter, 191
politics of memory, 257
pollution, 181–198
Portenoy, Russell, 27
positive injunctions, 71–72
postscandal phase, 245, 249–263
PricewaterhouseCoopers, 135, 190
prison sentences, 4, 10–11, 101, 159, 197
professional failure, 155
profit maximization, 53, 221–223, 265
psychological safety, 227–229, 261–262
psychopathy, 20, 52, 57–59, 100
Purdue Pharma, 2, 26–30

Rand, Ayn, 107
rank-and-yank systems, 67–69, 167–168, 177, 236, 242
Reagan, Ronald, 13–14, 54–55
reality
  confabulation and, 24, 33
  construction of, 22–33
  distortion of, 5, 25–33, 35, 79, 99, 226, 249, 268
  frames and, 22–24, 29–30, 33, 42
  narratives and, 24–26, 29–30
  tunnel vision and, 42–44, 52, 170
red flags, 266–267
Reeves, Keanu, 246

INDEX

Resch, Jürgen, 194
responsibility
  accountability and, 41, 255–259, 267–268
  diffusion of, 32, 65, 78, 93
  displacement of, 31–32
  holistic responsibility, 219–224
  importance of, 20, 267–268
  moral responsibility, 223
Richard, Stéphane, 159
rigid ideology
  antidote to, 219–224
  examples of, 53–56, 87–88, 107–108, 128, 147, 163, 166, 176, 206, 216
  explanation of, 5, 52–56
  holistic responsibility and, 219–224
  understanding, 269
risk management, 136, 139, 222–225, 230–233, 258–263
Rosendorff, Adam, 98–99
rule violations, 4, 20, 58, 64, 74, 157, 191, 231, 237, 240, 268–269

S&P, 14
Sackler, Richard, 28–29
safety
  analysis of, 161–179, 252
  ensuring, 174–179, 252
  occupational safety, 216, 227–229, 238, 261–262
  psychological safety, 227–229, 261–262
Samsung, 200
San Francisco Municipal Transportation Agency, 108–109
Sartre, Jean-Paul, 49
scandals
  after the fall, 2–3, 6, 83–84, 120–126, 249–263
  analysis of, 5–8, 12–18, 49–50, 265–269
  bank scandals, 1–4, 6, 49, 60, 62, 125–142, 224, 250
  cost of, 2–3

fraud and, 3–7, 10–14, 56, 62, 67–68, 89, 100–103, 115–121, 125–142, 159, 184–198, 229
  hidden dynamics of, 12–18, 23–24
  impacts of, 1–24, 51–84, 249–263, 265–269
  looking back on, 251–252
  moral healing and, 253–257
  newly occurring scandals, 265–266
  postscandal phase, 245, 249–263
  red flags about, 266–267
  small scandals, 266
  solutions for, 6–7, 24, 30–33, 219–263, 269
  subliminally occurring scandals, 266
  therapy strategies, 8, 48, 85, 119
  warning signs of, 245–246, 249, 266–267
  see also specific scandals
Schacter, Beth, 56, 108
Schein, Edgar H., 225–226
Schering-Plough, 89
Schimke, Otto-Julius, 76
Schmidt, Oliver, 197
Scholem, Gershom, 18
Schumpeter, Joseph, 13, 54
Scientific American (magazine), 27–28
scientific management, 206, 217
Securities and Exchange Commission (SEC), 101, 140
shareholder, 129, 134, 146, 169, 216–217, 236, 266
shareholder value, 53, 141, 163, 179, 219, 221–223, 269
Shelley, Mary, 41
shifting baselines, 81
Shinkansen, 63–64
Shultz, George, 86
Shultz, Tyler, 97, 99–100
Sidecar, 106
Siemens, 64, 90, 96–97, 100–101, 233, 238, 258

INDEX

Silicon Valley, 86–92, 102, 107, 112, 117, 120
Silicon Valley Toxics Coalition, 216
Sinn, Hans-Werner, 192
Skilling, Jeffrey, 10, 19, 48, 56, 67, 116
slippery slope
  antidote to, 220, 245–248
  ethical blindness and, 21–22
  examples of, 79–83, 100–102, 114–115, 139–140, 157, 169, 187, 190, 209, 246–248
  explanation of, 5, 8, 52–53, 79–83
  virtuous circle and, 220, 245–248
  warning signs of, 245–246, 249
Sloan, Timothy, 141
Smith, Adam, 14
Smith, Ted, 216
SNC-Lavalin Group, 229
"The Social Responsibility of Business Is to Increase Its Profits," 53
solidarity, 155, 211, 243–244, 256
solutions, 6–7, 24, 30–33, 219–263, 269
Sony, 200
Sorensen, Mikael, 234
Southern Weekly (newspaper), 206
Southwest Airlines, 178
speak-up culture, 78–79, 100–103, 137–139, 167–179, 186–187, 220–245, 250–262
stand-up culture, 3, 122, 220, 242–245
Stanford University, 85, 267
"Stealing in the Name of Justice," 74
Stonecipher, Harry, 163–166
Stora Enso, 227
stretch goals, 63, 67. *See also* goals
Stumpf, John, 1–4, 125–128, 132, 136, 139–140
suicide
  attempts at, 7, 144, 152–155, 157–160, 200, 202–205, 210, 214
  incidences of, 7, 26, 143–144, 150, 157–160, 200, 202–205, 210, 214, 217

mass suicide, 26
preventing, 203–206
reasons for, 7, 143–144, 150, 152, 154–155, 157–158, 202–211
suicidal thoughts, 119–120
Suicide Disclaimer Agreement, 204
Suneja, Bhavye, 161, 179
"super pumpedness," 115–119, 122
supply chains, 165, 214–216, 221
sustainability, 188, 191–193, 222, 227, 236–239, 259

Takeda, 239
taxi industry, 105–123. *See also* Uber
Taylorism, 206, 217
telecommunications, 10, 49, 143–160, 224, 243
teleopathy, 65
Temple of Apollo, 247–248
Tesla, 266
Thatcher, Margaret, 14
theory-induced blindness, 54
Theranos
  analysis of, 6, 49, 85–103, 224
  blood tests and, 85–103
  downfall of, 2–3, 100–103
  faked data at, 88–103
  fraud and, 89, 100–103
  laboratory testing, 86–102
Theranos Wellness Centers, 101
therapy strategies, 8, 48, 85, 119
Thinking, Fast and Slow (Kahneman), 54
Third Reich, 18
Tian Yu, 210
Tolstedt, Carrie, 4, 127, 129–130, 136, 139–140
Tour de France, 72–74
toxic leadership
  antidote to, 220, 224–227, 257
  examples of, 56–59, 94, 99, 117, 120, 123, 130–131, 139, 151, 168, 174, 187, 198, 208

INDEX

toxic leadership (*Cont.*)
  explanation of, 5, 52, 56–59
  speak-up culture and, 138, 168, 174, 187, 220, 224–227
  understanding, 267
Toyota, 181, 188–189
training programs
  bias training, 263
  bystander intervention training, 245
  ethics training, 69–72, 137–138, 223, 239, 257–258, 262–263
  leadership training, 226–227, 233, 262–263
  management training, 147–151, 226–227, 233, 262–263
  pilot training, 174, 177–178
  speak-up training, 226–227, 245, 256–257
transparency, 91, 105, 241, 255, 259
Trapp, Wilhelm, 76–77
Trivers, Robert, 102
tunnel vision, 42–44, 52, 170
Turbocharged Direct Injection (TDI) diesel engine, 185
Twitter/X, 266

Uber
  analysis of, 49, 105–123, 224, 243
  downfall of, 120–122
  fake accounts at, 114–115
  fraud and, 115–121
  meritocracy and, 107, 116–117
  transportation laws and, 105–115, 121–122
  TV series about, 56, 108
Uber Eats, 122
UberCab, 105–106, 108
UberX, 106
UK Post Office, 266
Ullrich, Jan, 73
unethical behavior
  behavioral change and, 235, 262
  decision-making and, 6–7, 20–24, 33, 62, 82–83, 249–250, 260–262
  drivers of, 261–262, 269
  ethical blindness and, 7, 19–26, 33
  moral decay and, 81–82
  survey on, 261–262
  types of, 19–22
  see also specific companies
unicorns, 87, 89, 102, 105–123
University of Chicago, 54
University of Lausanne, 6
University of West Virginia, 183
unrealistic goals, 48, 52, 63–66, 69, 90, 130–142, 147, 177, 188–189, 217–218. *See also* goals
upstanding conduct, 122, 220, 242–245
US Air Force, 66
USA Today (newspaper), 106

values
  decision-making and, 42, 235, 238–239
  ethical principles and, 131, 228–232, 235, 238–239
  reflecting on, 247–248
Vasquez, John, 137
verticalization of HR, 148–150, 156
victim dehumanization, 32, 132, 207–217
Vietnam War, 14, 31
Virgil, 50, 84
virtuous circle, 220, 245–248
Volkswagen
  analysis of, 6, 49, 181–198, 224, 226, 252, 258
  cheating and, 181–198
  downfall of, 2, 185–186
  emissions tests and, 181–198
  faked data at, 183–197
  fraud and, 184–198
  pollution and, 181–198
von Holst, Erich, 56–57
von Siemens, Werner, 233

INDEX

Walgreens, 89, 95–96, 101
Wall Street Journal (newspaper), 87, 100–101, 107, 236
war language, 60, 62, 160
warning signs, 245–246, 249, 266–267
Warren, Elizabeth, 1, 3, 126, 250
Waters, James, 228
Welch, Jack, 63–64, 66–67, 163–164, 166–167, 179
Wells, Henry, 125
Wells Fargo
    analysis of, 1–4, 6, 49, 125–142, 224, 250–251
    downfall of, 2, 140–142, 250–251
    fake accounts at, 128–135, 139–140
    fraud and, 3–4, 125–142, 159
    pressure and, 128–142, 159–160
    sales quotas and, 1, 125–142
Welsh, David, 232
Wenès, Louis-Pierre, 146–147, 157–159
Wharton School, 13, 56
Whistleblower (Fowler), 118
whistleblowers, 3, 267

White, Heather, 216
"Why good people do bad things" program, 262
Williams, Kevin, 57
Winfrey, Oprah, 72–73
Winterkorn, Martin, 181–188, 191, 226
Woike, Jan, 234
World Bank, 229
World Economic Forum, 221
World War II, 10, 96
WorldCom, 2

Xiao Qin, 206
Xiaomi, 200
Xu Lizhi, 200, 214

Yeats, William Butler, 268

Zappos, 235–236
Zeitgeist, 176
zero-sum meritocracy, 68, 116–117
zero-tolerance policies, 191, 232, 247
Zimbardo, Philip, 267–268
Zuckerberg, Mark, 55, 85

Guido Palazzo is a professor of business ethics at the University of Lausanne in Switzerland and a business advisor. His work has been published in leading management journals such as the *Academy of Management Review* and the *Academy of Management Journal*.

Ulrich Hoffrage is a professor of decision theory at the University of Lausanne in Switzerland. He is a highly cited psychologist who builds and tests models of bounded rationality to better understand how people decide and navigate in a social world characterized by risk and uncertainty.